WINNERS !

Winners! How today's successful companies innovate by
design/John Thackara
Copyright © 1997 by ECSC-EC-EAEC, Brussels-Luxembourg

ISBN 0 566 07954 2

John Thackara

WINNERS !

How Today's Successful Companies Innovate by Design

The European Design Prize,
a project of the European Union's Innovation Programme,
is organised by the European Design Partnership,
Agence pour la Promotion de la Création Industrielle,
and the Netherlands Design Institute.

Gower

11565977

Learning Resources
Centre

This book is published as part of the European Design
Prize 1997, which is an initiative of the Innovation
Programme of the European Union. The Netherlands
Design Institute has also contributed to this publication.

WINNERS! EDITORIAL TEAM
Editor and writer: John Thackara
Project editor: Jennifer Sigler
Assistant editor: Astrid Baxter-Holtman
Case studies: Andrew Baxter Associates
Where To Go Next editor: Yvon Gijsbers
Research: Alison Roberts, Karen Smith,
   Kristina del Carmen
Proofreading: Susan Hunt

DESIGN AND INFORMATION GRAPHICS
Opera Design (Ton Homburg and Sappho Panhuysen)
Typeface used: ITC Officina
Photographs (pp. 36, 78, 128, 282, 330, 332, 333, 382):
   Reinout van den Bergh
The robot appearing in the photograph on p. 282
   is from the collection of Guus Otto

PUBLISHER
Gower Publishing Limited
Gower House, Croft Road
Aldershot, Hampshire GU11 3HR
United Kingdom
t +44 1252 331 551
f +44 1252 344 405

Printed in The Netherlands by Giethoorn, Meppel

Contents

Urban equipment: tools for competing cities 128

The human factor: usability and safety 174

Working with wetware: technology and the body 234

The European Design Prize: 436

Where to go next: books, periodicals, websites, and organisations 456

Winners!

Artemide
(Italy)
Authentics
(Germany)
Bates
(Denmark)
Bulthaup
(Germany)
Dyson
(United Kingdom)
Fiskars
(Finland)
Hörnell
(Sweden)
Lafuma
(Spain)
Mediamatic
(The Netherlands)
Oken
(Spain)
Oticon
(Denmark)

Winners and finalists of the European Design Prize 1997

Finalists

AKG (Austria)
Allègre (France)
Amat (Spain)
Atlet (Sweden)
Blatchford
(United Kingdom)
Burkhardt Leitner
(Germany)
Burodep (Belgium)
Cable Print (Belgium)
Cifial (Portugal)
Daisalux (Spain)
DMD
(The Netherlands)
DVV/LesAP (Belgium)
Escofet (Spain)
Eurologic (Ireland)
Frequentis (Austria)
Gillet (Belgium)
Groninger Museum
(The Netherlands)
Gunnebo (Sweden)
Hirsch (Austria)
Holland Railconsult
(The Netherlands)
Holmhed (Sweden)
Hultafors (Sweden)
ITG (United Kingdom)
JCB (United Kingdom)
Limar (Italy)
Magnus Olesen
(Denmark)

MDS (Ireland)
Mediacom (Ireland)
Moviluty (France)
Neuromag (Finland)
Norton (Luxembourg)
Novacor (France)
Octatube
(The Netherlands)
Olympus (Germany)
Optimom (France)
Össur (Iceland)
Partek (Finland)
Plustech (Finland)
Psion
(United Kingdom)
Rexite (Italy)
Rukka (Finland)
ScanView (Denmark)
Silampos (Portugal)
SkiData (Austria)
Stokke (Norway)
Swarovski (Austria)
Trintech (Ireland)
TVS (Italy)
Ufesa (Spain)
Unifor (Italy)
Vaki (Iceland)
Vinsmoselle
(Luxembourg)
Vitalograph (Ireland)

PREFACE

Edith Cresson

Design is a tool for introducing new products into our everyday lives, whether at home or at work. Design is what gives us the edge over our competitors. But design is also a cost-cutting tool: all designers are now trained to be artists and at the same time to use a wide range of materials, from the most traditional to the most modern, and to apply the techniques of value analysis, which, when properly used, simplify products.

For the head of a small or medium-sized enterprise (SME), design is also an excellent means of forging an in-house alliance — no mean task — between those involved in the conception of a new product: for the designer, it is second nature to get those responsible for marketing, development and production to work together; the designer of today knows how to reconcile imagination and industrial imperatives!

The best way to use design and designers, i.e. the way that does not confine this fertile function to the role of a window-dressing afterthought, is to impose this discipline as far upstream as possible, at the product conception stage.

The first stage in really introducing design into an enterprise and its products is not necessarily the recruitment of a salaried designer. Although this is frequently the case in Asia, SMEs can equally well call on the expertise of specialised consultancy firms, whose designers may well have received part of their training in another European country and are thus able to imbue their work with what a top designer has called "European cultural quality", which is much sought after by customers, especially those outside Europe.

We need only to look around us, and especially at the range of products presented in this guide — from the medical instrument to the pair of scissors, from the park bench to the toy — to realise that design is not a luxury. It is an essential element of the product which makes a vital contribution to its success by motivating people to buy it and giving them satisfaction in using it.

Through its support for this European Design Prize, the European Commission is contributing to the increasing realisation that design has a decisive influence on the success of the innovations which come on to the market.

The success of the products presented in this book, and that of the SMEs which have made the effort to design them, will encourage an increasing number of European enterprises to follow their example.

Edith Cresson is the European Commissioner
responsible for Research, Education and Training

This book is for anyone who believes small firms are where the action is in the new economy. Our theme is how successful companies use design to innovate — but not in abstract: we discuss innovation in the context of real companies, their products and services, and their new ways of working.

What all this adds up to is a colourful but complicated picture. Because the companies reviewed here respond to change in such a multitude of ways, it is hard to draw universal conclusions; there are no 'Five Rules for Successful Innovation' in the pages that follow. But they do contain talking points, data, and the encouragement that comes from from seeing how other companies have done it.

Innovation in Europe: the background

Innovation is one of those words that everyone agrees is important, but which means different things to different people. For our purposes, we take innovation to mean two things: first, the commercialisation of a technologically changed product in such a way that the new design delivers improved service to the user; and second, improvement in the way an item is produced — which may involve new equipment, new management and organisational methods, or all of these.

Whatever its precise definition, innovation matters — and not just economically. The European Commission's 1995 *Green Paper on Innovation* explained in ringing terms that "innovation is not just an economic mechanism, nor a technical process;

John Thackara

INTR

The new drivers of innovation

Social

- ageing population, demographic change
- new family structures, one-parent families
- changing consumer values
- the end of 'jobs', new patterns of 'work'

Market

- product differentiation
- customisation
- usability and safety
- environmental limits

Technology

- technology and the body
- microchips and smart materials
- intelligent manufacturing
- smart logistics
- the Internet and online communications

ODUCTION

innovation is above all a social phenomenon through which individuals, companies, and societies express their creativity, needs, and desires".

The prospect of an 'innovation deficit' therefore causes great concern, at least in Europe. The European Commission has advocated a number of remedial actions, including technological development, training, improving the availability of venture capital, and streamlining the administrative framework of national and European regulations affecting business.

The European *Green Paper* was followed in November 1996 by an *Action Plan for Innovation*. This called for specific actions: first, to foster an innovation culture; second, to establish a legal, administrative, and financial environment favourable to innovation; and third, to gear research more effectively towards innovation.

This book, as part of the European Design Prize (which is a project of The European Commission's Innovation Programme) is just one contribution towards the objective of fostering an innovation culture. It describes how today's successful companies innovate by design.

Knowledge-sharing among peers is the main reason for the Prize. Through selection processes in seventeen countries, companies are identified that use design to innovate in exemplary ways; once they are found, the Prize generates a variety of communications which tell the companies' stories as widely as possible — in the expectation that managers and designers in other companies will be encouraged and inspired by their example. As well as this book, the EDP involved the European Design Industry Conference (EDIS) for senior managers of the 64 companies that were finalists and winners of the prize; a website (www.design-inst.nl/edprize/); a travelling exhibition that visits a number of countries; and widespread media coverage.

Entrepreneurial flair and innovation are easier to describe than to teach. The European Commission harbours no illusions that an innovation culture can be legislated, or achieved by short-term measures. Of course, some steps can be taken by public authorities: they can improve education and training; they can make it easier for researchers and engineers to move around; they can foster best practice in the public sector; and so on. But the main way business cultures change is through the exchange of knowledge among those directly involved out there in the marketplace. Hence this book.

Why companies succeed

So what sets these winning companies apart? Innovation requires, in the words of the EU's Action Plan, "a state of mind combining creativity, entrepreneurship, willingness to take calculated risks, and an acceptance of some social, geographical, or professional mobility". Being innovative also demands an ability to anticipate needs, rigorous but flexible organisation, and a capacity to meet tight deadlines and to control costs.

There are nearly 16 million businesses in the 15 countries of the European Union, 99 percent of which have fewer than 50 employees. But although small, these companies account for over two-thirds of all jobs, and create the bulk of national wealth. Many of them are also innovative; according to *Enterprises in Europe,* a European Union report, 20-70 percent of them, depending on the country, introduced technological changes in their products or processes in the period between 1990 and 1992.

Research generated by the European Design Prize is the latest in a number of recent studies to throw new light on why some companies are able to innovate successfully. Another project, *Europe's 500,* recently concluded a five-year investigation of Europe's "most dynamic entrepreneurs". The companies identified grew by an average of 21 percent per annum, and increased employment levels by almost 160 percent, during a period of recession (the early 1990s) when the total

number of jobs in the economy fell. Other significant findings of the *Europe's 500*
project included:

- These dynamic companies were larger (the group average was 108 employees in
  1994) than the average SME (see chart below). This was to some extent due to
  the selection criteria, but it confirms the results of other studies which show that
  the strongest growth in employment occurs in companies with 100-250
  employees. (The average size of EDP winners is 233 employees).

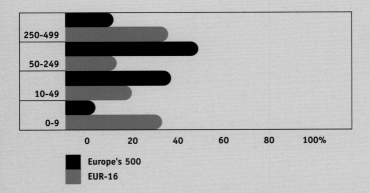

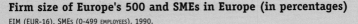

Firm size of Europe's 500 and SMEs in Europe (in percentages)
EIM (EUR-16), SMEs (0-499 EMPLOYEES), 1990.

- They were not particularly young: *Europe's 500* companies had been in business
  for 17 years on average (and four of them were established in the 19th century).
  EDP winners are a bit older, with an average age of 28.
- The majority of companies emphasised product differentiation rather than cost in
  their strategies — in marked contrast to strategies pursued by their competitors
  (see chart overleaf). The dynamically performing companies differentiate

principally on the basis of the quality of their product (48 percent), in the superior service they provide to their customers (33 percent), or on product appearance (14 percent).

	Europe's 500	Competitors
Low-cost leadership	21%	48%
Product differentiation	54%	22%
Cost focus	18%	25%
Differentiation focus	49%	19%

■ Europe's 500
■ Competitors

**Strategies pursued by Europe's 500 and by their competitors —
the majority of the companies have adopted a strategy that emphasises
product differentiation rather than costs.**
EUROPE'S 500.

- Almost two-thirds of their growth came by entering new markets at home and in Europe; relatively little of the growth (14 percent) came from existing markets.

- These dynamic companies are at least as concerned with *soft competencies* — marketing and human resources (and design) — as they are with *hard competencies* such as production and technology (see chart overleaf).

- The majority gave "customer orientation of employees" as the most critical success factor for further growth. But as the chart shows, the companies gave almost as much weight to logistics, knowledge of new technology, efficient production processes, quality of suppliers, feeling for market trends, and so on.

They acknowledged no single, magic ingredient among their success factors. Finalists in the European Design Prize had similar priorities: when asked which issue they thought most important as a theme for their conference, 81 percent of them said "customer relations".

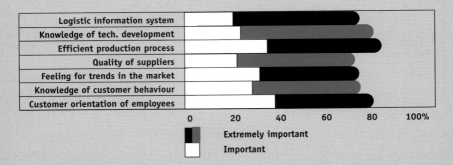

Logistic information system	
Knowledge of tech. development	
Efficient production process	
Quality of suppliers	
Feeling for trends in the market	
Knowledge of customer behaviour	
Customer orientation of employees	

0   20   40   60   80   100%

■ Extremely important
□ Important

Critical success factors: Europe's 500 companies are at least as concerned with 'soft' competencies - marketing and human resources — as with 'hard' competencies, such as production and technology
EUROPE'S 500.

• The dynamic companies are highly collaborative: 40 percent of them established some form of cooperation with other companies during the previous five years; (another finding was that team start-ups — rather than one-man bands — represented a higher-than-average share of the companies).

Another study, published in a book called *Hidden Champions,* by Hermann Simon, a professor at the London Business School, looked at the strategies of low-profile but high-performance German companies. Simon discovered that innovation was one of the pillars on which the world market leadership of his 'hidden champions' is built; many pioneered a new product or created a market. These companies made innovation an explicit priority not just in their products, but in every facet of their day-to-day operations. For them, innovation is not a spectacular jump into the future, but a continual and gradual process that never stops.

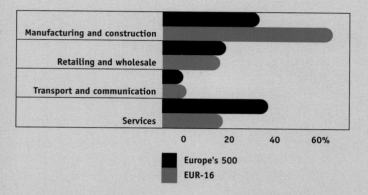

Sectoral Distribution
EIM Small Business Research and Consultancy.

Companies and technology
Innovative firms are known to collect and assimilate technological information enthusiastically — but the key to their success is in their capacity to exploit it immediately in new products. "Speed is God; Time is the Devil," goes Hitachi's company slogan.

Successful small companies in high-tech sectors are well aware that the careful design of the way things are made, and a development process that involves users 'online', accelerates time to market significantly. The design of logistics and distribution systems, for example, can greatly influence the whole cycle. And intelligent manufacturing, and the growing connections between its networks, ushers in the industrial infrastructure for 'mass production in lots of one'.

The organisation of research and development within the modern enterprise — as *The Economist* magazine put it, "wedding boffins to bureaucracy" — has been the subject of countless studies by consultants, business schools, and other academics. Commercial success is determined by the *quality of interaction* between research, technology, marketing, design, and communications on the one hand — and changes in the external world on the other. Getting that interaction right is what most preoccupies successful entrepreneurs. A common thread: how to run research, development, and marketing in parallel, rather than in linear sequence — the industrial equivalent of parallel processing in computer software and, for that matter, the human brain.

Innovation as software

Although innovation is, above all, a social process among people, the *Sloan Management Review* ran a fascinating analysis of the many ways that innovation processes can involve software. The analysis holds for almost every conceivable kind of product: ships, aircraft, cars, circuits, bridges, tunnels, machines, consumer electronics, buildings, refineries, chemicals, textiles, advertising, packaging, biological systems, buildings, dams, weaponry, etc.

There are four important consequences of this dramatic penetration of communications and software into innovation:

- First, as software and communications connect up with each other, and envelop participants like a cloud, researchers, designers, production engineers, logistics experts, and consumers should find it easier to communicate with each other.

- Second, if this infastructure can indeed break down the functional and disciplinary barriers that now impede, then removing obstacles (such as incompatible standards, or software platforms) becomes an economic and social priority, not just a technical one.

Innovation as software

Basic research
literature searches
databases
exchanges between researchers
laboratory experiments
analysis of correlations
modelling of complex phenomena
review of experimental results

Applied research
evaluation of basic research
results against:
market projections
economic forecasts and models
performance trajectories

**Development and design
(parameters, volumes,
engineering data)**
modelling in 2D, 3D
whole systems
subsystems
components
parts
tests

**Manufacturing engineering/
process design**
data gathering
anaysis/modelling of processes
testing of physical formats
modelling system usability
workflow process modelling
(people)
ditto for materials

**Interaction with customers and
users**
models and simulations
(products, contexts,
interfaces)
shared screens and usability tools
video, audio simulation, and
feedback capture
networks and groupware

**Post-introduction monitoring and
feedback to enhance:**
use
maintenance
addition of new features
logistics, distribution, and stock
control

**Environment-sensing and
connectivity to enhance:**
health and welfare services
utilities management
environmental quality (e.g.
lighting)
utilisation of domestic appliances

**Knowledge diffusion and
organisational learning**
visualisation of data
shared databases
websites
project management (groupware)
multimedia communication
adaptive interfaces

JAMES BRIAN QUINN, JORDAN J. BRAND AND KAREN ANNE ZIEN, *SLOAN MANAGEMENT REVIEW*, SUMMER 1996.

- Third, the 'softening' of innovation speeds it up. Software design productivity doubles every six years.
- Finally, the design of interfaces to this innovation 'medium' becomes a priority. There are currently fewer than 5,000 human-computer interaction designers in the whole world, and many of them have engineering or computer science backgrounds. If innovation is as important as policymakers claim, then interaction design needs to be made more of a priority.

Organisational skills   Innovative companies tend to organise

their activities in teams; the purpose of teams is to coordinate different disciplines through the life of a project. They recognise that innovation is a communication process within organisations, as much as between them, and that the best way to coordinate product conception, production, design, and distribution is to bring the specialists together from the outset.

Coordinating these different inputs is an art in itself: as any manager knows, you don't create a team just by locking a bunch of (probably incompatible) people together in a room. It is one thing to describe the benefits of teamwork, but getting teams actually to function effectively is another, much harder, matter. If the companies reviewed in this book are any guide, innovation is as much about attitude and context as it is about about systems. Small firms are by their very nature decentralised, adaptable, agile, and collaborative: that's what being small means! And being close to their customers fosters fresh thinking: they unavoidably interact continuously.

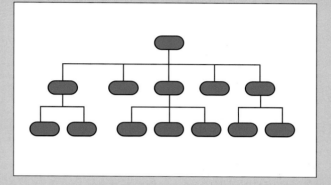

The industrial company
NETHERLANDS DESIGN INSTITUTE.

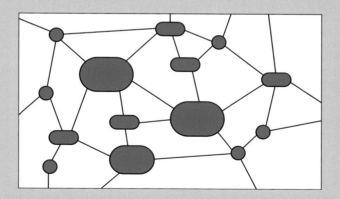

The knowledge-sharing company
NETHERLANDS DESIGN INSTITUTE.

Companies in the local community
Although globalisation still dominates the headlines, the vast majority of small and medium-sized companies operate within a radius of 50 km (30 miles). And despite those endless television images of computerised dealing rooms, much of the world's GDP is highly localised. In high-tech sectors, of course, even tiny firms need to think and act internationally; but local conditions, local trading patterns, local networks, local skills, and local culture, remain a critical success factor for many companies. Because innovation is a social process that exploits the skills and capabilities of all the people in a company, local conditions and local identity often shine through in the products of innovative firms.

Local knowledge and information was key 150 years ago when there were 80 different steps in the button-making industry; it is key today if you are a software company needing bright recruits from the local university. Long-established local roots, and human skills that are unique to a region, can be a powerful advantage when local companies venture onto the wider economic stage. Their ideal home base will contain craft-based workshops, consultants, law firms, accountants, distribution and logistics companies, advertising agencies, universities, research labs, database publishers, government offices, and professional and trade organisations.

The 'local is good' logic is reinforced by increasing competition among 'edge cities' for inward investment by those floating multinationals. Unique skills, clusters of specialised suppliers, and the synergy and dynamism that comes from their interaction are powerful attractors to itinerant multinationals.

The 'new consumer'
Communities are made up of consumers. Innovation is a social process that, to be effective, necessarily involves users and

consumers as active participants. That much we've been told a hundred times. But involving 'the consumer' is easier said than done: their needs and values are constantly changing. For example, the consumer spending downturn in recent years, which was blamed on 'the recession', may well turn out to be the signal of a more permanent change in values. Consumers are getting older and more environmentally aware — with the result that quality, durability, and value for money count for more than flashy short-life products and heavily branded goods. Consumers are also living in new ways. The one-person household, for example, will soon be more common than the nuclear family. By the year 2000, fewer than than 50 percent of households, at least in the industrialised West, will contain a father, a mother, and two children.

The possibility that many consumers, being older and wiser, might be bored with brands, and critical of the 'needs' so many products are supposed to meet, is frightening to contemplate. But contemplate it we must.

Age and demographics

The demographic revolution is the most profound driver of attitudinal change. By the year 2000, the world population of people aged 65 and older will be greater than the combined populations of France, Japan, and Germany, and there will be more than 115 million people aged 50 or over in the EU (with another 38 million in those countries that have applied for membership). And with life expectancy approaching 80, most Europeans can look forward to 30 years of active life beyond the age of 50.

In the United States, more people are 65 and over today than make up the entire population of Canada. In 1986, the average North American couple had more parents than children — a trend that is growing. *Modern Maturity* has one of the the largest circulations of any US magazine.

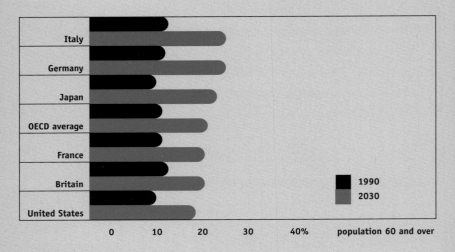

A grey future

The Economist.

In the past, 'the elderly' were either ignored by business, or treated as dependent and infirm. According to Roger Coleman, who leads the European Design for Ageing Network, this equation of age with disability is patronising and wrong. And James Pirkl, a leading North American expert, is contemptuous of what he calls the "myth of senility, which states that all older people are either disabled, decrepit, senile, or locked away in nursing homes". Frail elderly people, living in institutions, comprise less than five percent of the over-60s. And Anne Voshol, who runs the DesignAge programme at the Netherlands Design Institute in Amsterdam, explains that 'the elderly' do not exist as a distinct group with special characteristics. "What we are dealing with here is the most diverse group of people there is."

The elderly form a vast market: for example, people over 65 control more than 77 percent of all assets in the United States. The figure for Europe is not much lower.

The simplest way to think about older consumers is that 'they' are 'we'. Professor Pirkl argues for a 'transgenerational' design that bridges the physical and sensory changes associated with ageing, responds to the widest range of ages and abilities, and preserves the individual's sense of dignity and autonomy.

Design for our future selves, a report published by the European Design for Ageing Network, lists ubiquitous products that need to be modified right now: packaging that opens without the need to slice your hand open with a knife; elegant clothing that is easy to wear and maintain but still looks good; chairs that are easy to get out of; houses that can adapt to changing space and equipment needs; clear signs and labelling on buildings, vehicles and products in shops; cups, door handles, light switches, supermarket trolleys — the list is endless — that do not require the strength of a weightlifter, the eyesight of Superman, or the patience of Job to handle. We all need products that are sympathetic to the gradual decline in vision, hearing, and movement capabilities that affects us all in time.

'Elderly' consumers are also a good market for technology. A RAND study in the United States, for example, found that while only about ten percent of 'seniors' currently own a computer, and that a little over three percent use network services, these rates are growing at 30 percent and 46 percent annually — faster than the rates for any other group. Another study of 3,000 North American seniors by the Markle Foundation found that fully 30 percent of them felt "a strong need to keep up with the latest developments in technology" and even those aged 80 and over "care a lot about their ability to learn how to work new electronic products".

For older people, technology is a means — not an end in itself. It is a means, in particular, to better communications, which are more important than high-tech physical aids to the welfare of older people. Better communications can reduce the call made by older people on welfare services. In one experiment in Alsace, France, a network designed to help elderly people call up medical and social services was actually used more by elderly people to contact each other — with the result that calls on welfare services went *down* by 40 percent.

The future of work

Most of us try not to think too much about getting old, but the prospect of a life without work is harder to ignore. This confronts innovative companies with a profound change in the psychological profile and lifestyles of consumers. The design of products and services will necessarily be informed by new criteria.

Work is not just about earning money to buy products. "We work not just to produce," said Eugene Delacroix, "but to give value to time." Work has social, cultural, and personal, as well as economic meaning. For tens of millions of European adults, the idea of a 'steady job' is no longer a realistic prospect. Young adults, in particular, face a future in which they will live and work in wholly new ways. The OECD estimates that 35 million people are formally unemployed in the developed countries, and that 15 million more have given up looking for work; one third of these are young people.

The circumstances we face are neither temporary, nor the result of some unfortunate accident or cyclical downturn. Eric Britton, author of *Re-thinking Work*, says they are the direct result of the social and economic system we have set in place: "We have voluntarily created all the preconditions of a 'labour saving society' — and now we are surprised that there are large numbers of people 'out of work'."

So what happens to business when one third of the adult population is in its 'third age' and 50 percent does not have a job? Nobody knows. Perhaps our whole economic system will change, and we will begin to calculate labour as a value in products, not a cost. Perhaps we will reintroduce apprenticeships, and reorganise

Facts of working life — 2020 perspectives

- A society of abundance
- Market forces drive production side of economy
- Basic survival of all assured with or without a job
- Flexible 'career path' associated with every job
- Much more flexible work arrangements
- More complex compensation arrangements
- Possibility of simultaneous jobs with different employers
- Greater range of possibilities of work locations
- Flexible hours (daily, weekly, etc.)
- Decentralised work locations
- Objective (not product) driven
- Flexible work flows
- Flatter hierarchies
- Self-regulation of work habits
- Flexible teams
- Networking
- New incentive arrangements
- Less clear lines between work and education
- Blurred lines between work and 'non-work'

ECOPLAN, PARIS.

In the end, the job crisis raises
the most fundamental question
of human existence:
what are we doing here?
There is a colossal amount of work
waiting to be done by human beings
— building decent places to live,
exploring the universe, making cities
less dangerous, teaching one another,
raising our children, visiting,
comforting, healing, feeding one
another, telling stories, inventing
things, and governing ourselves.
But much of the essential activity
people have always undertaken to
raise and educate their families,
to enjoy themselves, to give pleasure
to others, and to advance the general
welfare is not packaged as jobs.
Until we rethink work and decide
what human beings are meant to do
in the age of robots and what basic
economic claims on society human
beings have by virtue of being here,
there will never be enough jobs.

RICHARD J. BARNET, 'THE END OF JOBS', HARPERS MAGAZINE, MARCH 1993.

education to favour time-based skills that take decades to master. Whatever happens, the new world of work changes the context for innovation profoundly, and we will all need to confront the changes this will entail.

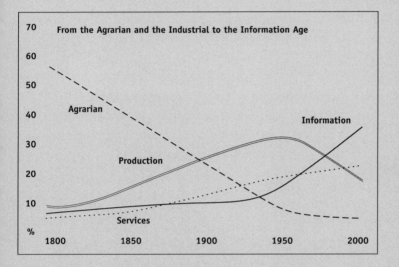

Development of Employment 1800-2000
Leo A. Nefiodow, *Der Fünfte Kondratieff* (Wiesbaden: FAZ/Gabler, 1990).

Design — an instrument of innovation

Innovation is about technological invention that reinvents the future — but it is also about the new products and services that respond to changes in the way we live. This is where design comes in as an instrument of innovation; design is a process that transforms raw technology into products or processes that people can actually use.

Design — like innovation — is one of those words which means different things in different contexts; despite decades of discussion, nobody has yet come up with a commonly accepted definition. Although many people perceive design to be all about appearances, design is not just about the way things look. Design is also about the way things are used; how they are communicated to the world; and the way they are produced.

There are as many kinds of design process as there are design disciplines, which is a lot. To the CEO of an airline, 'design' denotes the corporate logo applied to a thousand objects — from aircraft to sickbags. To the owner of a hairdressing salon, 'design' means the way someone's hair is cut — or, possibly, the wallpaper pattern that adorns the salon walls. To a brand manager, designers are responsible for the label on a can of baked beans — and possibly the dumpbin that trips you up in the supermarket. To an online Internet publisher, the 'design' of a website lies somewhere among its information architecture, its flow charts, its visual appearance, and the html software that makes it work.

Some companies hire designers to enhance a product whose function remains unchanged; others use designers to envision future lifestyles, and to simulate the products that will be needed to sustain them. Some companies have high-level 'design managers', who spend millions on design; other firms 'design' great products without ever hiring, or even hearing about, the concept of a professional designer.

The search for a universal definition of design is probably a waste of time. Can you define 'creativity', or 'organisation', or 'communication'? Probably not: but you know they are important.

The best way to understand the slippery, multifaceted nature of design is to read the case studies in this book. Each company here uses 'design' in a different way. Most — but not all — of their projects involve professional designers; they all interact in different ways with customers, technology, research, finance, marketing, distribution and logistics, as well as information technology.

But whatever design is, it must work. Despite its fuzzy profile, design is a big and successful service industry. There are nearly 10,000 design companies in the European Union (although they tend to be small: most have fewer than 25 staff, many comprise only two or three people); alongside these agencies are at least 150,000 staff designers employed by companies. At any one time, 180,000 students are enrolled in design courses somewhere in Europe; 30,000 graduate each year, and most of them find jobs.

Companies clearly believe design contributes to competitiveness, because they spend heavily on it: in 1993, 7.3 billion ECU ($9.5 billion) was spent on design royalties and fees. According to a 1994 study by the Netherlands Design Institute, from which these figures are taken, expenditure on design by governments, cities, multinationals, and small companies will rise to more than 12 billion ECU ($15.5 billion) by 2000. It could be more.

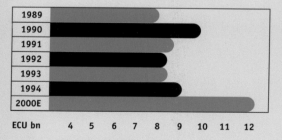

1989									
1990									
1991									
1992									
1993									
1994									
2000E									

ECU bn   4   5   6   7   8   9   10   11   12

Expenditure on design
NETHERLANDS DESIGN INSTITUTE.

Different companies use design for different ends. When asked "in which area does design deliver value to your company?", 87 percent of the companies that won the European Design Prize, or were finalists, replied: "the form of a product"; 81 percent mentioned the usability of a product; 62 percent was also concerned with corporate or brand communications; 43 percent said design enhanced their physical environment; and 35 percent quoted a whole range of other benefits, ranging from websites to environmental impact.

Although design manifests itself in many ways throughout industry, a feature common throughout is technological intensification. In the same way that every aspect of the innovation process may now be supported by software, design, too, is fast becoming technology-rich. Just ten years ago, many designers would get by with a pencil and a drawing board; today, the average European or North American design office — and remember, most contain fewer than 25 people — spends 24,000 ECU ($30,000) a year on computer hardware, software, and training.

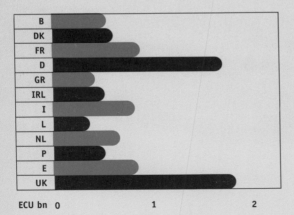

ECU bn 0   1   2

European design services expenditure
NETHERLANDS DESIGN INSTITUTE.

How the book works
From here on, WINNERS! contains four kinds of information. Each chapter begins with an analysis of a particular 'driver' of innovation. This is followed by short case studies in which some of the companies that have won or were finalists in the European Design Prize are reviewed. The stories illustrate how these companies have used design to innovate new products or services. A third level of content consists of statistical information and data; these charts and tables crop up throughout the book. At the end of the book, a section called *Where to go next* contains a fourth kind of information: a critical selection of books, magazines, organisations, and websites. This list includes references from the main texts.

How the companies were selected
Our pre-final chapter describes the background to the European Design Prize: the European Commission's Innovation Programme; the members of the EDP jury; and a list of the EDP's national organisers. This is followed by a 'Roll of Honour' in which previous winners of the Prize, plus the finalists and winners of the European Design Prize 1997, are presented, together with contact details and a description of what they do.

The companies reviewed in this book have been selected purely because their story is of particular relevance to our overall narrative. They were not selected on the basis of superior merit in relation to those other winners and finalists that are not reviewed. The status of all EDP winners and finalists is the same: they are all superlative European companies.

How to be Different:

Even in crowded markets, successful companies tend to compete by making their products different, not by making them cheaper. Europe's 500, the EU's fastest growing companies, for example, steer clear of low-cost leadership strategies by a factor of two to one.

REINVENT THE WHEEL

Low-cost leadership	21%	**Europe's 500**
	48%	**Competitors**
Product differentiation	54%	
	22%	
Cost focus	18%	
	25%	
Differentiation focus	49%	
	19%	

Alternative competitive strategies
EFER/Europe's 500.

But product differentiation is not exactly a secret weapon; most notoriously in consumer electronics, but in many other sectors too, new products are proliferating and differentiation has become more difficult. The relentless optimisation of everything from cars to steam irons means that most consumer durables deliver similar performance and functionality. And of course, "they all look the same". The result: many products have become commodities, and are marketed as brands, with enormous effort and cost being invested in their communications and packaging.

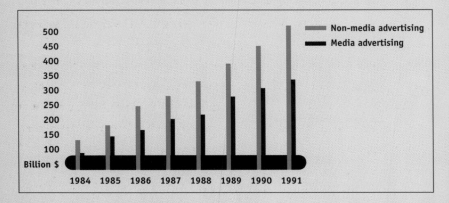

Growth in worldwide marketing services expenditure 1984-1991
WPP.

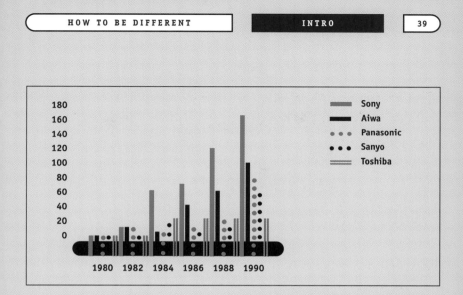

Products are proliferating, so differentiation is more difficult
ARTHUR D. LITTLE.

This 'me too' squeeze is one reason why marketing and packaging design had such a boom during the late 1980s. When consumers were prosperous and undemanding, making products look different, even when they were not, seemed an easy option. But today's consumers value performance over puffery; this is why the recession in consumer spending has not gone away. Values have changed.

The companies profiled in this chapter have faced up to this challenge and manage to be different in surprising ways: they reinvent the wheel. They step back. They return to square one. They ask stupid questions. They doubt the obvious. They reject received wisdom. In short, they manage to make their products different even when it seems inconceivable that any improvements are left to be made. Some of these products have been around for thousands of years.

These successful companies immerse themselves in the contexts in which their products are used. They look at performance, ergonomics, aesthetics, maintenance, safety, and manufacturing, of course. But these companies think about more than what their products do, they also consider what products mean in their contexts. Making such cultural connections is one of the inputs of design; it can act as an interface allowing technical and social factors to interact.

Collective Intelligence

In professional and industrial markets, where products and systems have not become commodities, the rules of competition are more clear-cut: the best product usually wins, assuming it is supported by excellent after-sales service and support. But traditional barriers to entry — capital-intensive production facilities or ownership of a specialised technology — are less effective now that technology is mobile and innovation so fast. So the only thing a company has that cannot be bought or copied is the knowledge and creativity of its people.

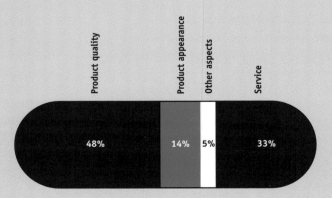

Product quality — 48%
Product appearance — 14%
Other aspects — 5%
Service — 33%

Main sources of differentiation

EFER/EUROPE's 500.

This chapter is therefore less about new product concepts than about finding new ways to exploit a company's human skills and expertise — the intelligence of its customers, as well as that of its staff — continuously. As Tom Peters, the American management guru, so memorably remarked, "There is no such thing as a product business anymore."

In *Hidden Champions*, Hermann Simon's study of 500 obscure companies (developers of machines to stick labels onto bottles, large living trees, glass showcases for museums, industrial coffee-roasting technology, screws and nuts) that are nonetheless world leaders in their particular sectors, he found that all were older (on average, 67 years old), slower growing, and in more stable markets than expected. "They owe their success not to one specific factor," writes Simon, "but rather to the sum of their implementing many small moves slowly and consistently to improve their performance."

Successful companies reinvent their products continuously. All the time. Every minute of the day. Not in big bangs, but in thousands of tiny steps. Companies that rely passively on pre-existing market information, or that make assumptions about what customers want without involving them directly in the development process, or that hire a designer to 'make it different', are the companies that reinvent the wheel pointlessly. *Difference* has no value if it is not also *better*.

The companies profiled on the following pages exemplify these rather obvious lessons. The story of **Hultafors** proves that even a product that has evolved over 50,000 years, like a hammer, can be made better. Confronted with fierce competition in Europe's 1.4 billion ECU tools market, Hultafors stood back and asked some seemingly silly questions: "Who uses hammers, for what purpose, and how?" And they discovered that there was still room for improvement.

Knives have been around for almost as long as hammers. The French company **Laguiole** brought in a big name designer, Philippe Starck, to update its products, its factory, its shops, and its packaging — and, in truth, to attract media attention. But Laguiole also emphasised to its customers the importance of traditional craft skills — in one case, 40 separate operations — to the quality of its knives.

Like these innovators, **Lamy**, the German pen company; **Allègre**, the French baby products manufacturer; and **Rexite**, the Italian producer of home and office accessories, exemplify how collective design thinking can add value to archetypal products. And the story of **Stokke**, once a conservative furniture company, shows what happens when a company really looks twice at how and why its products are used. What Stokke discovered, when it went back to design basics, was that many cultures — the Bedouin, the Japanese before 1945, millions of people in Africa to this day — don't use chairs because they inhibit the body's natural tendency to move. The startling but seemingly obvious revelation that the human body moves but most objects do not, was the basis for a revolutionary chair design.

When a deep, tacit understanding of a product and its market exists in a company; when communication with customers is real; when development teams, including designers, step back and ask basic questions from new angles; when they mobilise the expertise to answer them; and when they organise the creation of real or simulated product prototypes to test the waters; when these conditions exist, then yes, it is possible to reinvent the wheel.

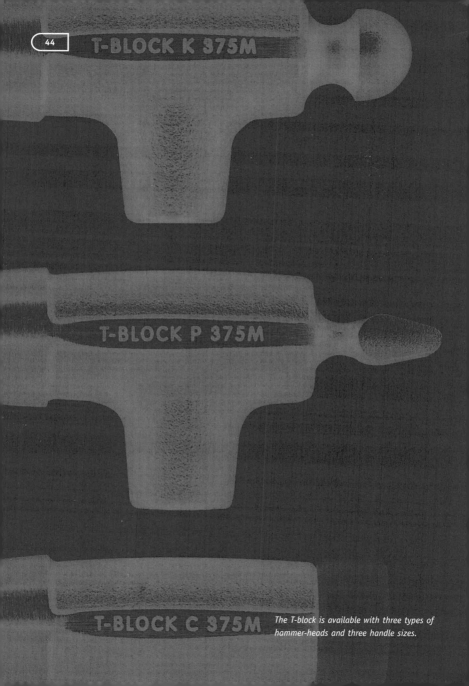

T-BLOCK K 375M

T-BLOCK P 375M

T-BLOCK C 375M

The T-block is available with three types of hammer-heads and three handle sizes.

GETTING A GRIP

More than 3 billion ECU worth of new hand tools are introduced onto the market each year.

INDUSTRIAL DISTRIBUTION SUPPLEMENT, DECEMBER 1992.

Hand Tools

Hultafors
"It's the best thing that's happened to hammers in 50,000 years," says Bo Jägnefält, managing director of Hultafors, a Swedish hand tools manufacturer. A complete rethink of the concept of the hammer has resulted in a new ergonomic tool that reduces accidents and strain injuries.

A few years ago, Hultafors joined several other companies, including car makers Saab and Volvo, in a project to understand and reduce the number of injuries caused by the use of hand tools in their industries. It quickly became evident that the most dangerous tool was the traditional hammer. The shapes of many hammer handles are in fact unsuited to the human hand, causing people to grip them too tightly, which can lead to inflamed joints or strained muscles, ligaments or tendons. The force of the blow when the hammer head hits the surface, along with the recoil and the rotation of the handle when the hammer bounces back, also increase the risk of hand and arm strain. Clearly, a new, ergonomic design had been long overdue.

To tackle this problem, Hultafors teamed up with the Ergonomi Design Gruppen, a design office renowned for its pioneering work on the ergonomics of hand tools. Together they

developed the T-Block hammer. Its handle is designed for optimum grip where tasks demand both power and precision. Its head is hollow and filled with small steel balls, which relieve the shock caused by each blow, reduce recoil, and minimise rotation of the handle. A counterbalance at the end of the handle improves control over the tool, reducing the risk of accidents. To ensure that the hammer-head does not come loose, a steel tube through the handle connects it to the counterbalance.

The new hammers come in three handle sizes and several hammer-head weights to suit different hands and tasks. "At last," says Bo Jägnefält, "we've made the first hammer that's really designed for human hands."

The head of the T-block is filled with small steel balls to relieve
shock, reduce recoil, and minimise handle rotation.

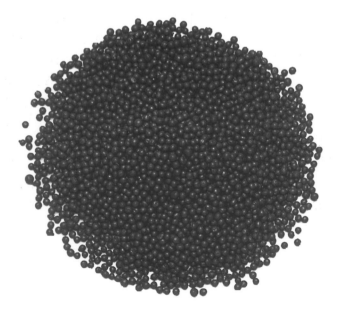

The first stone tools were made in Africa about 2 million years ago. 'Choppers', as they were named by anthropologists, were made by hitting two stones against each other.

COMPTON'S INTERACTIVE ENCYCLOPEDIA (COMPTON'S NEWMEDIA, INC., 1995).

Traditional hammers are not designed for the modern person. The situation has actually grown worse during the past century because hammers are now mass-produced. In the old days, the smith would start by measuring the person's hand and arm, so that he could better tailor the hammer to suit the individual. Traditional industrial production of hammers presumes that all users look the same, because the starting point for mass-produced hammers is a man-sized hand.

ENGINEERING HAMMERS (BROCHURE), HULTAFORS.

A complete rethink of the concept of the hammer has resulted in a new ergonomic tool that reduces accidents and strain injuries.

In Norse mythology, the god Thor
was the embodiment of thunder and chief god of war.
Generally portrayed as a crude, bearded warrior who
was capable of drinking copious amounts of alcohol,
Thor was armed with a hammer which returned to
his hand after he had hurled it at his enemies.
According to popular legend, this hammer was given
to the giant, Thrym, who built the god's residence.
When Thrym became its owner,
he demanded the goddess Freya as his wife
in exchange for the hammer. Thor pretended to be
Freya and regained his prized hammer.

THE 1995 GROLIER MULTIMEDIA ENCYCLOPEDIA (GROLIER INC., 1995).

STAYING SHARP

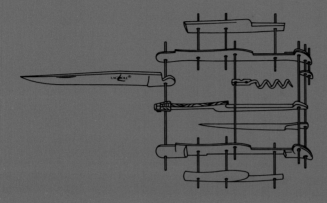

Winner '92!

Knives

Laguiole
From dagger to working knife to popular penknife to highly cherishable *objet du désir:* the Laguiole Knife has come a long way in the past hundred years. But its most recent phase is most remarkable.

More than a century ago, in the tiny village of Laguiole in the Aubrac, in southern France, the artisan Pierre-Jean Calmels transformed the local dagger into a folding knife. It became extremely popular, and over the years many new features were added — an awl for shepherds and a corkscrew for *patrons* and *pères de famille,* for instance. The knife soon gained an excellent reputation, and Calmels started to refine it, using horn, wood and ivory to give it a more attractive finish.

During the reign of Queen Elizabeth I in the late 16th century, some wealthy English people had begun to carry a small case containing a rudimentary cutlery set. However, it wasn't until almost 100 years later that the majority of European and American people began to use cutlery for eating food. Until that time, they had almost always used their fingers.

But the knife's popularity backfired: the market was soon flooded with imitations and in 1950 the village workshop closed its doors for the last time. Though similar knives continued to be made in nearby Thiers, the 'real Laguiole' faded into oblivion...

Or so it seemed, until, in 1987, the village was put very decidedly back on the map by Calmels' great-granddaughters, who reopened the family shop and led what was to be a phoenix-like renaissance of the Laguiole Knife. Philippe Starck designed the new factory, which can be recognised from afar by the giant blade sticking out of the roof.

Since then, without sacrificing the craftsmanship involved in making the perfect knife, production has increased dramatically — the firm now produces some 200,000 knives a year. Laguiole still makes the traditional folding knife, but the company's recent success has resulted mainly from its adoption of design as an instrument of renewal. Many new varieties have been contributed by highly acclaimed designers like Starck, Yan Pennor, and Eric Raffy. This approach has improved both the appeal and the performance of the product, while respecting its unique spirit and heritage.

Packaging plays an important role in making each knife a desirable object: the traditional range is presented in gift boxes designed by Yan Pennor, while the newer knives come in special, customised cases.

The Laguiole Knife was recognised as one of the fifteen most representative products of French design at a 1989 exhibition at the Cooper Hewitt Museum in New York. By using design — of products, packaging, architecture, and communications — as its primary tool, Laguiole has bridged a rich history with contemporary values to make an unexpected come-back.

Three recent Laguiole models, including knives designed ▶
by Philippe Starck (middle), and Yan Pennor (bottom).

WRITING STRAIGHT TO THE POINT

Winner '88!

Writing Instruments

Lamy Ever since Cro-Magnon man and woman starting drawing on the walls of the Lascaux caves, writing tools of one sort or another have been part of our lives. Even now, despite the advent of computers, life without the pen would be unthinkable. "Pens are very personal objects," says Manfred Lamy, chairman of Lamy, Germany's foremost maker of writing instruments. "People can be very fussy about what they write with." Lamy has successfully exploited this intimate aspect of pens, using design to transform a traditional tool into a new, but still timeless object.

Lamy started making fountain pens in Heidelberg in 1930, and now sells in every major market in the world. It places great emphasis on the practicality of its products and on the use of the very latest writing technology. "We work for all market segments," says Lamy. "We make pens for schoolchildren as well as for managing directors. Our products are not intended to be status symbols, but to be products with the 'added value' of design. That is our trade mark."

Manfred Lamy introduced design into the firm in the 1960s, inviting Gerd Müller to design a pen in the Bauhaus style. The spartan-looking Lamy 2000 is now a design classic.

The Safari.

In 1959, a year after its introduction, 53 million BiC Crystal ballpoint pens were sold in the UK. Today over 12 million BiC Crystal pens are sold daily worldwide.

GEOFF TIBBALLS, *THE GUINNESS BOOK OF INNOVATIONS* (LONDON: GUINNESS PUBLISHING LTD, 1996).

More recently, in 1990, in a move to enter the high-price segment, Lamy developed its 'designed by' concept. The result was the Persona, designed by Mario Bellini and reminiscent of Art Deco. "It brought a touch of elegance and sensuality into our somewhat austere and 'Bauhaus-ish' thinking," says Lamy.

The use of star designers, however, is exceptional at Lamy; the company is now working with teams of designers recruited through restricted competition. The new Spirit range of very slim ballpoint pens and pencils represents Lamy's latest achievement. The entire casing comprises a single piece of stainless steel, formed into an austerely cylindrical, highly polished sleeve to surround the mechanism. A decorative perforated pattern ensures a good grip. Due to its slimness, the Spirit fits unobtrusively into pockets and bags, and is meant for making notes rather than for extended periods of writing.

Since winning the first European Design Prize in 1988, Lamy continues to demonstrate its skill in using design to make an archetypal product into something different.

% SHARE BY VALUE 1992: BALLPOINTS 34% FOUNTAIN PENS 17% FIBRE TIPS 13% ROLLER-BALLS 12% STANDARD/ MECHANICAL PENCILS 15%

The Lamy Spirit: the entire casing is made of a single piece of stainless steel.

UNDERSTANDING BABY TALK

Baby Products

Allègre In 1990, after 30 years of making baby bottles and feeding utensils, the French company Allègre Puériculture made a strategic decision to break out of the monotony of its field, where packaging and decor had become the sole marks of identity, and escape the price war that had brought profitability to a standstill.

With substantive differentiation as its goal, Allègre boldly brought design to the forefront of its activities, expanded its marketing team, and began to ask its customers — parents, hospitals, day-care centres, and most importantly, through behavioural studies, babies themselves — what they really wanted, and where standard products fell short.

This research revealed many shortcomings in the whole range of baby products. "We saw that standardised products weren't meeting parents' expectations at all," said Jean Paul Allègre, the company's managing director. "So we decided to set up a range with a distinctive appearance and functionality that would fit into the parent-child environment more harmoniously."

Allègre's baby bottle is intended to be natural, comfortable, and accessible to the child.

With the MBD design agency, Allègre brought new life to its primary product, the baby bottle. Its form, inspired by the shapes of the aquatic world — fluidity, movement, and ease of integration — is intended to express a sense of physical and psychological well-being; to be natural, comfortable and accessible to the child.

Most importantly, Allègre improved the baby bottle by developing an 'anti-drip nipple system' which allows easy preparation and cleaning and minimises leakage during transport.

Allègre's packaging and communication tools aim to assist parents and simplify selection. Products are coded not according to age, but according to developmental phases — lying down, sitting, and standing.

Following its success since taking these steps in 1990 — turnover has increased by 77 percent — Allègre has introduced a more formal innovation programme with regular improvement and expansion of its entire range of products.

Aquatic shapes inspire the company's whole range of products, from potties to baby bath seats.

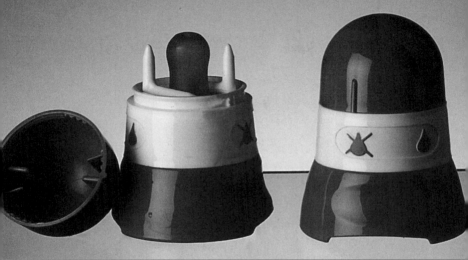

Allègre's patented 'anti-drip nipple system' allows easy preparation and cleaning and minimises leakage during transport.

In France, it is estimated that 40% of baby lotions and skin-care creams and 55% of baby shampoos are used not by babies, but by women.

LIE BACK AND WORK

Chairs

Stokke Human beings are not made for sitting down for long periods of time. And if they must, the last thing they should do is try to sit still. This is the message from the tiny village of Skodje between the fjords and the mountains of Norway's west coast. From here, the furniture company Stokke Fabrikker distributes its revolutionary chairs all over the world.

Established in 1932 as a traditional furniture company, Stokke's outlook shifted in the 1970s when the company began to examine the impact of a sedentary lifestyle on health and productivity. Stokke took a fresh look at sitting, redefined it as a potentially active rather than a passive condition, and developed its 'philosophy of movement'. For years, industrial design had really been design for a streamlined industrial process rather than for human bodies in their infinite variety. Stokke was now putting people before process and began to develop chairs that stimulate, rather than inhibit, our natural need for movement and variation.

Stokke's first breakthrough was the Tripp Trapp, a wooden chair for babies and children. Designer Peter Opsvik conceived it in the late 1970s as the chair that grows with the child: the height and depth of the seat and footrest are adjustable. The Tripp

Trapp is intended to encourage the freedom, independence, and diversity children need during meals and play.

In 1986, Stokke decided to leave traditional furniture behind and concentrate exclusively on the philosophy of movement, with Peter Opsvik as its leading designer. His ideal is that people can use a single chair to sit in many different positions — upright, lounging, or even hanging. The latest generation of Stokke chairs — first the Variable and recently the Gravity — are based on the principle of a wheel finding its natural balance. Each chair rests on curved runners, so that a small shift of position is enough to make it move and rediscover its optimum balance.

The versatility of Stokke's furniture makes it suitable for use in both home and

office environments, a distinction which is becoming increasingly blurred as workers become more mobile and the office functions primarily as meeting place. Digital Computers has incorporated Stokke's furniture into its open-plan office landscape: "When we lie down during meetings," says Jonny Johansson of Digital, "we're much more open to one another's arguments. We communicate better."

The Variable rests on curved runners so that a small shift of position is enough to make it move and rediscover its optimum balance.

The Tripp Trapp was conceived in the late 1970s as the chair that grows with the child.

Czapek Creativ, an advertising agency in Innsbruck, Austria, is one of many companies incorporating Stokke's furniture into a more relaxed vision of the workplace.

There is evidence that a horizontal position improves lateral thinking.

STEVE CONNOR, *SUNDAY TIMES*, UK, OCTOBER 1996.

According to Link Resources, **43 million Americans** **worked at home on at least a part-time basis at the end of 1995.** **This number is thought to be increasing at 5% per year.**

M.J. HIMOWITZ, 'SETTING UP YOUR OWN HOME OFFICE', *FORTUNE*, JULY 10, 1995.

GOOD TIMING

Clocks/Home and Office Accesories

Rexite   "Ever since it was invented," says Rino Pirovano, managing director of Rexite, "time has refused to stand still. How can we possibly be serious about anything as flighty as that?" In line with this philosophy, the Italian manufacturer of home and office accessories has made a virtue of necessity, turning the inexorable ebbing away of our lives into a light-hearted experience. Rexite continually reinterprets the abstract concept of time. With their unconventional shapes and colours, Rexite's playful clocks exploit this fact to combine precision with pleasure. They tell us it's time to relax.

Rexite makes extensive use of plastic. The company started in 1968 as a producer of injection-moulded plastics and metal components for various industries. Since both moulds and components were produced in-house, it acquired considerable technical know-how in this field.

In 1978, Rexite began to collaborate with architects and designers to develop an original collection of contemporary home and office accessories, including desk organisers, picture frames, coat racks, waste paper bins, and free-standing shelving units. Using technologically advanced materials and innovative designs, Rexite's range of classic everyday products show how it is possible to give age-old concepts a fresh, contemporary feel.

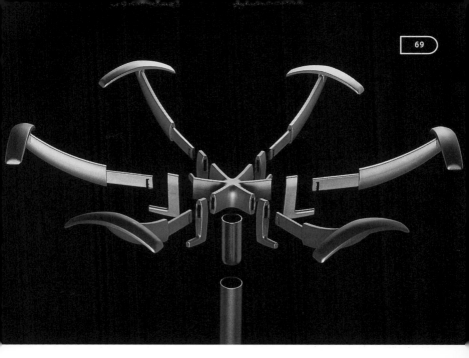

▲ Rexite's table alarm clock was inspired by a colourful warrior's helmet which was kept by Julius Caesar as a trophy.

Telling time is a simple technical
problem, but unfortunately the clock
is a rather obscure perceptual device.
Its first widespread use in the
thirteenth century was to ring
the hours for clerical devotions.
The clock face which translated time
into spatial alteration came later.
That form was dictated by its works,
not by any principle of perception.
Two (sometimes three) superimposed
cycles give duplicate readings,
according to angular displacement
around a finely marked rim.
Neither minutes nor hours nor half
days correspond to the natural cycles
of our bodies or the sun.
And so teaching a child to read
a clock is not a childish undertaking.
When asked why a clock had two
hands, a four-year-old replied,
'God thought it would be a good idea.'

KEVIN LYNCH, QUOTED IN DONALD A. NORMAN, *THE DESIGN OF EVERYDAY THINGS* (NEW YORK: DOUBLEDAY, 1988).

Winner '97!

Vacuum Cleaners
Dyson

THE BAGLESS
VACUUM CLEANER

Viruses

Pet hairs

Pollen

*Inefficient bag vacuum cleaners leave
harmful dust and allergens behind.*

Dust mite faeces

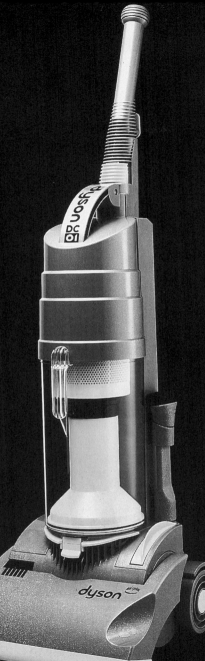

The Dyson upright model:
always perfectly balanced.

When, in 1901, the Scotsman Hubert Cecil Booth watched a newfangled dust-blowing machine in action, he was amazed at its inefficiency. Why not, he thought, reverse the process? In a single stroke, he had invented the vacuum cleaner. Today it is hard to imagine civilised life without this magnificent invention. But even the best of ideas are open to improvement.

From the beginning, vacuum cleaners have been equipped with bags to collect the dust they suck in. The tiny pores in these bags are intended to trap the dust and let air pass through. But ordinarily, after cleaning just one room, dust clogs these pores and blocks the air flow, reducing the cleaner's suction by as much as 50 percent. And these bags are certainly not known for their ease of use: they tend to tear, they're often awkward to install, and it is difficult to remove them without letting dust escape. So, reasoned British designer James Dyson, the best invention after the vacuum cleaner itself must surely be the bagless vacuum cleaner.

In 1993, he set up Dyson Appliances Ltd. and started manufacturing a revolutionary type of vacuum cleaner based on what he calls 'dual cyclone' technology. Instead of collecting dust in a bag, the Dyson appliance uses centrifugal force to spin it out of the air stream in two

The Dyson spins out large debris in the outer cyclone and finer dust in the inner cyclone, at speeds of up to 924 mph.

stages (or cyclones), at air speeds of up to 924 miles per hour — faster than the speed of sound! This system allows air to pass through the machine clean and unobstructed, so that suction remains optimal. Besides cleaning more efficiently, the Dyson removes twice as many allergens and particles from the air as conventional cleaners, providing welcome relief for asthmatics. It also avoids the problem of bad odours: the particles that cause smells are trapped away from the air stream and therefore cannot be blown back into the room.

The Dyson vacuum cleaner also represents a breakthrough in ergonomic design. It comes in two models, upright and compact. The upright model is always perfectly balanced, so when held at 45°, it feels almost weightless. And the notorious instability of cleaners when used on stairs becomes a problem of the past with the compact model, designed to 'hug' each individual step. In both models, the height of the cleaner-head adjusts automatically to the carpet or floor so that bending down to operate a dial or switch is unnecessary.

Dyson believes that a product whose form reflects and reveals its technology will 'excite the customer'; the bin in which the dust and rubbish is gathered is transparent. "You can watch the product at work and see when it's full," says Dyson.

One in five of those employed at Dyson is engaged in engineering or design activities. Dyson combines these disciplines and has invested heavily in CAD modelling machines, rapid prototyping machines, high-speed cameras and other testing equipment. The designers are involved in all aspects of product development to ensure a sound connection between form and function. "Successful products are those that are both different and better," says James Dyson. "It's the designer's job to improve the technology and rethink the entire purpose and function of the product in order to maximise performance and satisfy the customer to the highest possible degree." Dyson has clearly shown how design can deliver uniqueness and functionality, helping a company to outsell makers of more conventional products. Dyson's success is reflected in its annual turnover, which increased thirteenfold in just two years (1993-1995), with estimated turnover in 1996 of 84 million ECU.

The compact model, designed to 'hug' each step,
solves the problem of instability on stairs.

CUSTOM

Mass Production in Lots of One

ISATION

For the best part of 100 years, the basic process of industry has been the mass production and distribution of more-or-less standard goods and services. This system has been run by experts in mass communications, mass advertising, mass marketing, global design, and worldwide distribution. The most successful practitioners of mass-everything business are today's multinational corporations (MNCs); the least successful are small businesses which operate on a limited scale, or in niche markets, or for consumers they know personally.

Now that mass thinking and mass acting are out of fashion, and something called 'customisation' is in, these small firms are suddenly fashionable, too. Which is one reason why so many big firms want to be small again.

The quality quest
Although customisation is in all the headlines, it seems only a short time since we were told that *quality* was the way to win. Now quality is the beginning, not the end — a condition of entry into the market. At least quality can be measured: it means 'no faults'. And that's what we now get. We enjoy a dazzling level of quality in a vast array of products and services — from cars and courier services, to pizzas and clothes. So why are the rules changing once again?

The main reason is that quality, having become systematised, no longer differentiates products and services from each other. Consumers have become spoiled for choice among perfectly-performing products. All those quality techniques worked — the checklists, bar charts, histograms, graphs, Pareto analyses, regression and failure mode analyses, quality function deployments, scatterplots, benchmarking, and so on. Such techniques delivered value — extraordinary value, in historical terms — but once established, they basically removed pain from the consumer experience. However, these techniques have one fatal flaw: they do not deliver a direct relationship with the customer.

I was reminded of this simple truth when looking for a reliable car mechanic recently. The Yellow Pages listed thousands of them, many of whom boasted quality certificates and impressive authorisations by official-sounding bodies. But in the end I opted for two guys in a railway arch round the corner; the fact that I live one minute away is an effective incentive for them to do good-quality work. And they do. Dealing direct is the best quality assurance technique I know.

Customisation is a logical response to the evolution of mass society towards something more complex. But a return to pre-industrial modes of production is not imminent. An economy in which every product is made to order by a rugged old craftsman with an apron, sitting behind a workbench, working with ancient tools, makes an appealing advertising image — but it is a fantasy.

In the real world, customisation is a *range* of responses to new market and technological conditions. These responses include increasingly specialised products or services; flexible and targeted distribution systems; new ways of organising work that bring consumers and producers closer together; and information networks that dissolve boundaries between the firm, its suppliers, and customers.

In this chapter we look at the different approaches to customisation adopted by our profiled companies, and examine the kind of infrastructures they deploy in order to implement them.

Mass-producing customisation

The business airwaves are now filled with talk of a 'one-to-one' economy, the end of mass production, and the dawn of customisation. Management theorist Henry Mintzberg (writing in the Fall 1996 *Sloan Management Review* with his colleague Joseph Lampel) has measured the clamour: "Between 1971-1980, an average of twenty articles on customisation appeared annually; after 1990, the annual figure now averages 2,234." So customisation is now a fully-blown fad. But in the real world things are not, of course, so simple — despite a temptation to replace one extreme with another. Mintzberg and Lampel spotted the danger first: "Customization and standardization do not define alternative models... but rather, a continuum of real-world strategies."

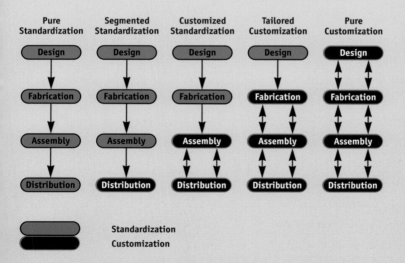

A continuum of strategies

Joseph Lampel & Henry Mintzberg, *Sloan Management Review*, Fall, 1996.

The modern economy can support quite a few 'pure customising' businesses — jewellers, tailors, cooks, gardeners — and writers. But only quite a few. A population of 5.6 billion people — soon to be ten billion — will not be fed, sheltered, clothed, kept healthy, moved around, educated, and entertained, by purely manual, one-to-one means. Neither will a post-modern mood-swing against mass society undermine the economic logic of large-scale production.

Even in capital goods, which always entail some customisation, the pressure to standardise is enormous. The number of different power plants, building systems, and railway engines continues to diminish. At the opposite extreme, in the vast software industry, a similar pressure to standardise is evident. The high cost of programming — a new computer program can involve millions of man-days of programming input — has prompted an intense search, in a field called object-oriented programming, for 'patterns' or repeatable ways of doing things.

The interesting companies profiled in this chapter do not cling proudly to nineteenth-century ways of doing things; they operate somewhere between the two extremes of standardisation and pure customisation at different points in their design, fabrication, assembly, and distribution operations. They strive to be ultra-adaptable but also to produce ultra-leanly. The exemplary technical quality of their products and services is the result of naturally close links to customers, not of enchantment with a theory of customisation.

Take the example of **Bulthaup**, a German kitchen company. You would think designing a kitchen would be a simple enough process, but not for this firm. Everything, down to the smallest detail, is scrutinised for its ergonomic efficacy, driving all sorts of tiny modifications. Bulthaup thinks about kitchens not as products, but as living environments in which people's lifestyles are changing constantly. This means that the company's kitchens have to evolve continuously, too:

materials, surfaces, storage, handles, utensils — all evolve as a result of direct input from customers about how they wish to prepare, cook, and serve food, sit, eat, talk — and even do the washing up.

This level of product innovation, variation, and responsiveness to customer needs, costs money. Bulthaup's kitchens are famously expensive. But the company urges customers to evaluate the value-for-money of their investment against time. And, as is shown by the example of **DMD**, a small Dutch producer of low-price household products, if your overheads are low, you can still afford to specialise.

A picket fence of patents
Customisation is not an engaging strategy for companies with proprietary technology. For David McMurtry, chairman of Renishaw — and of the European Design Prize jury — the economies of scale, and profits, associated with standardisation can still be exploited. "We surround our products with a thicket of patents, and prosper as the only game in town." If the thicket is penetrated by agile or weighty competitors, Renshaw simply moves on.

This strategy demands a high and continuous level of investment in costly research and development which is not feasible for most companies outside the specialised high-tech sectors. But it's the sheer speed and unpredictability of the new economy that makes the erection of legal barriers unviable as a strategy to many companies. Connie Bagley, a professor at Harvard Business School, told *Inc.*magazine (October 1996) that "in the post-Netscape world it might take 18 months to get a patent on a product that has a 12-month life cycle. By the time you get the damn thing litigated, it's meaningless." That's why, say Bagley and others, people are focusing less on proprietary technology and more on 'first-mover advantage' — the development of skills and infrastructures for continuous, rapid innovation rather than a reliance on legal firewalls.

Mass production in lots of one

True customisation — substantive, two-way interactions between suppliers and customers — resembles the economic relationships that prevailed before industrialisation; but the scale and complexity of the infrastructure that makes customisation possible in the new economy today, changes the nature of the process. Oliver Morton, in a seminal piece for *The Economist* (5 March, 1994), calls it "mass production in lots of one".

So what does it mean to design for customisation? First, customisation needs connectivity — effective communication between and among the players. In the past, the productive enterprise, whether it was one person making things to order, or a factory with a production line, was fixed. This is no longer so. As production becomes more fluid, and design technologies have started to interact with flexible manufacturing and prototyping technologies, a fairly direct informatic connection between the company and the consumer emerges, and it becomes possible to create unique objects to order.

True customisation demands that consumers be active participants in the development process, and close to the core processes of the business. This demands a new kind of infrastructure involving a flat organisation and new work processes.

Most important of all are new distribution concepts. Logistics is one of the least glamorous but most potent support systems for continuous innovation and customisation. As Martin Christopher, Britain's first professor of logistics emphasises in *The Strategy of Distribution Management,* "logistics is a bridge between demand creation and physical supply". Logistics is a much more significant economic activity and much more economically important than most of us realise. According to Christopher, the distribution sector typically accounts for one-third of Gross Domestic Product in developed economies.

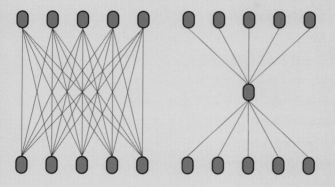

The effect of an intermediary in the marketing channel
Martin Christopher, *The Strategy of Distribution Management,* (Oxford: Butterworth-Heinemann,1986).

The relationship between logistics and customisation boils down to this: logistics makes products available. In this sense, logistics is more easily understood as an advanced form of customer service. The process of managing the movement and storage of materials, components, and finished inventory from suppliers, through the firm, and on to the customer, is a process. And a complicated one: Martin Christopher lists a staggering 22 elements of customer service (see box).

Competitive logistics: a short list of your next

tasks if you decide to compete on distribution and customer service

- frequency of delivery
- time from order to delivery
- reliability of delivery
- emergency deliveries when required
- stock availability and continuity of supply
- orders filled completely
- advice on non-availability
- convenience of placing order
- acknowledgement of order (feedback)
- accuracy of invoices
- quality of sales representation
- in-store merchandising support
- regular calls by sales representatives
- manufacturer monitoring of retail stock levels
- credit terms offered
- customer query handling
- quality of outer packaging
- well-stacked pallets
- easy-to-read use-by dates on outers
- quality of inner packaging for in-store display
- consulting on new product development
- regular review of product range.

MARTIN CHRISTOPHER, *THE STRATEGY OF DISTRIBUTION MANAGEMENT* (OXFORD: BUTTERWORTH-HEINEMANN, 1986).

...and a less-than-simple way to organise them

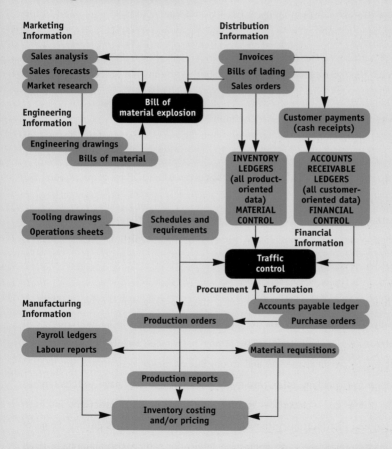

Customisation demands an integrated flow of information in the business

MARTIN CHRISTOPHER, *THE STRATEGY OF DISTRIBUTION MANAGEMENT*, (OXFORD:BUTTERWORTH-HEINEMANN, 1986).

Judging be de luxe

Relatively few companies will opt for pure customisation — but impure varieties can be extremely profitable. France's luxury goods industries are a case in point. A few decades ago, a top-class boutique in the *huitième* in Paris would subsist on the custom of perhaps 150 regular clients; today, one of Louis Vuitton's three Hong Kong shops alone might cater for that many customers off the morning flight from Osaka. During the bubble economy of the late 1980s, Vuitton's Hong Kong managers even had to install marshalling pens, complete with light refreshments, where anxious shoppers waited their turn.

In Paris today, business is booming. Any manager interested in degrees of customisation would enjoy a visit to Hermes' delightful flagship store at 24 Faubourg St. Honoré. It is filled with a cheerful, babbling, multiracial throng throughout the day, falling over each other to buy a small, exquisite but undoubtedly expensive scarf, bag, or bathmat. The atmosphere is one of exclusivity; but the objects are made by what Françoise Jollant, former design director of Louis Vuitton, calls "industrial craftsmanship"... It's a far cry from the days when a *Comtesse* might pass an elegant hour or two on a single purchase.

Hirsch, an Austrian manufacturer of watchstraps, evokes many of the sensibilities cultivated by French companies; its literature is filled with references to artisans, 230 years of tradition, ancient craft skills, straps hand-made in 60 different stages, natural materials, personal service, and so on. But on closer examination you realise that although the company offers variety, it does not actually make watchstraps to order. What it does do — cleverly — is offer 100 models in 2,000 variations and have a production and distribution system that can deliver those orders quickly. Some of these are made-to-measure — an impressive service for people with abnormally-sized wrists, but still not *true* customisation. Hirsch also has an advanced technology

Towards pure customisation

1. Fashion accessories
2. Leather goods/luggage
3. Shoes
4. Cosmetics
5. Furs
6. Clothing (excluding lingerie)
7. Watchmaking
8. Jewellery
9. Lingerie
10. Perfumes

11. Cars
12. Private jets
13. Yachts
14. Motorcycles

15. Champagne
16. Spirits
17. Wine

18. Crystalware
19. Silverware
20. Chinaware

21. Furniture
22. Household fabrics
23. Lighting
24. Upholstery

25. Catering
26. Hotels
27. Restaurants

28. Musical instruments
29. Camera/hi-fi/video/sound equipment

30. Stationery
31. Books
32. Printing

33. Smokers' paraphernalia
34. Florists
35. Bodycare products

McKinsey & Company Inc., France.

division which explores new materials and processes that deliver greater comfort, durability and adaptability to decorative finishes — hardly the stuff of a medieval workshop!

Mass luxury means big business. High financial stakes explain why the luxury sector, particularly in Europe, can present two such gloriously contradictory faces. Its glossy public image, preened and pampered by remorseless promotion, is suffused with the glow of history. Expensive brochures, classy advertising, cultural and sporting sponsorship, and legions of well-drilled lieutenants, promote the idea that these companies are the last havens on earth of quality and integrity.

I am reminded of the sublime assertion to me once, by Hermes' man in London, that "Hermes does not know the meaning of marketing." The same manager also reminded me that in respect to Hermes products, 'less is more'. I had to agree. At £3,500 upwards for one of Hermes' celebrated Grace Kelly handbags, a *lot* more.

Direct marketing is not customisation

Direct marketing is not customisation — although the big marketing agencies would have us believe as much. The social and economic changes that foster customisation do explain the recent success of direct marketing: at a time when mass advertising is ceasing to be cost-effective, targeted communications have grown strongly during the 1990s. But 'direct' here is one-way direct: it overwhelmingly focuses on the generation and exploitation of sales leads, and is seldom a source of serious input to product development. Although sales people may talk about customers, most marketing people talk about sales *figures*. To them, the bottom line is that 'customers' are basically just data.

The structure and processes of direct marketing speak for themselves. In America, in 1995, the average citizen received 950 pieces of direct mail. Quantities in Europe are lower — the UK household figure is 90, for example — but however 'targeted' these bits of paper might have become, they are *one-way* communications. The language of the direct marketeers gives the game away, too: "We are moving from broadcast to broadcapture," says one such, John Orsmond, in the *Financial Times* (28 June, 1995); "every service request, every complaint, every sales enquiry, and every order, can help fuel the database."

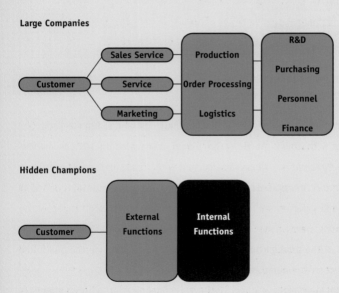

Hierarchies vis-à-vis the customer in large companies and the Hidden Champions
HERMANN SIMON, *HIDDEN CHAMPIONS*, (HARVARD BUSINESS SCHOOL PRESS, 1996).

Customers	86.7%
Trade Fairs	68.0%
Competitors	60.7%
Trade Journals	48.7%
Market Surveys	36.0%
Suppliers	35.3%
Patent Offices	34.0%
Universities	33.3%
Research Institutes	24.7%
Technology Transfer Agencies	16.0%
Trade Associations	14.0%
Data Banks	14.0%
Congresses	11.3%
Consultants	6.0%
Banks	5.3%
Chambers of Commerce	4.7%
Newspapers	4.7%

Importance of sources of information

HERMANN SIMON, *HIDDEN CHAMPIONS*, (HARVARD BUSINESS SCHOOL PRESS, 1996).

'Fuelling the database' may well pile up facts about customers, but it is not the same as interacting with them. As Hermann Simon discovered in his fascinating analysis of *Hidden Champions,* "Close interaction with customers requires direct distribution, a flat and integrated organisation, and extensive contact between customers and non-sales personnel." Dumping direct mailshots through the door, or 'fuelling the database', meets none of these criteria; such activities do nothing to enhance the quality of the product being sold, and nothing to enhance the quality of the relationship between the company and its customers.

One company that does achieve direct, two-way communication with its clients is **Vitra**, a manufacturer of high-end furniture. Vitra is legendary in Europe for its skill at attracting, and keeping, the interest and attention of the architects who specify office furniture for their clients. Nothing Vitra does is anonymous. Its owner, Rolf Fehlbaum, hires the world's most famous architects to design 'antenna buildings' on his company's campus near Basle. These designer-follies, which include a chair museum and a fire station, attract the attention of the world's architectural media and enjoy massive coverage. Thousands of architects and architecture students make their way to Weil am Rhein to see them. The exercise is not just about marketing the Vitra name; Fehlbaum enjoys the company of architects (his customers) and has genuine enthusiasm for innovation. His design patronage cleverly enables him to mix with architects on equal terms; he is a client more than a salesman.

A similar cosiness between the company and its clients characterises **Burkhardt Leitner**, a manufacturer of exhibition systems (also from Germany). Every communication by the company — its brochures, its annual report, the clothes worn by its managers, its advertising, and certainly the design of its products — mimic the aesthetic preferences and visual language of the architects and designers who specify or order Leitner's systems for clients. There is no 'we' and 'they' — just 'us'. The same goes for the Spanish company **Amat**, which emphasises its attention to craft processes and an early tradition of metalworking, and for **Cifial**, in Portugal, which somehow prospers in the tough building products market.

Customisation: it bothers brands

If the differences between direct marketing and customisation are distinct, the gap with brand-based marketing is even wider. Brands are based on values, not on the material quality of products or services. As writer Dennis Hayes puts it, "Brands are constructed according to a marketing sociology that treats consumers as an amalgam of lifestyle constructs; it is informed by assumptions about the social values, beliefs, fantasies, and dreams of consumers which are attached to commodities through the medium of advertising." The thing is that consumers are now wise — and increasingly hostile — to these complex and expensive communications. Most customers today want performance and difference — but they do *not* want to pay for a barrage of communication. The closer customers get to suppliers, the less interested they are likely to be in paying good money for a 'concept'.

A sea change is certainly evident in academic and consulting circles. Brady and Davis, in a famously vitriolic article in the *McKinsey Quarterly,* criticised the value of ever more costly brand advertising, "which often dwells on seemingly irrelevant points of difference"; of promotions "which are often just a fancy name for cost-cutting"; and of large marketing departments, which, far from being an asset, "are often a millstone around an organisation's neck".

Most marketing professionals are structurally isolated from the trend towards customisation. A survey by the British Chartered Institute of Marketing in 1994 found that only a quarter of marketing departments in larger companies were responsible for customer service, and only 31 percent were involved in quality programmes.

Designing customisation

Flat organisations, new distribution channels, and close contact between customers and producers are processes, and these processes have to be designed. Historically, manufacturing effectiveness has been viewed in terms of the physical flows of materials... but viewing manufacturing in terms of information flows will be central over the next decade. Customisation will be delivered, to varying degrees, by information systems that support adaptive production. The result will be evident in the product — but the means will be achieved by the continued move away from matter to service.

Customisation checklist

- Connectivity among all players
- Consumers active participants in development processes
- Technologies and processes are adaptive
- Flat organisation; few steps between supplier and user
- Fast, effective service, not price
- Integrated operational management to optimise processes
- Design and manufacturing know-how
- Close mesh with suppliers
- Smart distribution and logistics
- Retail alternatives to reduce transaction costs
- Time-based skills

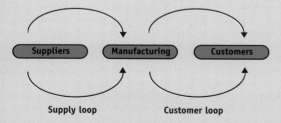

Supply loop   Customer loop

Supply and customer loops in the information system

HERMANN SIMON, *HIDDEN CHAMPIONS*, (HARVARD BUSINESS SCHOOL PRESS, 1996).

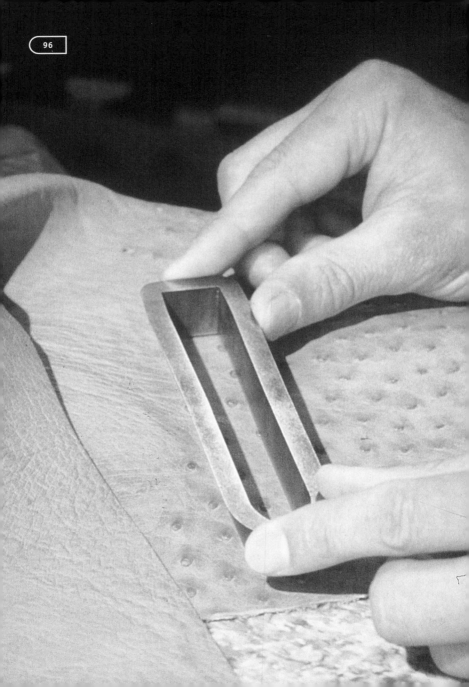

TRADITION IN AN INSTANT

Watchstraps

Hirsch "It is to be hoped," wrote a Hamburg professor in the 1920s, "that the modern fad for wearing a timepiece on the wrist — the part of the body that is not only the most mobile but is also subject to the greatest fluctuations in temperature — will soon disappear!" The trend stuck, of course, and Hirsch, the Austrian manufacturer of watchstraps, has revolutionised the market, turning what was once an insignificant 'add-on' into a valued product in its own right, and providing millions with a subtle way to express individual character and style.

Hirsch has given the strap totally new functional and aesthetic characteristics by introducing, for instance, the world's first waterproof leather watchstrap and the world's first allergy-free strap. By providing original straps for major brands of watches, Hirsch also exerts considerable influence on fashion in this field.

The company was founded in 1765 by master tanner Johannes Franz Hirsch, and traditionally made only leather watchstraps. But by 1990, when the 100 millionth Hirsch watchstrap was produced, 15 million were made of plastic. And these are no

ordinary plastic straps: Hirsch's Advanced Technology Division has developed and patented a special technology called Skinline, which enables the application of individual colour-printed designs on thermo-plastic core materials. This film protects and finishes the high-grade plastic core, resulting in a scratch and abrasion-resistant surface.

Despite these developments, leather remains Hirsch's primary material; its leather collection contains 100 models in no fewer than 2,000 variations. Drawing on its long experience in leather crafting, the firm developed its Artisanal line, an exclusive range combining traditional craftsmanship — each strap is made by hand in 60 steps — with sophisticated logistics and distribution methods, ensuring that each special request can be produced and delivered in a matter of days.

An Artisanal watchstrap is clearly intended as a form of personal expression. "Owners of valuable and unique watches expect nothing less from their straps," says Hermann Hirsch, the company's president. "We guarantee an infinite choice of models and styles. No wish is too grand. And the more unusual the request, the more enthusiastically our team sets about fulfilling it."

Two hundred and thirty years of traditional skills, broad insight into the functionality and aesthetics people want, and a pursuit of quality that has led to the award of the only ISO 9001 certificate in the watchstrap business, all justify Hirsch's position as market leader with a timeless product in a time-bound world.

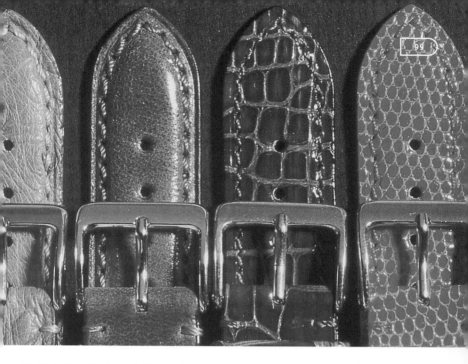

Hirsch's leather watchstrap collection contains 100 models in no fewer than 2,000 variations.

Hirsch makes extensive use of automation which means that personnel can deal with individual requests in minute detail.

LIMITED INGREDIENTS, INFINITE VARIETY

Exhibition Systems

Burkhardt Leitner

The game of Spillikins — or Pick-Up-Sticks — is one that requires precision and control. Players must try to remove a single match from a chaotic heap without dislodging any of the others. Featured in the logo of Burkhardt Leitner constructiv, Spillikins symbolises the company's philosophy and approach to problem-solving. "Each customer that comes to us, brings along a bundle of questions, problems, and demands, and drops them on our desk," says the company's founder, Burkhardt Leitner. "Step by step, we then try to sort them out, finding order in chaos and providing enlightening solutions."

This young German company develops and produces exhibition and display systems, basing its design approach on the functionalist tradition of the Bauhaus. It was established in 1993 by a man who founded his first, very successful company at the tender age of 21. Why start again? "I was curious," Leitner says; "I wanted greater freedom to create and develop new ideas."

Over the past three years, Leitner's new company has introduced ten separate systems onto the market, each incorporating high-quality materials and a flexible modular structure. They consist of prefabricated elements that can be easily assembled to create countless variations of exhibition spaces. The systems' simplicity of form and function belie the complexity of the constructions they enable. Through the ingenious use of specially developed links and hinges, they can be tailored to each customer's exact wishes. "Each time, the result is unique," says Leitner, who playfully compares the modular principle of his system with Chinese cuisine, which manages to conjure up an infinite variety of dishes from a limited number of ingredients.

Leitner's products range from the impressive Max system, for exhibiting large-scale objects, to the compact and portable Joker system, which comes with a specially designed suitcase-on-wheels so that it can be transported and assembled anywhere.

"Design," says Leitner, "forms the foundation of the company, and is linked directly to all other business activities." When a new product is being developed, designers, marketers, product managers, buyers, and planners sit down together to work out the strategy to be followed. "Our approach is one of calm, clear analysis," says Leitner. He views his systems as a means to an end: clear-cut, practical, and refined — "with just as much design as is needed, no more and no less."

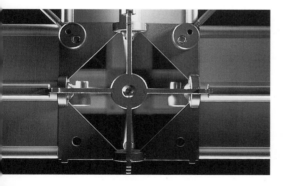

The stainless steel connectors and aluminium supports of Burkhardt Leitner's Pila system.

The compact and portable Joker system comes with a suitcase-on-wheels.

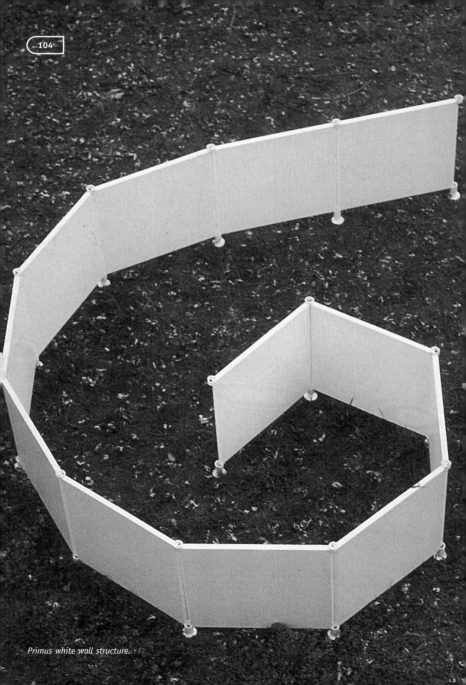

Primus white wall structure.

Max beechwood wall with ceiling trellis.

Junior shelving system.

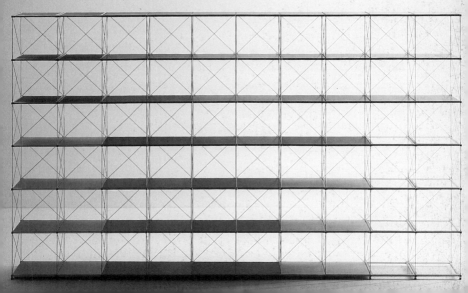

BACK TO THE KITCHEN

Winner '97!

Kitchens

Bulthaup

The English cookery writer Elizabeth David once remarked that the kitchen should be "the most comforting and comfortable room in the house". Traditionally a space of warmth, cosiness, and appetising smells, the concept of the 'family kitchen' went out of style earlier this century, and the efficient 'fast food factory' became the norm. The German company Bulthaup has tracked and influenced the changing cultural implications of the kitchen for 30 years. Today, Bulthaup is at the forefront of those aiming to make the kitchen once again the heart of the home.

The company's philosophy is one of continuous innovation, combining insight into changing trends, demands, and lifestyles with the latest technological advances. Following its pioneering 1982 study, Kitchen for Living, Bulthaup set about 're-installing people' in the kitchen. Having built up a distinguished reputation as a manufacturer of high-quality kitchens, Bulthaup tackled this objective in a number of ways.

First, it re-examined the ergonomics of the kitchen, re-adjusting work top heights to provide maximum comfort while cooking. It introduced the new (and subsequently much-imitated) concept of the 'food preparation island' and the stainless steel 'kitchen workbench'. Its products are designed to reflect higher, almost professional standards in terms of functionality and appearance, knowing that people who take their work seriously also tend to regard their hobbies — including cooking — in the same way.

Second, the company brought back natural, high-quality materials. Chipboard, plastic and enamel were replaced by natural and laminated wood, stainless steel, aluminium, granite, and glass. "The aesthetic aspect of natural materials is also important," says Günther Schertel, one of Bulthaup's directors. "The wood grain, for example, gives immense vitality and creates a natural environment which mellows pleasingly over time."

The launch of Bulthaup's System 25 in 1992 was an important milestone. This new design incorporated the latest insights into changing attitudes, habits, and tastes. The result was a comprehensive, flexible system of interchangeable modules, produced in a wide spectrum of colours and materials. Based on a 25 millimetre grid, the system can be customised to fit successfully into the most awkwardly shaped spaces. "It's an unfortunate fact that most kitchens are far from ideal when it comes to the shape of the space available," says Schertel. "We just have to make sure our systems are versatile enough to cope with that."

More recently, in 1994, Bulthaup introduced a range of kitchen tables, benches and chairs, with an emphasis on ergonomics, comfort, and quality of materials that matches that of the company's kitchens. With these products, the social function of the Bulthaup kitchen comes more fully into its own.

Bulthaup accepts that the market for its kitchens is limited. "We've adopted a selective marketing strategy, aiming at high-income, well-educated, family-oriented people who are seriously into cooking as a hobby," says Schertel. "These are people who are after quality and authenticity in their lives on many levels. We aim to provide that authenticity by concentrating on the essentials, both technological and cultural — all of which create a timelessness which is highly appealing to those whose working lives are lived in the 'now'."

Germany is the world's largest single market for expensive kitchens, with total sales of 1.2 billion ECU a year. This makes Germany's market six times larger than the US market for expensive kitchens, after adjusting for differences in population.

FORBES, VOL. 156, NO. 4, AUGUST 14, 1995.

A recent survey found that **27.9%** of consumer panellists are doing more cooking at home than 2 years ago and **50%** are doing the same amount. About **21.4%** are cooking less. Approximately **24.8%** of consumer panellists said that frozen convenience products enable them to eat at home more often, while refrigerated convenience products were cited by **34.7%**.

FROZEN FOOD AGE, VOL. 44, ISSUE 6, JANUARY 1996.

Enrollments in non-professional cooking schools are up over 50% since 1990, according to Dorlene Kaplan, author of The Guide to Cooking Schools. Kaplan, who reports sales of her book have quintupled since its first printing in 1989, says there are more than 700 high-quality cooking schools in the US now, and estimates they take in roughly 1.5 million pupils a year.

SUZANNE OLIVER, 'LET'S MAKE SAUSAGE TOGETHER', FORBES, VOL. 155, NO. 6, MARCH 13, 1995.

1962–1992

Bulthaup's products are designed to reflect almost professional standards in terms of functionality and appearance.

The Vitra Design Museum contains one of the most extensive collections of modern furniture with more than 2,000 objects.

FOR YOUR SITTING PLEASURE

Winner '94!

Design Chairs

Vitra Established in 1950, Vitra is now a well-known and successful German manufacturer of high-quality, high-design furniture for offices, the public sector and the home market. Its products are developed through collaborations between famous designers and a 30-person in-house product development team. By commissioning the best creative talents from different countries and cultures, the company has produced a continuous stream of 'classics'. The essence of Vitra is its talent for creating the right climate — the working spirit — to inspire great achievements from such personalities.

Vitra still produces many of the chairs that Charles and Ray Eames designed in the fifties and sixties. "The Eames' works have inspired our design understanding like no other," says Rolf Fehlbaum, managing director of Vitra. In the 1960s, the company worked closely with Verner Panton, a collaboration which resulted in the world-famous plastic Panton chair. Since the late 1970s, Vitra has worked with Mario Bellini, who created office furniture inspired by the domestic world rather than the machine-filled office environment.

The 1980s saw Vitra embark on a quest for improved office seating. The company began extensive experimentation with furniture designers Antonio Citterio, Philippe Starck, Borek Sipek, Frank Gehry and others. Gehry's cardboard chair, Little Beaver, came out in 1987. Citterio's designs for office chairs brought new aesthetics to the office at a time when office chairs were becoming more luxurious, colourful, and decorative. He set a new reductive trend, using simple geometry and clearly visible technology. Philippe Starck designed Vitra's famous Louis 20 stacking chair, a typical mix of Starck's freshness and elegance with Vitra's technological and ergonomic know-how. Borek Sipek, a romantic among contemporary designers, showed that office furniture does not have to be cold, spartan and rational; that 'emotion' does not exclude function.

In the 1990s, Vitra began to focus on 'the office of the future'. In association with Ettore Sottsass, Andrea Branzi, and Michele de Lucchi, Vitra embarked on the project Citizen Office to undertake a critical study of the office world and create scenarios that are more conducive to creative work and cooperation. The confinement and dullness of today's office, they say, does not correspond to the reality of human thought and behaviour. Their proposals for new office furniture break through the strict rationale of the modern office. Recently, Vitra started working with Alberto Meda, the first result of which is the Meda chair, presented in 1996.

Vitra's deep commitment to design extends beyond its products to its architectural and cultural philosophy. Its complex of buildings in Weil am Rhein include various contributions by noted architects, including Grimshaw, Gehry, Ando, Siza, and Hadid.

The Vitra Design Museum, an initiative of the company, was designed by Frank Gehry and opened in Weil am Rhein in 1989 as an independent institution. The search for early works by Charles and Ray Eames formed the beginning of the collection. The museum now contains one of the most extensive collections of modern furniture with more than 2,000 objects. It regularly loans its furniture to other museums for exhibitions and attracts up to 50,000 visitors each year.

The chair is one of humankind's oldest products. It is surely a token of Vitra's remarkable achievement that in the half century of its existence it has managed to find new 'classics' in such a well-worked field. ▶

The works of Charles and Ray Eames have inspired Vitra's design understanding as no other.

A TOLEDO TRADITION: FROM SWORDS TO CHAIRS

Aluminium Chairs

Amat The medieval town of Toledo, one of the most tangible expressions of Spain's long and rich cultural tradition, provides a fitting name for one of Spain's most notable design successes of recent decades: the Toledo chair, designed by Jorge Pensi and manufactured by Amat of Barcelona, is the first outdoor chair to be made of anodised cast aluminium, using a new polymerisation technique to achieve its perfect finish. Since its introduction in 1988, the chair has won numerous awards, and sells worldwide.

In the ancient world, the city of Toledo was renowned for its fine swords; Amat's simple and elegant aluminium chair represents a modern continuation of that early metalworking tradition. With its clean lines, its simple, lightweight construction, and its practical convenience, the Toledo chair has become a legend in its own lifetime, symbolising the importance of Spanish industry and design in the world market.

The path that led to this happy state of affairs was far from easy, however. Amat was founded in 1944 as a small family business specialising in the manufacture and marketing of metal furniture, mainly for the contract market. But after 40 years of operating as a traditional furniture company, Amat made a strategic decision in 1984 to bring design to the forefront of its activities, where it would play a key role in all processes and decisions. "Persistence and determination were required to counteract traditional thinking at first," says Conrad Amat, the company's managing director, "but the effort has been well worthwhile. Introducing new design products alongside our existing product range and developing our corporate image have led to improvements throughout the company."

Amat's R&D department now devotes special attention to the possibilities offered by new materials, technologies, and production techniques in view of market trends. The company always has several projects under consideration simultaneously, and is linked to some 15 external design studios, ensuring the continuous input of new ideas.

Amat's decision to adopt design as a guiding principle has paid rich dividends: the company has more than doubled its exports since 1990. "We no longer talk of design as an objective," says Conrad Amat, "we think of it as a vocation."

The Toledo chair and table, designed by Jorge Pensi, are made of anodised cast aluminium: a world first.

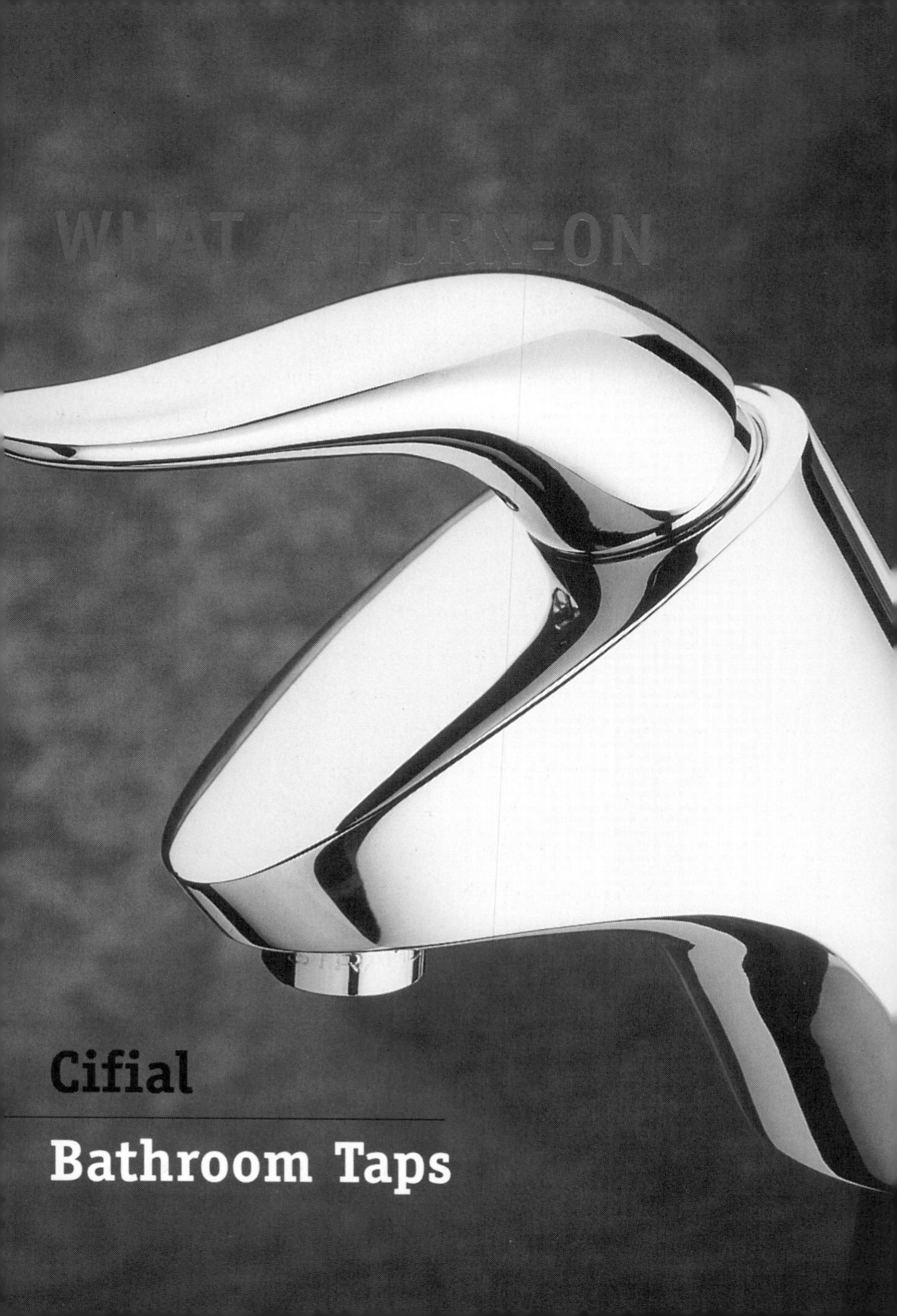

WHAT A TURN-ON

Cifial

Bathroom Taps

When Cifial won the prestigious Design for Industry prize in Portugal in 1996, the judges were not just acknowledging the quality of the company's products; their thinking was equally influenced by the tough environment in which this 58-year-old company operates. Few industries are tougher than the building industry when it comes to cost control, sticking to old ways of doing things, and suspicion of fancy notions. Despite this inhospitable environment, Cifial has managed to invest in new ideas and technologies more or less continuously since its inception in 1928. The result is a product range that holds its own even in highly competitive export markets such as Germany, France, and the United Kingdom. From this solid base, the Portuguese company is now exporting to the United States and, using an important foothold in Macau, East Asia.

"Innovation is the basis of our strategy," says Cifial's managing director Ludgero Marques. "Our aim is to be at least national market leader in taps and bathroom accessories, brass fittings, and security locks. These are extremely demanding markets from a technical and functional point of view — and we can only keep ahead by continuous investment in research and design." Cifial has invested heavily in computer-aided design and automated manufacturing systems, and upgrades the training of its 470 employees regularly, in order to ensure that new ideas are transferred rapidly into marketable products. Cifial has developed specific expertise in brass die-casting at low pressure; it also places special emphasis on the achievement of high-quality surface finishes using physical vapour deposition (PVD) techniques.

"Design is an essential part of the innovation process for us," says Marques, "because although we have several areas of special technical expertise, that expertise only helps us compete when it is embodied in products that our customers, who in general are very demanding, will find desirable."

DMD
_____

Household and Interior Products

THE MISSING LINK

In the Netherlands, most of which is ten feet below sea level, being dry is more than a matter of comfort: it denotes the difference between life and death. So it is surprising to hear, in the case of a new collection of household objects called Droog Design — literally 'dry design' — that "saleability and producability are never a criterion for selection". Even more surprising is the enthusiasm with which Teake Bulstra, whose company DMD produces objects with the Droog Design label, praises "wayward Dutch designs for which there is hardly any industrial basis".

But DMD — it stands for Development, Manufacturing, Distribution — reckons there is a significant niche market internationally for the out-of-the-ordinary household artefacts which Dutch designers dream up with such flair. It's not a big market — DMD turned over less than one million ECU in 1995 — but it is widely spread. The five-strong company trades with most European countries, and the critical success of a recent exhibiton at the Museum of Modern Art in New York has now opened up the North American market, too.

In the new economy there is undoubtedly a need for new kinds of intermediary connnections between independent designers, networks of small production units, various physical and virtual distribution channels, and customers. Whether the international avant garde is an economically viable niche for any company outside rich and rather pampered Holland is a moot point. But one thing is certain: no other finalist in the European Design Prize is like DMD, which imposes "no restrictions... all products are born purely from the designer's personal perspective".

DMD can also be seen as a small research lab. Its recent activities include experiments in new uses for synthetic fibres, in collaboration with the aviation and space laboratory of the prestigious Delft University.

DMD's series of Droog Design soft vases.

URBAN

EQUIP

"Duisberg likes experimenters... there's room here for unconventional thinking." This advertisement, in a recent edition of the *Far Eastern Economic Review*, featured the English architect Sir Norman Foster set against the backdrop of a new high-tech building. Who has heard of Duisberg? Not many people, even in Europe, it has to be said. And that's the point. As a small provincial German town, with a tradition of small to medium-scale engineering enterprises, a good local beer, and not much else, Duisberg is unexceptional. But the city felt a strong urge to get onto the international map — which is why it commissioned an expensive building from Foster and then advertised the fact in an international business magazine.

The reason for this urban self-promotion is a new but intense phenomenon: competition between cities. Investment, jobs, and prosperity have become so 'fluid' and mobile that old cities are competing against new ones, and new ones are competing against each other. In Europe, an estimated 300 smaller cities and regions are in a race for investment and jobs; a similar situation exists in the USA, where the movement of people and capital from East to West, and from North to South, has unleashed a frenzy of competition among obscure towns with names like Manchester-Nassau, West Palm Beach, Raleigh-Durham, Portsmouth, Huntsville. These 'edge cities'

Tools for competing cities

MENT

Glasgow's competitors: a league table of cities

Primary	Secondary (American)	Secondary (European)
Amsterdam	**1** Baltimore	Dortmund/Düsseldorf
Antwerp	Boston	Duisberg
Barcelona	New York	Cologne
Birmingham	Pittsburgh	Liverpool
Bremen	**2** Dallas	Paris
Essen	Indianapolis	Rotterdam
Hamburg	St Louis	
Lille	St Paul	
Lyons	Seattle	
Manchester	Vancouver	
Marseilles	**3** Chattanooga	
Milano	Denver	
Napoli	Louisville	
Torino	Portland, Maine	
Valencia	Richmond	
	Salt Lake City	
	San Antonio	
	Tampa	
	Tulsa	

Glasgow's marketing strategy clearly identifies and ranks its European competitors — and also keeps an eye on comparable US cities

GLASGOW DEVELOPMENT AGENCY.

promote themselves as the latest 'hot spot' and constantly jockey for position in league tables. A league higher, and internationally, 40-50 medium-sized cities of one million or more people see each other as competitors. And that's quite apart from the better publicised rivalry between the financial centres of London, Frankfurt, New York, and Tokyo. The smaller, younger pretenders may indeed be fighting hard for market share, but many of the world's big capital cities, after a period of defeatism, have renewed self-confidence and are gearing up for a period of 're-densification' and renewal.

All these cities are committed to continuous investment in the hard and soft aspects of their urban infrastructures: showpiece 'antenna buildings'; transport and information systems; cultural buildings and infrastructures; small items of urban equipment. Each wants to be different, smarter, first. This chapter is about the context for a rapid growth of innovation in urban design at all levels; it is followed by case studies about one group of firms — those in the urban equipment market — and how they use design to compete.

Strange attractors
Historically, the success and prominence of cities and regions was economically determined: some cities were the nexus of trade routes, some had ports; others were noted for the exploitation of nearby raw materials, or a tradition of artisanal skills; some developed because they were easy to defend militarily. All this appeared to change during the 1980s and early 1990s with the advent of globalisation. A perception grew that economic power was less and less rooted in a *place*. Investor pressure, interacting with rapid flows of capital, forced companies constantly to move production around in search of low-cost materials and cheap labour. Whole countries, like Mexico, could be denuded of investment capital overnight.

As competition between cities grew, cities embraced the concept of marketing, and in extreme cases began to think about themselves as brands. At first, many cities were persuaded that communications alone might help them succeed; they acquired logos, slogans and corporate identities, many of them, to put it mildly, unimaginative: "Glasgow's Miles Better", "EuroLille", and the like. Although advertising and design consultants did good business peddling these surface treatments, city fathers soon realised that communication campaigns alone were ineffective unless they were accompanied by genuine improvements to the 'product'.

Civic leaders proceeded to evaluate more seriously the features which really mattered to inward investors: the local economic and political situation; the availability of financial incentives; their particular location and physical communications; telecommunications infrastructures; the quality of the labour force; and the availablility of education and training to upgrade it. Cities also looked afresh at the quality of life, and began to re-assess the natural environment and local cultural activity as important competitive assets.

Cities discovered that different types of companies value different combinations of these factors. One report, *Regions of the new Europe,* drew up a shortlist of the regions to which a hypothetical company, planning to locate a Research & Development centre in Europe, might choose to go. The researchers looked at the size and quality of the Research & Development sector, at skill levels, transport and telecommunication links, and at geographical location, before coming up with a list of 16 economic regions (see box). The list, which would be different for other kinds of businesses, emphasises the complexity of the task facing urban renewers.

The ideal location of a Research and Development centre

Emphasis is given to the size and quality of the R&D sector, skill levels, reasonable international transport and telecommunication links, and a relatively central location.

- Bavaria, Germany
- Centre East, France
- Denmark
- East Anglia, UK
- Flanders, Belgium
- Ile de France, France
- Lombardy, Italy
- Mediterranean France
- North Rhine Westphalia, Germany
- Scotland, UK
- South East England, UK
- Stockholm, Sweden
- North East Switzerland
- Vienna, Austria
- Wallonia, Belgium
- West Netherlands

ERNST & YOUNG, *REGIONS OF THE NEW EUROPE*, 1995.

Cultural infrastrucure The cultural identity of a place is another important factor for mobile companies. Which makes recent signs of a resurgence of ancient cultural-economic entities all the more fascinating. The Hanseatic League, for example — originally a 12th-century alliance of entrepreneurs and traders which dominated trade in Northern Europe between 1350 to 1450 — has been re-invented as Hanze Expo. The mission of Hanze Expo, a grouping of cities and trading entrepreneurs, is to link what is known as the Baltic Rim (St Petersburg, Tallinn, Riga, Rostock) to Northern Germany and Holland. Then there is the "Heidi Line", a trade promotion effort based on ancient trading routes from Munich through Switzerland, down through France to Barcelona and on to Madrid. Another example: 17 Spanish cities were made capitals of new (and sometimes invented) regions as a device to help them market 'culturally specific tourism'. (Tourism is now the world's fourth largest industry and its largest single employer).

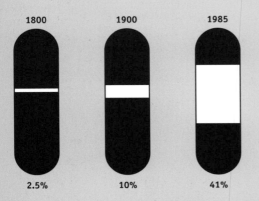

1800   1900   1985

2.5%   10%   41%

Urbanisation: Percentage of world population living in cities
PONTING.

1800	20
1900	160
1985	2250

Urbanisation: Number of people living in cities (millions)
PONTING.

1800	9
1900	27
1985	230

Urbanisation: Number of cities with population over 1 million
PONTING.

The search for tourist business did not just stimulate a rediscovery of ancient political and cultural ties; but cultural building projects like museums and art centres also became popular as a means of enhancing the 'soft' aspects of a city's resources during the 1980s. France created a *Direction du Développement Culturel* to make cultural development agreements with individual municipalities; Brest, Grenoble, and Bordeaux spent 15-20 percent of their budgets on architectural and public spaces. In Holland, the new Groninger Museum — a Dutch nomination for the European Design Prize — was intended explicitly to promote this regional city as a tourist destination and centre of cultural, economic, and administrative activity.

The success or failure of these ambitious programmes — versions of which were repeated throughout much of Europe — is hard to judge: many of them were postponed or cancelled outright as the worst recession for decades ravaged much of the European economy during the early 1990s. A similar pattern was evident in Japan. But, on balance, the consensus — in Europe at least — is that these cultural engineering strategies were a worthwhile investment.

Place still matters

The context for competition between cities continues to change at extraordinary speed. Cities face new challenges as the distance between the producers of products or services, and their users, shrinks. Sophisticated distribution and logistics systems, computer-integrated manufacturing and design, new materials, and direct marketing have changed fundamentally what it means to design, produce, distribute, or sell a product or service.

The transformation of business processes means that a good geographical location does not always carry as much weight as it once did. But place still matters. Location is one more edge that smart entrepreneurs can capitalise on.

So what are the new competitive features of a city? In her influential book *World Class*, Harvard University professor Elizabeth Moss Kantor says they are built around a golden triumvirate of world-class resources: "concepts, competence, and connections". Cities, she argues, should develop these three assets to link their local population to the global economy. They should aspire to be a place where new ideas can be generated by interactions among a variety of disciplines and cultures; to be a place where some production skills are concentrated; and above all, to be a place which, if it does not possess a skill or competency itself, has links to a place which does.

Place versus space

For that to happen, two things are needed. People must want to stay in your city, rather than in someone else's; but good transport links are also important.

Airports, for example, have replaced Central Business Districts as the epicentre of office development in many towns. Virtual corporations are big users of airports. The growing amount of business carried out across national boundaries has fuelled demand for meeting rooms, exhibition and showroom facilities, business centres, and other non-travel-specific facilities — inside, next to, under, and on top of, most new airports. Among literally thousands of projects to upgrade or build new airports around the world, a large majority involve the development of office, meeting, exhibition, and trade facilities — many of which will be used by people who never fly. The Spanish furniture company **Oken**, for example, is doing fantastic business in big airports providing seating systems!

The problem for many regions is that there are going to be too many airports — and airports are rapidly becoming unattractive to sophisticated citizens of the information economy. Quite apart from the sheer pressure of crowds, security issues make it less and less comfortable to be there. The Swedish company **Gunnebo** was nominated for the European Design Prize because its security and access control hardware is beautifully made — but the psychological pressure remains intense.

In his book *The Fall of Public Man*, the American writer Richard Sennett quotes in horror a planner who described his local airport as a "traffic-flow-support-nexus". "For 100 years and more," writes Sennett, "we have seen that when public space becomes

Factor	%
Easy access to markets, customers or clients	60%
Quality of telecommunications	59%
Quality of transport infrastructure	57%
Cost and availability of staff	35%
Gov. tax policies and availability of fin. incentives	30%
Availability of office space	27%
Value for money of space	22%
Languages spoken	17%
Quality of life for employees	14%

Importance of business location factors, in % of all respondents
HEALY & BAKER'S SURVEY 'EUROPEAN REAL ESTATE MONITOR 1990'.

a derivative of movement, it loses any independent experiential meaning of its own. On the most physical level, these environments of pure movement prompt people to think of the public domain as meaningless... It is catatonic space."

The contradiction is this: as communications improve, more and more people will choose to travel less and less — at least for work. There are already signs, such as a plateauing of business travel, that workers in the new economy will choose to avoid these 'environments of pure movement' as much as possible. Forty million Americans now work at home using computers. These teleworkers will increasingly choose to live in places that afford the most pleasant facilities for themselves and their families. The mass exodus of Americans from Southern California to places like Phoenix and Montana is evidence of this trend. Regional towns and cities are discovering that the way to attract high-income families and businesses is to rediscover the traditional planning values like 'community' and 'comfort' — in combination with investments in state-of-the-art telecommunications infrastructures.

In transport, as in other sectors, the role of IT is likely to be symbiotic, more than it is revolutionary; it complements and multiplies journeys at least as much as it replaces them. Rather than fantasise about a car-free world in which we all sit at home in front of computers, a sensible strategy will attend to practical ways of making existing cities more habitable and easier to use.

Semiotic pollution
Countless modern writers have described the alienation people feel in modern cities. Psychologists have discovered a reason for it: having a clear mental picture of an environment contributes to one's mental well-being, and such clear pictures are often absent in modern cities. They are hard to 'read', and that makes people feel uneasy.

There are both physical and perceptual ways in which cities can be made more comfortable. Architects, having picked up these distress signals from alienated citizens, have been trying for some time to make buildings physically more 'transparent'. The Dutch company **Octatube** has made their job a good deal easier by developing glass wall systems that enable buildings to be radically demassified.

Perceptually, there are different ways to read and locate yourself within a city. In some ideal situations, like Paris or Manhattan, you can read the streets directly: when they are organised on a grid or around huge boulevards, it's usually easy to get oriented. If the plan itself orients the visitor, it is not necessary to add on complicated signs and information systems. In other cases, changing patterns of trade, the rise and fall of different economic interests, and the impact of new technologies on mobility and communications render the shape and processes of cities ever more complex. In cities like London, which grew out of an agglomeration of villages, and which are now overlaid with increasingly dense traffic and pedestrian circulation systems, no obvious grand plan is visible at street level, and you need a map — or a sign. Our increasingly mobile and culturally jumbled world has created a strong market for signs whose meanings are universally understood. **Daisalux**, a Spanish company, is among a throng of suppliers developing universal sign languages for use in public spaces.

In other words, a city does not just speak through its hardware. A multimedia sea of business and commercial information plays an important role in the way we experience a place. Posters; signs; bumper stickers; shop windows; neon displays; slogans on t-shirts, hats, and trainers; discarded packaging; carrier bags; sales messages on vehicles; billboards; newspapers in the gutter; radio commercials blaring out of cars; logo-covered dirigibles; junkmail under windscreen wipers; old men carrying sandwich boards; newspaper vendors wearing lapel buttons; leaflets sticking out of letter boxes; the ubiquitous Big Mac cartons.

These layers of information are barely touched in planning or architecture schools, and receive insufficient design attention from the city fathers — except as the 'trash' problem — even though ordinary people frequently complain about this 'semiotic pollution'. Occasionally people measure it. When he was about to start advertising Absolut Vodka in New York a few years ago, its importer decided to analyse the 'media environment' surrounding the typical yuppie vodka drinker in Manhattan. Researchers set out to measure the quantity and type of commercial messages to which a typical consumer was exposed. On the first morning of the first day, they lost count when the total for most subjects shot over the 400 mark. That's 1,000 or more messages a day.

Hardware matters — but it's 'soft', too

Planning and information strategies for our cities will continue to evolve: the re-design of both hard and soft infrastructures is a continuous process, subject to changing demands. But as Mies van de Rohe pointed out, "God is in the details". The debate will rage forever about the design of public space and large buildings — but nobody disagrees that a city's small hardware can always be improved. These small, mundane *things* probably influence our feelings about a city as much as the big spaces and buildings do, but subliminally. The children's playground equipment sold by **Kompan** in more than 40 countries is a good example; so are the paving systems and concrete benches made by **Escofet**, another small company that has made a big contribution to the success of Barcelona, a place which is lifting itself up to become one of the smartest cities in Europe.

Hardware matters, too:

- Interchanges, stations, stops and ranks
- Roadmarkings, bollards, kerbstones, bins
- Flags, banners, landmarks, icons
- Stairs, lifts, trolleys, bannisters
- Signs, nameplates, leaflets, notices
- Doors, gates, windows, entrances
- Streetlamps, floodlights, information and warning signs
- Play equipment, parking meters, fire hydrants
- Doorbells, knockers, letterboxes, mats
- Shelters to dart between; covered arcades to loiter in; awnings to stand under
- Chairs, benches, tables, stools
- Floors, paving, pathways
- Fences, barriers, cones, barricades

INDUSTRIAL DESIGN IN THE URBAN LANDSCAPE.

A ROUND DETAIL IN A SQUARE WORLD

Winner '94!

Playground Equipment

Kompan "A round detail in a square world, and with a heart for children," that's how the Danish company Kompan describes its design concept. The company supplies outdoor playground equipment to kindergartens, schools, parks, and recreational centres in more than 40 countries.

Through play, children develop not only their physical coordination, but also the social skills they will use for the rest of their lives. Kompan's products are designed to stimulate children's natural play patterns, encouraging interaction and cooperation in 'real life' scenarios. "We gently turn play into an unconscious process of learning," says the company, "helping to develop physical, social, cognitive, and emotional skills."

Kompan's equipment and toys are remarkable for their bright colours and fantastic, organic shapes, designed to encourage children to play, and to distract them from drab urban or institutional settings. "Outdoor play areas for children should have a balanced blend of the natural landscape and good equipment. By offering a variety of types of play activities and even small play houses, we aim to enable children to create their own landscape and social environments."

Kompan produces playground systems for various age groups. Mosaiq, for instance, is designed to encourage two to six-year-olds to explore the world around them with all their senses. Produced in various heights and degrees of difficulty, the system contains imaginative elements to suit many stages of development: houses to explore and hide in, towers, slides, bridges, climbing nets, fire-fighter's poles, sandpits, and other features to provide challenge and experimentation.

For children in the four to eight-year age group, Kompan produces Oasis, a system that offers excitement, speed, and movement, but also moments of quiet. Oasis is extremely flexible: thanks to its modular structure, 34 different standard combinations are possible, and a whole range of nets, connecting elements, tower heights, and extensions is available for each. Children can climb, jump, swing, hang, and slide; Oasis helps to strengthen their muscles and joints, as well as improve their concentration and physical coordination.

Kompan's choice of wood as its basic material is based on environmental and aesthetic considerations: it is a renewable resource and its texture and warmth make it appropriate for children. Of course, durability is an important factor, and Kompan is continuously working to enhance this aspect, particularly through the development of weather-resistant coatings.

With its clear, bright colours, Kompan's wooden playground equipment has a special message for children: it signals warmth and comfort, helping children to feel at home right away. "The shapes and colours that we've used for the past 25 years aren't affected by fashion. They form a language of simplicity that children everywhere understand." By approaching the world of play from the point of view of children, and understanding their physical, social, and emotional needs, Kompan has successfully created a superior range of children's playtime classics.

Kompan even makes small playhouses, enabling children to create their own environments.

The extremely flexible Oasis system has 34 different standard combinations.

Kompan's toys are remarkable for their bright colours and fantastic, organic shapes.

A NEW URBAN LANGUAGE

Urban Furniture

Escofet

Escofet, a Spanish company with a noble tradition, has taken up the challenge of meeting the thousands of demands citizens make on their cities by adding architectural value to urban furniture, pavements, and facades. "Our strategic objective," says Emilio Farre-Escofet, the company's managing director, "has been to recognise the importance of the urban environment and meet people's needs for a better quality of life."

Escofet was founded in 1886 in what was then Spain's most modern city, Barcelona. Antonio Gaudi had begun building his elaborate *Templo Expiatorio de la Sagrada Familia*, and preparations were under way for the great exhibition to be held in 1888. As the city expanded from the old quarters to what was to be known as the 'Ensanche', Escofet acted as a go-between, linking market requirements —

hydraulic cement mosaic floors for flats — with artistic and creative trends, utilising first-class products of the highest material and aesthetic quality. In subsequent years, Escofet introduced 'vibrazo' floors in Spain.

Then, in the years following the Second World War, and particularly since the early 1960s, Escofet began to focus on urban landscaping and paving. When in the 1980s and 1990s, Barcelona's urban development again flourished when the Olympic Games came to the city, Escofet responded to the new mood. There was a growing consciousness of the cultural importance of the city, its rich architectural heritage, and the role of design in the urban setting. Using a daring new moulding technique for cast stone designs, Escofet expanded into the world of architectural concrete facades and street furniture, and introduced a whole range of products for the urban landscape, including benches, lampposts, planters, and litter bins. "We aim to provide elements that emerge as landmarks when you walk through the city," says Farre-Escofet, "things that give identity to the landscape, that become part of people's daily lives and their collective consciousness, and gradually become assimilated into the history of the city itself."

Since its foundation, Escofet has aimed to link industry to architecture and design. Today, it employs a large number of designers, working in a culturally diverse atmosphere, maintaining the creative synergy that characterised the company at the end of the 19th century.

It is Escofet's policy to provide added value in the widest sense: it has successfully introduced mass-produced, high-quality industrial products at affordable prices which surpass their functional requirements. "Cities imply culture, memory, and innovation," says Farre-Escofet. "We have sought to be sensitive to cultural supply and demand. By creating a new urban language with our products, we believe we can make a significant contribution to the quality of life in the modern city."

Escofet introduced a whole range of products for the urban landscape using a daring new moulding technique for cast stone designs.

The great American sociologist William H. Whyte argues that cities lose their centres to inner-city ghettoisation for very specific reasons. When pedestrians are subordinated to cars and when there are no places to sit down, watch and be watched, an exodus is likely and urban dereliction sets in.

WILLIAM H. WHYTE, *CITY: REDISCOVERING THE CENTRE* (LONDON: DOUBLEDAY, 1988).

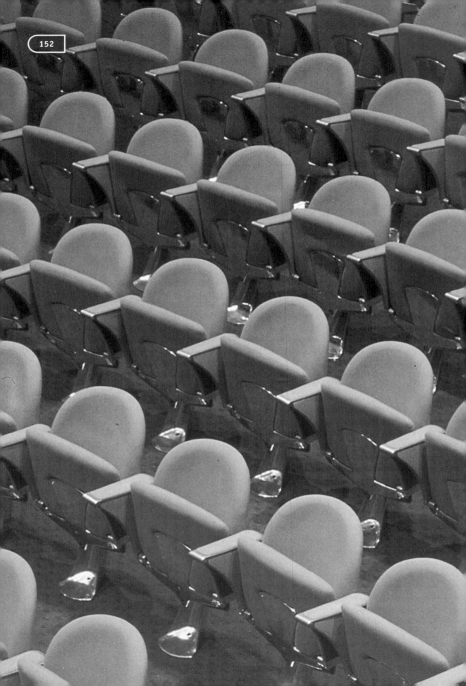

COMFORT AND STYLE

Winner '97!

Seating Systems

Oken

Oken is a young Spanish company that designs, manufactures, and markets seating systems for public spaces, like offices, airports, schools, and auditoriums. "We look for solutions to seating problems which maximise comfort and quality," says Joan Tó Padullés, Oken's managing director. "And by quality, we also mean the product's relationship with its surroundings."

Oken's design approach is to blend the rational with the non-rational: technical and industrial know-how have been combined with more human insights from ergonomics, culture, and the concept of service. "We apply design as a global and integral concept to all parts of the firm," says Tó Padullés, "from the initial idea of a product to our corporate image. In fact, to a large degree we attribute our success to design." This approach has allowed Oken not only to create innovative products that meet customers' demands, but also to differentiate its products from those of its competitors by making them more and more recognisably 'Oken products'.

The creator of four out of five items in the Oken catalogue is Josep Lluscà, a designer whose stated ideal is to put a product at the service of the human being.

The Marlene system combines comfort with good looks.

"It's a philosophy we wholeheartedly endorse," says Tó Padullés. "Lluscà's experience and his skill at balancing the technical with the cultural, not to mention his social commitment to the product, have played a decisive role in helping to shape Oken's present identity."

Oken's seating systems are made using advanced Spanish aluminium technology — among the best in the world. The company also adapts advances made in related fields: Oken's upholstery techniques, for instance, have been borrowed from the automobile industry.

Since it was founded in 1989, Oken has grown considerably, both in number of staff and turnover. Tó Padullés credits this to the excellent relationship the company has with its customers and the way its range of products is continually adapted to the needs of the market. "Innovation is one of the things that drive the company," says Tó Padullés. "The main challenge for our firm is to systematically improve everything that can be improved, from the product and the production process all the way through to the management structure of the firm itself."

Oken's Aria system is specifically intended for auditoriums. The beechwood used in the design gives it a friendly appearance.

Oken looks for solutions to seating problems
which maximise comfort and quality.

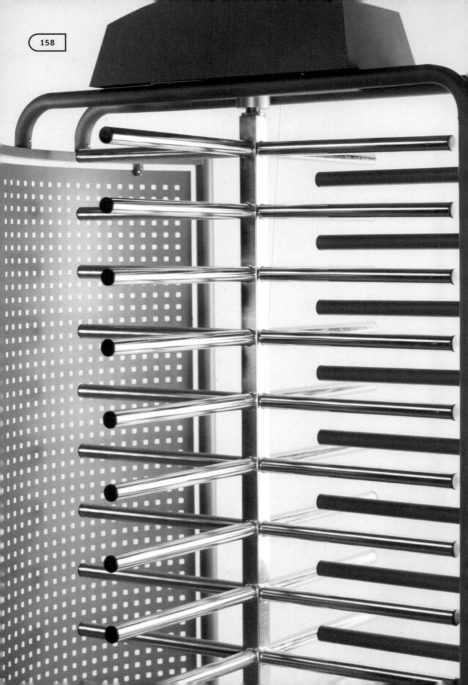

SAFE PASSAGES

Access Control

Gunnebo Theft, armed robbery, sabotage, and industrial espionage are threats businesses need to take seriously. Equipment for controlling access to buildings and sensitive areas therefore has to meet high demands. But the entrance to a building must also be inviting, open, and efficient: those who are authorised to enter must be able to do so quickly and easily.

Gunnebo Protection from Sweden specialises in access regulation for both private and public areas. "Banks, offices, museums, public transport, sports stadiums have very different needs," says Staffan Grimbrandt, Gunnebo's managing director. "The level of security required, the numbers of people passing through, and the importance attached to aesthetics are just a few of the factors we have to take into account." Accordingly, Gunnebo has developed products and systems suited to a variety of situations.

The company groups its products into basic, medium, and high security levels. At the basic level, relatively simple types of access control — revolving entrance gates, tripod turnstiles, and automatic gates — are designed to regulate large flows of people. The TurnSec, a fully glazed revolving entrance gate, allows only one person through at a time. It can be connected to a control device, such as a card reader, to check people's authorisation and then let them pass. Another model, the WingSec, can accommodate small trolleys and wheelchairs.

For peak times, when many people need to move through an entrance quickly, Gunnebo has developed the SpeedSec. Passage through the gate is regulated by a number of strategically located photocells which, together with contact mats in the floor, ensure that only one person per signal is allowed through. A new development is the TriSec, an elegant, noiseless tripod turnstile which locks if an unauthorised person tries to pass.

Gunnebo's medium-security-level products include manual and automatic revolving doors and turnstiles for use at places like offices, banks, or airports. Gunnebo produces the RevoSec, a glazed manual revolving door, and for more stringent control, the AutoSec, which admits people only after they have been checked by a card reader or other control device.

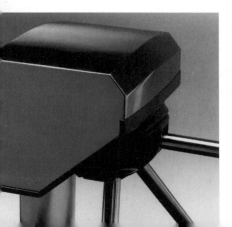

For environments where security overrides all other considerations, Gunnebo makes automatic revolving security doors and automatic security booths which enable complete surveillance and checking

The TriSec is an elegant, noiseless tripod turnstile which locks if an unauthorised person tries to pass.

The TurnSec is a fully glazed revolving entrance gate.

procedures. Maximum security is offered by the HiSec security booth: after passage has been approved, the first of two curved sliding doors opens, the visitor enters the booth and the first door closes; after the visitor has been approved in a second authorisation check, the second door in the booth is opened to allow entry. It can be combined with electronic systems for detecting metal or radiation.

In all its products, Gunnebo applies its revolutionary disc-brake technology, resulting in smooth, silent, and maintenance-free products. Advanced technology, combined with attractive and functional design, has enabled Gunnebo to offer made-to-measure protection without neglecting the vital psychological function of an entrance. "After all," says Grimbrandt, "you don't get a second chance to make a first impression."

A 32-metre high frameless glass facade for the lobby of the Citicorp skyscraper in Hong Kong (opposite: under construction)

GLASS HOUSES

Structural systems

Octatube

Some of the very 'latest' technological ideas are, in fact, quite old; they were just too far ahead of their time when they were thought up. Space frames, those complex geometrical structures used to form glass roofs over atriums in prestige offices, covered walkways in shopping malls, and vast domes over sports stadiums, were actually first conceived by Alexander Graham Bell back in 1907. But it wasn't until the advent of sufficient computing power in the 1970s that the idea became a practical possibility.

At that time, Mick Eekhout, a young architecture student, at Delft University in the Netherlands, became fascinated by such lightweight structures and their sculptural possibilities in architecture. In 1982, he founded a company called Octatube Space Structures to exploit these ideas. This Dutch company now designs and produces dome structures, space frames, and glazing systems for buildings, and is market leader in three-dimensional space structures in the Netherlands.

Octatube's aim is to advance building technology by developing innovative concepts and systems and

The music pavilion in Haarlem: an inside view.

implementing them in specific projects. The company's earliest products were 'stressed membrane structures', or tents. This type of structure had been developed in the 1960s by Frei Otto, who used it to create the cable-net roofs at the Munich Olympic Games in 1972. Octatube developed several of these tent structures for shopping malls, temporary canopies, and umbrella roofs.

The development of Octatube's space frames took off in 1984, when the Tuball-Plus system was developed. This system combines structural tubes and glazing profiles in a single cross section, enabling the creation of flat glazed space frames, cylindrical roofs, and domes. The visual aspect of the space frame was improved in 1985 with the Flowtube system, which resulted in more streamlined nodes.

The 1990s saw the success of Octatube's revolutionary Quattro system, in which the glass panels themselves form part of the structure, eliminating the need for frames entirely. The panels are structurally supported by metal connectors and stabilised with slender superstructures. The first large frameless Quattro glass facade was created for the Hong Kong Citicorp skyscraper in 1991. Octatube has also developed the world-patented Quattro Seismic Resistant system for earthquake-sensitive zones.

In all its new projects, Octatube cleverly combines architectural, structural, and industrial design and has shown itself capable of taking on any of the challenges it may come across in these fields. This approach allows the company to produce well-built spatial structures to the highest standards of design.

The Tuball-Plus space frame system was used for the music pavilion dome in Haarlem, the Netherlands.

Space frames, those complex geometrical structures used to form glass roofs over atriums in prestige offices, covered walkways in shopping malls and vast domes over sports stadiums, were actually first conceived by Alexander Graham Bell back in 1907.

GUIDING THE WAY

Emergency Lighting and Signage

Daisalux

What do the Ancient Egyptians, Sumerians, early Chinese, Minoans, Zapotecs, North American Indians and the mysterious former inhabitants of Easter Island all have in common with the inhabitants of the late-twentieth-century global village? They've all used pictograms or ideograms — the precursors of current writing systems — to convey messages.

In our increasingly mobile, culturally jumbled, and safety-conscious world, signage — especially for emergency situations — must be universally understood and quickly processed. Daisalux, a firm from the Basque country in northern Spain, has recently launched an innovative signage system, called Myra, comprising over 180 pictograms and a luminaire. Appropriate for diverse settings and situations, they can be used wherever there is a need for emergency lighting or active signage — hospitals, sports centres, hotels, and department stores.

Conceived by Josep Lluscà, who designed all of Daisalux's recent emergency lighting systems, the Myra's simple, elegant shape creates what Lluscà describes as a "shy visual dialogue" with its architectural surroundings. The luminaire can be built in or surface-mounted, and can be checked and operated by computerised building management systems.

Daisalux also designs and manufactures emergency lighting systems in flexible configurations which can be easily integrated into specific architectural

environments. Zenit, for example, is a discreet emergency luminaire for large spaces. It uses a high-performance lamp with tempered glass, specifically

Zenit is a discreet emergency luminaire for large spaces.

The Myra signage system, conceived by Josep Lluscà,
comprises over 180 pictograms.

The Argos system is ideal for spaces where aesthetic considerations are important.

developed for emergency lighting, and has visual indicators to warn of malfunctioning lamps.

For public and private spaces where aesthetic considerations are important, Daisalux has developed the Argos system. "There's nothing Platonic about the relationship of the Argos with its environment," quips Llusca. "It 'cohabits' with its surroundings, combining restrained expressivity with articulated polyvalency."

Daisalux, founded in 1989, has successfully breathed new life into a sector in which design had previously played a marginal role. "Design is a basic element in our business strategy," says José Antonio Fernández de Arroyabe, the company's managing director. "We've been able to make emergency lighting as attractive a proposition as any other type of lighting."

Daisalux's commitment to innovation can also be seen in the company's organisation. The management has been structured to facilitate more efficient product development and quality control. It has also developed software to help architects, interior designers, and product designers integrate emergency lighting into their projects. "The R&D department and the design team form the heart of the company," says Fernández de Arroyabe. "But they couldn't succeed without the total involvement of management, the right working atmosphere, and proper investment in equipment and new systems."

The R&D department and the design team form the heart of Daisalux.

How to avoid

1 Do nothing afternoon. 2 O careful where out for all ob use one of the fingers out of baby. 8 And do

The Human Factor:

and SAFETY

an accident:
t 5:00 in the
 in July. 3 Be
you go. 4 Look
ects. 5 Do not
e. 6 Keep your
t. 7 Don't be a
't go home.
USABILITY

1

Do nothing at 5:00 in the afternoon.

12:00 am
1:00 am
2:00 am
3:00 am
4:00 am
5:00 am
6:00 am
7:00 am
8:00 am
9:00 am
10:00 am
11:00 am
12:00 am
1:00 pm
2:00 pm
3:00 pm
4:00 pm
5:00 pm
6:00 pm
7:00 pm
8:00 pm
9:00 pm
10:00 pm
11:00 pm

Diurnal distribution of accident occurrence
HOME ACCIDENT SURVEILLANCE SYSTEM (HASS), UK, 1994.

2 Or in July.

January
February
March
April
May
June
July
August
September
October
November
December

Monthly distribution of accident occurrence

Home Accident Surveillance System (HASS), UK, 1994.

3

Be careful where you go.

The Netherlands	1991	0.8
Great Britain	1993	1.2
Finland	1993	2.0
Denmark	1992	2.5
Germany	1992	3.0
USA	1992	3.0
Greece	1992	3.3
France	1993	3.9
Belgium	1992	3.6
Ireland	1992	4.0
Spain	1993	4.9
Italy	1991	5.7
Portugal	1992	5.7

Fatality rates (per hundred thousand employees or employed people)

Eurofact.

If a product line generated ten million failures in the field each day, consumers would boycott it, and its manufacturer would go bust, right? Wrong — at least, if the product is a computer. Or a video recorder. Or a digital car radio. Or a telephone. Or a can-opener. Or a misleading door handle. They fail constantly. Who has not experienced at least one glitch, frustration or failure with such a product within the last 24 hours? A computer crashing; a phone call disconnected; a TV programme un-recorded; a load of laundry unrinsed; a car radio scrambled? It's incredible that we put up with it.

The signs are that our patience is finally wearing out. There are two reasons for a big attitudinal sea change. The first is experience; many millions of people are now on to their second or third computer or digital telephone; they no longer tolerate products they can't use. The second reason is money: research has revealed the huge hidden costs of hard-to-operate machines and systems. Poor usability can have an adverse impact on the bottom line.

But usability problems are not just about incomprehensible telephones, or computers that mess up our minds; poorly-designed products can also hurt the body. And as European consumers get older, usability will be among their top priorities when deciding what to buy.

This chapter explores both the physical and mental aspects of usability, and shows that the two, though often managed separately, are intimately connected. By using design to make their products usable, the companies portrayed on the following pages have gained a competitive edge in their diverse markets.

Safety and usability were not sexy subjects until modern statistics figured out the costs of getting them wrong. According to figures from the Industrial Society in the UK, injuries and dangerous incidents cost companies an average of five percent of gross trading profits each year. Considering that up to two-thirds of dangerous

The Hidden Costs of Industrial Injuries

1. Cost of time lost by injured employee.
2. Cost of time lost by other employees who stop work to assist injured employee.
3. Cost of time lost by foreman, supervisors, and other executives investigating the cause of the accident, finding other people to do the injured person's work, preparing official reports, attending hearings and so on.
4. Cost of time spent by first-aiders (excluding hospital staff).
5. Cost of damage to machines, tools, or other property in the process.
6. Incidental costs of lost production.
7. Costs under employee welfare and benefit systems.
8. Cost of full wages on employee's return to work before full recovery.
9. Costs of lost profit on productivity of injured employee and idle machines.
10. Costs arising from excitement or lower morale of other employees.
11. Overhead costs of lost production caused by accident — heat, light, rent, etc.

incidents are thought to go unreported, five percent may even be an underestimate. And most of these costs, hidden or otherwise, are uninsured. According to studies by the Health and Safety Executive in the UK, uninsured expenses, such as plant damage, legal costs, production delays and investigation time, can be up to 36 times greater than the cost of insurance premiums.

In this context it is ironic that many managers of small businesses perceive safety strategies to be expensive. It is true that compensation claims are much smaller in Europe than they are in the United States, where companies spend an estimated $110 billion in workers' compensation claims each year; but even if you don't buy the usability-as-competitiveness argument, it undoubtedly costs less to design usability problems out in advance than to pay for the consequences when you don't.

Ergonomics (in the US it is known as 'human factors') is about designing for the interaction between workers and their workplaces, between consumers and their appliances, between system operators and their systems. In one US analysis of 75,000 accidents, 88 percent were found to be caused by unsafe acts; ten percent by unsafe

Look out for all objects. 4

	Shipbuilding and repairing	Construction	Older factories	All Industries
Fall of persons	157	286	243	686
Struck by falling objects	151	162	263	576
Step on/strike against objects	302	267	983	1552
Caught in/between objects	134	112	504	504
Contact with hot substance/objects	19	10	60	88
Others	40	50	204	295

Industrial accidents by type of accident
MINISTRY OF LABOUR, REPUBLIC OF SINGAPORE, 1995.

conditions; and only two percent by unpreventable causes. Most accidents are blamed on 'human error', but the fundamental principle of ergonomics is that the vast majority of such errors occur when a workplace or product has been poorly designed.

This principle applies as much to steam irons as to aircraft cockpits, but it remains curiously neglected in the consciousness of industry. Since World War II, ergonomics has been used for the most part defensively; its original aim was to stop people from making mistakes. But during the past ten years, the competitive significance of human factors or ergonomics has impressed developers of modern technology; many high-tech firms have begun to emphasise usability and user-friendliness as desirable attributes of their products.

But most companies still find it hard to get usability onto their agendas. At a product strategy seminar for the bright young engineers of a well-known Japanese company that makes video cameras, every designer and marketing person in the room described negative consumer feedback to the overabundance of functions and buttons on recent products; but the company's engineers were oblivious to this bad news; they seemed to be competing with each other to add even more functions to make their products even 'better'.

Many companies regard 'making a product usable' as something that happens downstream in the development process; they specify the product's functions; they consult engineers about how it will work, and will be made; and then they bring in an ergonomist or a designer to sort out how it will be used. But usability cannot be added on; it must serve as both a starting point and a goal, with functions and production configured to achieve it. User-centred design belongs upstream.

But there is also a motivation problem: 'usability' sounds so lifeless and disembodied — yet another of the unenticing 'must-dos', like safety, or quality, that managers confront daily. It sounds important, but it doesn't sound like fun.

Don Norman's Principles of Usability Design

- Make sure that the user can figure out what to do, and that the user can tell what is going on.
- Make it easy to determine what actions are possible at any given moment.
- Make use of constraints.
- Make things visible — including the conceptual model of the system, the alternative actions, and the results of actions.
- Follow natural mappings between intentions and the required reactions; between actions and the resulting effect; and between the information that is visible and the interpretation of the system state.

DONALD A. NORMAN, *THE DESIGN OF EVERYDAY THINGS* (NEW YORK: DOUBLEDAY, 1988).

Don Norman's famous books (listed at the back) are one way to make the subject of usability more inspiring. Another is to look at successful companies like **Atlet**, a Swedish maker of fork-lift trucks and materials handling systems. Usability makes Atlet tick. The company believes that beyond causing accidents, poor usability is a sign of inefficiency in a system. In logistics, as the distribution of goods becomes increasingly complex and time-sensitive, inefficiency hurts profits. And ergonomics, according to Atlet, is the best way to prevent it in warehouse trucks and their drivers.

A concern for system efficiency also drives innovation at **JCB**, a British company famous for its bright yellow diggers. Modern building processes combine capital intensity with time-sensitivity; builders literally cannot afford the downtime caused by avoidable accidents.

While for business usability translates into efficiency and productivity, for consumers it can mean health, comfort, and quality of life — particularly if products relate to sports or leisure activities. **Lafuma**, a French manufacturer of backpacks and camping gear for hikers and mountaineers, employs a climber-ergonomist whose skill at scaling cliff-faces is complemented by her expertise in kinesiology. **Swarovski**, an Austrian company that has been making high-end telescopes and binoculars for more than 50 years, continuously enhances the handling qualities of its products; they must be lightweight, well-balanced, easy-to-grip, and noise-dampening. Even gardening has become a high-tech laboratory for new materials and advanced ergonomics; the Finnish company **Fiskars** has developed a revolutionary rotating handgrip for its secateurs that will be hard for its competitors to match.

Tools for the mind

Designing interactions between our bodies and hardware tools is a complex business, but these challenges are not new. Tools for the mind are a different matter: it is one task to design out the causes of a strained neck, and quite another to prevent the stress that comes from using a computer that doesn't think like we do.

Products designed by **Siedle**, a German manufacturer of entryway communications systems — speakers, intercoms, video-phones, etc. — have to be understood and used by a wide variety of users, both residents and visitors. Such systems need to give people a clear mental picture of what they do, and simple controls to use them. "In entryway communication, it is easy to understand what a door does," says the company; "we aim to make our systems just as clear."

Clarity, in an area like air traffic control, is not just desirable; it is crucial. The Austrian company **Frequentis**, which develops voice communication systems for air traffic control, is obliged to make its man-machine interfaces flawless. The company takes a clear stance on this extreme usability requirement: "The machine shall be adapted to the user, not the other way around". In aviation, 'the machine' is in fact a global medium in which objects (aeroplanes) pass through overlapping communication systems. The complexity is staggering; the need for safety absolute.

Until recently, the costs of usability errors were hard to measure. But in his book *The Trouble With Computers,* Thomas K. Landauer estimates that if every software program were properly designed for usability, productivity within the service sector would rise by four to nine percent annually. Professor Landauer also calculates that the average computer interface has some 40 flaws; correcting the 20 easiest of these yields an average improvement in usability of 50 percent. Where inputting data is involved, companies (often using other computers) can measure the performance of human operators; the more enlightened of them then look critically at the workplace and procedure design to see how the job can be made easier; others simply use the data to put pressure on their staff to improve performance.

Such 'scientific' methods applied to the study of human factors are inhumanly dry. 'Use' becomes abstract, and social context disappears. In the same way that people in white coats with stop watches gave 'industrial efficiency' a bad name, some human factors specialists seem to find it easier to observe and measure their fellow subjects rather than to understand them.

John Seely Brown, vice-president of Xerox PARC in California, has long opposed the tendency of human factors to be overly abstract. "Designers," says Brown,

5

Do not use one of these.

Article/Category	Number of Accidents
1. Construction feature	40,986
2. Unspecified article	18,719
3. Furniture	17,236
4. Person	12,279
5. Clothing/footwear	9,815
6. Outdoor surface	8,476
7. Building/raw materials	8,315
8. Cooking/kitchen equipment	7,136
9. Furnishings	6,169
10. Food/drink	5,854
11. Animal/insect	5,556
12. DIY tools/machines	4,007
13. Transport	3,756
14. Personal care items	3,630
15. Container/wrapping	3,402
16. Built feature	2,979
17. Washing/cleaning equipment	2,642
18. Sports equipment	2,545
19. Water/sanitary system	2,387
20. Ladder/support equipment	2,000

Categories of products involved in most home accidents

HOME ACCIDENT SURVEILLANCE SYSTEM (HASS), UK, 1994.

"should engage more closely with the social contexts in which products are used, and with the ways that communities of users interact with technology." Brown tells a famous story about a new photocopier that Xerox engineers were convinced would destroy the competition. When colleagues protested that the machine was too complicated to use, engineers would not listen. At last, they were shown a video in which two middle-aged men were trying, and failing, to copy a document. "The punchline was that both of these guys were Nobel laureates," recalls Brown. "Only then could we persuade the engineers that if the smartest guys in the world couldn't operate it, perhaps the product was not so usable after all."

Hand/fingers	2043
Lower limbs	472
Upper limbs	383
Head/neck	256
Foot/toes	241
Multiple locations	227
Trunk	203
Eyes	124
Other	38

6
Keep your fingers out of it.

Industrial accidents by part of body injured
MINISTRY OF LABOUR, REPUBLIC OF SINGAPORE, 1995.

Only when users are made part of the design and development process can their changing needs and behaviours be incorporated into a product. To design something, and then 'try it out' on a 'user' is to miss the point. Of course, many marketing-led and market-wise companies maintain continuous contact with representative customers, whether they be individuals or organisations, but the customer's role in these relationships has traditionally been that of an intelligent guinea pig. Such relationships are one-sided; the customer reacts, but does not propose.

7 Don't be a baby.

0-4	
5-14	
15-24	
25-44	
45-64	
65+	

Relative frequency of accidents by age group
HOME ACCIDENT SURVEILLANCE SYSTEM (HASS), UK, 1994.

Today, enlightened human factors designers are sensitive to the situations in which products are to be used, and to the ways in which context influences people's behaviour. This emphasis on context has prompted many companies to get rid of usability labs; they reckon that few customers spend their normal days peered at by video cameras through one-way mirrors. Observation changes the user's behaviour.

But people also behave differently when given new tools; designing for the user means anticipating that the user and the product will *both* change. "We are forever being made and remade by our own inventions," says Derrick de Kerckhove, director of Toronto's McLuhan Programme. "Any technology which extends or amplifies the sensory, motor, psychological, or cognitive functions of the mind cannot fail to have an impact on the way we process information — and hence on the way we behave."

This lesson has been well-taken by an Irish company, **Mediacom**, which makes systems for video conferencing. Realising that the more technology we have in our lives, the less we want to see it, and the less time we want to spend learning to use it, Mediacom resolved to make its system 'convivial' by reducing its physical presence

Jakob Nielsen's Ten Usability Slogans

- **Your best guess is not good enough.**
- **The user is always right.**
- **The user is not always right.**
- **Users are not designers.**
- **Designers are not users.**
- **Vice presidents are not users.**
- **Less is more.**
- **Details matter.**
- **Help does not.**
- **Usability engineering is a process.**

JAKOB NIELSEN, *USABILITY ENGINEERING* (BOSTON: ACADEMIC PRESS, 1993).

and minimising its computer look and feel. Making technology 'invisible' became, in an unusual twist, the best way to make it user-friendly.

Usability guru Don Norman agrees with the need to put people first. His job at Apple Computer is to merge industrial design with behavioural considerations. Norman finds that trying to solve problems in isolation makes for bad design, as does expecting a single expert to provide answers. "Designing usability requires extremely different talents. You need someone with good visual skills; someone who is a good prototyper; someone who knows how to test and observe human behaviour. These skills are very different and it's a very rare individual who combines all of them."

But a multi-disciplinary design team will not in itself guarantee usability. The whole innovation process has to change; as John Chris Jones, a pioneer in user-centred design, observes in *Re-Designing Designing*: "It is unlikely that 'design participation', the sharing of the process of design with those affected by its results, will make much difference until the nature of designing is itself changed — by transferring responsibility from designers to makers and users." Such a change is happening spontaneously in computing, where software designers are the makers, and the users, of their products, and where external users can be in direct and continuous contact via the Internet with the designers. As computers and smartness permeate more products and environments, this online connectivity between user and designer will increase. "This shift in responsibilities between user and designer is a good model," says Professor Jones. "It's a change from the specifying of geometry, or physical form, to the making of a context, a situation, in which it is possible for us all to determine the geometry ourselves."

8 And don't go home.

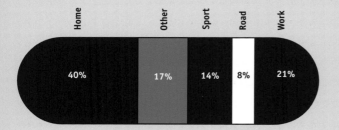

Places where accidents requiring medical treatment occur
Home Accident Surveillance System (HASS), UK, 1994.

ON THE SAFE SIDE

Construction and Agriculture Machines

JCB In the construction and agricultural world, skid steer loaders have always been useful, but notoriously dangerous machines, because the operator had to climb in and out through the front window. Many operators were killed or injured while using skid steers; they would get caught between the loader frame and the arm bucket, or slip while trying to scramble over the bucket or crawl over the controls and levers.

JCB, a long-standing British manufacturer of heavy equipment for handling, construction and agricultural sectors, delayed entering the skid steer market for many years, precisely because the conventional machines were so unsafe. "Safety has always been one of our primary objectives," says Michael James Edwards, managing director of JCB Special Products Limited, established in 1986 to complement the traditional JCB range. "We didn't want to sell a machine that would cause more injuries, so we developed the Robot, the world's safest skid steer, which allows the operator to enter and exit through a side door." The design of the JCB Robot is unique in that it has only one loader arm instead of two which, traditionally, were needed to support the digger. It was the presence of these two arms that had prevented side access to the driver's cabin and had caused so many accidents. The new single-armed loader matches the productivity of the twin-arm loaders, but its compact size, its versatility, the improved visibility it offers, and its extra safety features — seat belts, restraint-activated brake, grab handles, etc. — also make it ideal for non-professional use.

The concept and design of the single loader arm has been carried over to another break-through JCB machine, the JCB Loadall telescopic handler. The single arm allows a full-sized cab to be mounted centrally on a compact machine, combining good visibility with excellent manoeuvrability, performance, and stability. Using the technology of the Robot skid steer, JCB has also developed the world's smallest backhoe, a machine with a loader on the front and an excavator on the back.

The Robot was acclaimed "Top Product of 1993" and won the "Best Manufacturer's Safety Award" in 1994 for its innovative approach to the problem of unsafe skid steer machines.

JCB calls the Robot the safest skid steer in the world.

The JCB backhoe loader.

A person working in

for 20 years has a on

as the result o

SAFETY AND HEALTH PRACTITIONER, VOL. 14, ISSUE 3, MARCH 1996.

The JCB Robot skid steer loader, with its various attachments.

e agricultural sector

n 565 risk of dying

an accident.

Safe?

Because traditional skid steers had two loader arms, operators had to climb in and out through the front window, which resulted in many accidents.

JCB developed a skid steer with a single loader arm
which allows the operator to enter and exit through
a side door.

Safe!

REACHING FOR EFFICIENCY

Warehouse Trucks

Atlet

Atlet developed prototypes to simulate drivers' movements in its swivelling driving seats. The seat reduces twisting to a harmless level and tilts backwards automatically during high stacking.

In recent years, the distribution of goods has become increasingly complex and time-sensitive. Order flows are accelerating, placing higher demands on those at all levels of the distribution process, including the drivers of warehouse trucks.

Atlet, a Swedish company established in 1958, develops and manufactures electric warehouse trucks for indoor use. "It's our philosophy that the truck is only part of a complete logistics concept," says Knut Jacobsson, founder, and now Chairman of the Board of Atlet. With new products for loading, unloading, stacking, and picking, Atlet can offer the user high-performance trucks, low operating costs, and excellent ergonomics. Together with the analysis and simulation tool Logistic Analyser, a Windows-based computer program used to advise customers on complete storage solutions based on computer simulations of future storage costs, Atlet now has a unique package of hardware and software for the 'total logistics solution'.

From the outset, the business concept has been to provide innovative materials-handling solutions and high-quality products, with an emphasis on usability and safety. Design has played a key role in achieving these goals. As a developer of some of the first ergonomic reach trucks, as early as 1968, and recipient of several industrial design awards, Atlet continues to emphasise ergonomics as "the most important factor influencing the efficiency of the truck and the driver."

Order picking is one of the toughest jobs around. An individual may need to lift up to 15 tons of goods in a single shift.

In a 1987 research project, Atlet measured the strain on drivers by attaching electrodes to various muscles.

Currently, Atlet produces a complete series of reach trucks, including the brand-new Tergo Truck, the result of a six-year research project by four major Swedish companies on the problem of stress injuries suffered by side-seated truck drivers. The project revealed that most stress injuries were caused by repetitive, and often abrupt movements of the head; the combination of bending the neck and turning the head puts an unacceptable strain on the neck and back of the driver. To eliminate this problem, the Tergo incorporates a swivelling seat with automatic seat-tilt and arm-rest controls. Like the whole range of Atlet trucks, the Tergo is constructed from a total of only 3,000 standard components, as opposed to the 10,000 or more used by most others.

"Atlet plans to continue with its effort to reduce overall logistics costs by further developing its simulation software for warehouse planning to give more efficient handling solutions." Increased efficiency, better ergonomics, and higher levels of productivity will be the result.

The Tergo is constructed from a total of only 3,000 standard components.

The cost of injuries

- **Absence due to sickness**

Sick pay **96 ECU**/day

Associated costs **66 ECU**/day

- **Lower productivity**

0.5 hour/day **2,160 ECU**/year

1.0 hour/day **4,320 ECU**/year

- **Rehabilitation/physiotherapy**

2 hours/week **1,830 ECU**/year

- **Increased staff turnover**

Employment costs, training, etc. **9,000 ECU**/person

- **Classified stress injuries and/or redeployment**

12,000 ECU/person

The sternomastoid muscles in the side of the neck are under strain when the head is tilted backwards, which occurs mainly doing high lifts with a conventional reach truck.

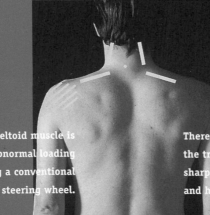

Turning of the head and neck was measured with a fixed camera.

The deltoid muscle is subjected to abnormal loading when using a conventional steering wheel.

There is often a heavy load on the trapezius muscles from sharp twisting of the head and heavy steering.

Wrist movements were also measured on the Tergo truck to check that the new controls did not introduce any undesirable movements.

A sideways-seated driver
of a conventional warehouse truck
typically turns his or her head
up to 1,000 times an hour.
More than half of these twists
are of 45° or more.

Industry experts estimate that
Germany's 'Big 8' producers of
Garden Dwarfs lost some 16 million
ECU in sales in 1994 to Polish rip-off
artists, whose imitations of these
ceramic bearded men in pointed caps
sell for a fraction of the price.

JESSICA SKELLY, 'THE WAR OF THE GARDEN DWARFS', *FORTUNE*, VOL. 131, NO. 3, FEBRUARY 20, 1995.

THE SCISSORS TRICK

Gardening Tools

Fiskars "A rose is a rose is a rose," said Gertrude Stein. If asked to comment on pruning tools, she might have remarked that "secateurs are secateurs are secateurs". And the Finnish firm, Fiskars, founded as an ironworks in 1649, would simply call her uninformed. Today, Fiskars' vast range of clippers, pruners, and loppers, each designed for a specific purpose, disproves any simplistic view of gardening tools.

For pruning roses, for instance, there are the soft-grip pruners; for cutting branches (up to four or five centimetres thick), there is the by-pass lopper; and then there are the cut-and-hold floral shears with their flexible mechanism to hold the cut flower firmly in an upright position after cutting, and the hedge shears and grass shears and the universal loppers for a thousand-and-one jobs around the garden...

The creation of customised families of products like these, ergonomically designed for particular tasks, has become a Fiskars speciality. The company learned early on that it could create consumer demand by producing various kinds of scissors: for cutting cloth, leather, cigarettes, paper, rubber, lamp wicks, poultry, not to mention a range for children and a wide variety of general-purpose and hobby models. Since then, this technique of producing ranges of highly differentiated products has been successfully extended to many related segments of the consumer market. Fiskars calls the technique its 'scissors trick'.

One of the company's recent triumphs has been its Handy axes, launched in 1993. The range consists of six axes, each for a different purpose. Fiskars generated the need for these by providing its customers with advice on how and when to use each type of axe: a heavy cleaving axe for chopping logs, a smaller one for chopping wood for the sauna, and so on. The axes are so popular that an entirely new use has arisen: "Thanks to their good looks, they've actually become popular gift items," says Fiskars' managing director, Stig Malar. "They're now collectables."

But there's more to these axes than good looks. Their impact strength is much greater than that of traditional axes and the shafts are made of an unbreakable material. In Finland, they quickly became one of Fiskars' best known products, while in the UK, they were chosen as 'Product of the Year' by *DIY Week,* a national trade magazine.

To support its outlook that gardening ceases to be pleasant when one becomes exhausted or injured by using inappropriate equipment, Fiskars devotes great attention to ergonomic design, working in close cooperation with the Department of Industrial Safety at Tampere University of Technology. The shafts of Fiskars' spades, for instance, are supplied in various lengths: a shaft of the correct length (which depends on the height of the user) allows the user to work more efficiently without bending over, thereby preventing back strain.

Fiskars also makes extensive use of Nyglass glass fibre to make products lighter yet more efficient and stronger

Fiskars makes six handy axes for various purposes, and will soon release the seventh in the series — a compact, short-shafted camping axe.

than traditional tools. Other tools, like those in the Ergo-Lite series, have swivelling handles to solve the problem of tools twisting in the hand. And the Softouch range of scissors, shears and pruners, with soft moulded grips and greater handle leverage, has been acclaimed by the American Society on Ageing and honoured with a design award from the US Arthritis Foundation.

By following a strategy of developing ergonomic concepts, applying them to a variety of product categories as well as creatively adapting existing products for sale in new segments, Fiskars has successfully positioned itself at what is literally the 'cutting edge' of a growing market.

I use scissors to cut pizza.

Strange but true, and it works.

RICHARD YOUNG IN CONDENET'S *EPICURIOUS FOOD MAGAZINE* (WWW.EPICURIOUS.COM).

*In addition to the classic model,
Fiskars produces a range of scissors
designed for particular tasks.*

THE HAPPIER WANDERER

lafuma

Winner '97!

PRO
4807

Outdoor
Activity Gear

Lafuma

Though people have always ventured into the great outdoors in search of beauty and tranquillity, challenge, and adventure, the numbers leaving the cities for outdoor leisure activities and adventure holidays are growing by the day. But nature alone cannot guarantee true happiness for the modern wanderer; comfortable, weatherproof clothing and practical equipment have become prerequisites for outdoor comfort and popular products for everyday use.

The French company Lafuma is well-positioned to take advantage of this trend. With 65 years of experience, it has firmly established itself as a leading name in backpacks and is gaining an equally strong reputation for its clothing and camping gear.

Lafuma aims to create ergonomic and technically fine-tuned products for a wide range of activities, and to offer an optimum mix of performance, quality, and affordability. Lafuma's starting point in all its product development is its customers — their needs, interests, and the trends which influence their preferences. "We try to follow our customers as their lifestyles develop and change," says Philippe Joffard, Lafuma's managing director. "We benefit from the experience of our technical advisers and product designers who use these products themselves." Lafuma has also set up what it calls *L'Observatoire de l'Air du Temps,* a market research programme to monitor the latest trends and developments in its field.

One way Lafuma has kept ahead of its competitors is by improving the backpack, its flag product, by integrating an 'airstream system' to solve the problem of heat and moisture build-up

The three Lafuma brothers started producing backpacks in 1930.

between the pack and its wearer. Available in radically different designs, sizes and colours, Lafuma backpacks are tailored to the individual's build, needs, and purposes. "We have streamlined our products to correspond more precisely to specific outdoor activities," says Joffard. "For example, a small pack that is designed for a mountain biker might be slightly different from one for a rock climber." Lafuma's 'new-style school bag', with an ergonomic waist-belt, is one recent variation of the backpack that has become popular for everyday use.

The company's range now includes products for mountaineers, hikers, climbers and campers. For this last group, Lafuma produces ultra-light circular tents made of a waterproof, 'breathing' material, which can be set up in less than two minutes. And when campers are not inside their tents, they can sit outside on one of Lafuma's Pop-up outdoor chairs, designed to be collapsible, compact, easy to carry, and of course, comfortable.

As a manufacturer in the outdoor sports business, Lafuma is attentive to environmental issues — from the treatment of waste-water within the production units to adopting a green policy for packaging. The company has also participated in the restoration of various outdoor campsites, trails, and shelters.

Furniture, including the collapsible Pop-up chair, accounts for one third of Lafuma's turnover.

While the sports market is known to be difficult, the outdoor niche is undergoing rapid growth. Despite total market drops of 9%, the backpack has experienced a rise of 4%.

NIELSEN, 1994.

STALKING DEER AT DUSK

Optical Instruments

Swarovski

Hunters, hikers, and bird-watchers are not usually deterred by a bit of rain or rough weather, though their visibility may be reduced. Everyday binoculars are little help in poor light, and, to be of practical use, more specialist precision equipment must be compact, lightweight, and durable enough to survive rough conditions.

Swarovski, an Austrian company with five decades of experience making high-quality optical instruments for both the professional and amateur markets, produces a range of binoculars, telescopes and rifle scopes which combine the latest in optical technology with sturdy, ergonomic design. "We give priority to the simple but logical formula 'form follows function'," says Gerhard Swarovski, the company's managing director. "We make sure our instruments are not only of exceptionally high quality in their functioning, but also that this quality is expressed through their appearance."

Several of Swarovski's products have been designed especially for use under poor lighting conditions or at night. The compact infrared night vision telescope, for instance, maximises all available light (from the stars, the moon, or a nearby town) to give a clear image. Using a camera adaptor, it is possible to take excellent photographs through the telescope. Other products, such as the binoculars, make use of a patented multilayer coating developed by Swarovski to reduce surface reflection from the lenses. Normally, up to eight percent of light falling on a lens is reflected, resulting in a loss of contrast in the image.

Swarovski's Laser Range Finder uses invisible laser impulses for fast, precise range measurement.

The Night-Vision Observation Telescope functions solely with residual light and can be used with a camera adaptor for night photography.

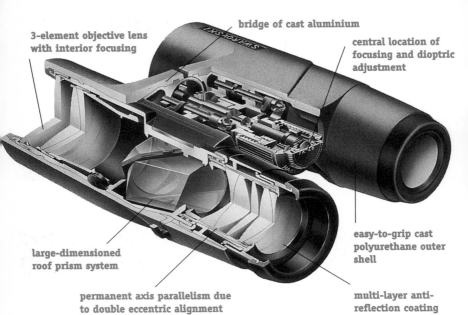

3-element objective lens with interior focusing

bridge of cast aluminium

central location of focusing and dioptric adjustment

large-dimensioned roof prism system

permanent axis parallelism due to double eccentric alignment

easy-to-grip cast polyurethane outer shell

multi-layer anti-reflection coating

The effect of Swarovski's coating is a clear, bright image with a full range of contrasts.

In order to judge how far away particular animals or birds are, gamekeepers and hunters often carry range-finding equipment which measures the time it takes for a transmitted laser pulse to be reflected back from a distant object. To lighten the load, Swarovski developed a rifle scope with an integrated laser range-finding function — the world's first. The distance appears in the view finder, accurate to within two metres over a distance of 600 metres.

By continually looking for ways to use new technology to meet its customer's special ergonomic needs, this traditional firm has managed to stay ahead in its field. "Tradition's a fine thing," says Gerhard Swarovski, "but it can become a burden unless you continue to develop. Our founder, Daniel Swarovski, used to say, 'Constantly improve what's good'. We like to think we've made innovation part of our tradition."

Swarovski's Habicht range of rifle scopes are available with steel
or light alloy scratchproof surfaces. They are watertight, recoil-
proof, and offer a bright, colour-true image.

2

Anwaltskanzlei
Roland Schwarz

Sprechzeiten
Dienstag - Freitag
9 - 12 Uhr
und nach Vereinbarung

GRAND ENTRANCE

The Siedle Intercom 3000, used for internal office communications, keeps phones free for external use.

▼

Winner '92!

Communication Systems

Siedle "Mr. Watson, come here; I want you." When on 10 March 1876 Alexander Graham Bell made the first telephone call, his words got no further than the next room. Now, although telephone signals cover the globe, much of our 'distant' communication still takes place within a single building.

Siedle, a German manufacturer of high-grade communication systems, has rationalised internal communication so that a single system can fulfil all the functions of speech communication, entryway systems and access control. Siedle's impressive product range is modular in structure: all the components can be used separately, but, in

keeping with changing demands, are easily upgradeable to form part of a more complex system. This modular 'open-ended system product', with clear and consistent styling and graphics, forms the basis of Siedle's design concept.

Entryway communication is a major focus for Siedle. "The doorway is extremely important, both from a security and an image point of view," says Eberhard Meurer of Siedle's design department. The Vario entryway speaker has been on the market since 1981 and is already a classic — functioning as both an identity marker and a communication tool. In conjunction with the speaker, Siedle offers labels with names, titles, opening hours or company logos. Combined with a movement sensor, a video camera, or a code lock, it provides optimum security.

Siedle's video system, available in colour or black and white, overcomes the problem of visitors standing out of range. The camera, controlled from the monitor, can move up and down and from left to right, so that the whole area can be scanned properly and even small children cannot slip by unseen. The colour monitor has an adjustable tilt angle to optimise vision from every point of view. The monitor can be equipped with a memory module, which allows images to be recorded. The system can be programmed, for example, to take a picture whenever the door bell is rung. With every picture, the date and the time is recorded.

The company's new system telephone T611-10 literally combines it all. The system not only covers entryway, in-house, and public network communication, but can also be used to open or close doors, switch lights on or off, or even to control heating. It is suitable for both homes and office buildings and, like all Siedle's products, can be made to measure. "Our products are conceived with one aim in mind," says Meurer, "to make people's lives easier."

▼ *The scanning capability of Siedle's door telephone solves the problem of visitors standing out of camera-range.*

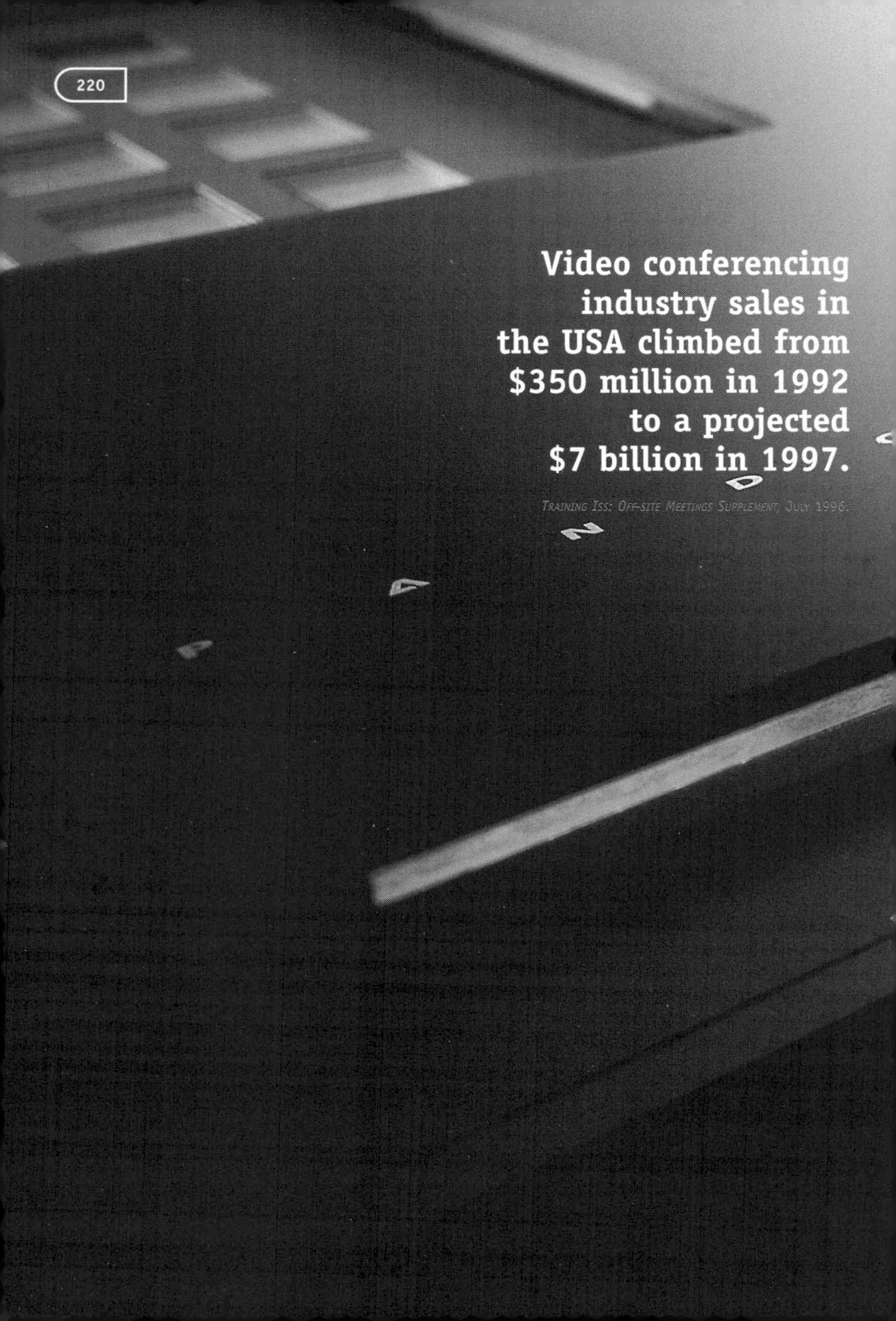

Video conferencing
industry sales in
the USA climbed from
$350 million in 1992
to a projected
$7 billion in 1997.

TRAINING ISS: OFF-SITE MEETINGS SUPPLEMENT, JULY 1996.

Video Conferencing Systems

Mediacom INVISIBLE ENGINE

As technology and its many applications become omnipresent in homes and offices, they threaten to clutter our lives; physically, through the accumulation of hardware, and mentally, through the complexity of their operating systems. In order to increase our efficiency — to serve as time-saving tools rather than inconveniences — technological appliances should 'disappear' into their surroundings, be straightforward to understand, and simple to use.

Mediacom is an example of a company applying design to minimise technology's physical presence and maximise its usability. Just established in 1995, this Irish firm is active in the world of modern technological applications — videoconferencing, multimedia communications, and interactive information systems. Its products are used for corporate conferencing, distance learning, hotels, and telemedicine.

Mediacom's Pandora Video Conferencing System is a sophisticated product with an extremely simple interface. "Pandora is designed to appeal through performance, style, and simplicity," says John Coburn, the company's managing director. Conceived as an 'engine' for easy and flexible integration into any audio-visual environment, it links up with existing in-house systems and is unique in that it uses the conventional telephone keypad as its user-interface console, making it look deceptively simple. Each key is a programmable back-lit display allowing standard numerical figures and text to be

In Texas, telemedicine techniques have reduced doctor-patient consultation and diagnostic costs from an earlier average $150 to $52 each.

Managed Healthcare, vol. 6, issue 4, April 1996.

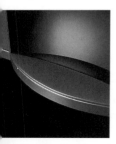

shown. Graphic icons indicate special control keys.

"Using design to innovate was neither easy nor pre-planned for Mediacom," says Coburn. "To be honest, we didn't realise beforehand how much it could contribute to competitive differentiation." Experience taught Mediacom that design could bring together engineering and marketing skills and form an integral part of the business planning process. "We were really 'design peasants'," says Coburn. "We're grateful to our design partners for daring to get involved with us."

Mediacom now pursues a total quality programme, demonstrated through the application of structured design and development methods. Its principal emphasis on innovation and customer orientation supplements its key objective to deliver products that are unique, competitively different, and enduring as performance leaders in their fields.

Mediacom's Pandora Video Conferencing System is designed for easy and flexible integration into any audio-visual environment.

Do

...wear solid colours, keeping in mind that light blue shirts or blouses look better than white.

...begin the interview with a smile, since you won't be able to shake hands.

...keep in mind that there will be a half-second delay in transmission; participants need to listen more carefully as a result.

...behave as though talking to a television with ears — and remember, the other party can hear everything unless the mute feature is turned on.

...always check time zone differences when scheduling.

Dr. Karl Magnusson, Florida International University.

HOW TO TEL

Don't

...be late. Besides being obviously rude, it's costly.

...wear clothes, scarves, or ties with busy patterns — they're distracting. Also avoid jewellery or cuff links that clink next to the microphone.

...make too many movements; while normal movement is fine, excessive gesturing will wash out on the screen, since data transmission is not as complex as on television.

...forget that you're talking to a real person like yourself. Concentrate on the interview, not on the technology.

...forget to thank the other person.

ONF R NC

IMMACULATE INTERFACE

Voice Communication Systems

Frequentis

The world is filled with invisible information systems. One area in which the proper functioning of such systems is crucial to our safety is air traffic control. With air space becoming increasingly congested, our lives depend on flawless communication.

"Air traffic control is a field that can't afford errors," says Hannes Bardach, managing director of the Austrian company Frequentis Nachrichtentechnik. Frequentis started producing voice communication systems (VCSs) soon after World War II, and today uses state-of-the-art technology to develop telephone and radio communication systems, receivers and transmitters for air traffic control, remote control systems, and controller working positions. It is among the world's leading companies in its field.

"Air traffic controllers sometimes have to work in stressful situations," says Bardach. "The man-machine interface to the VCS is therefore one of the most important parts of the system. Our goal is to make it immaculate," he says. "Even though VCSs are complex systems, they don't have to be complex to operate. We make sure that the machine is adapted to the user, and not the other way around." To coordinate and develop its expertise in this area, Frequentis has established a 'human factors competence centre' to study the man-machine interface.

From the start, Frequentis involves the air traffic controllers themselves in the design of new communication systems. This cooperation has led to many improvements in VCSs, including the development of a flat screen with 'tactile feedback', which has replaced the traditional, less reliable key panels. The smooth surface of the new screen with colour display incorporates reliable touch-screen buttons and also saves space through the layered structure of each panel.

Some 1,200 aircraft crisscross India daily; 40% — or nearly 500 — fly over Calcutta, creating a high level of congestion.
The largely antiquated air traffic control system is showing cracks.

Air Transport World, Vol. 31, Issue 5, May 1994.

Frequentis makes sure that the "machine is adapted to the user, and not the other way around."

Frequentis recently developed and installed the first fully digital voice communication system in the world (the VCS 3020). This extremely flexible system has a capacity of up to 2,000 connections and is already very successful. Because rapidly changing traffic situations require flexible communication methods, the possibility of splitting functions has also been implemented as a standard feature, allowing the controller to use radio and telephone simultaneously, for instance, using the right earphone for one function and the left earphone for the other.

In addition to the development, production, and marketing of voice communication systems, Frequentis provides services, such as maintenance, training, and consultation. "At Frequentis, quality management is a corporate objective," says Bardach. The company invests 15 percent of its turnover in research and development of new technologies and products. Its aim is to make sure that now and in the future we can fly safely around the world.

Statistics of the Global Aviation System

**International passengers:
261,000,000**
Domestic passengers: 851,000,000
**International freight carried:
(tons) 8,400,000**
**Domestic world freight carried:
(tons) 8,900,000**
**World's scheduled airlines had an
estimated operating revenue of
$203,400,000,000**
Jet aircraft in IATA fleets: 7,536
**Propellor aircraft in IATA fleets:
1,151**
Average age of aircraft (years): 10.2
**Total kilometres flown:
13,502,000,000**
**Total aircraft departures:
12,184,000**
Total hours in the air: 22,574,000
**Number of airports in the USA:
16,000**

Lost in Space (De Grafische: Haarlem, 1995).

Touch Panel Demo V 1.12 (c) 1994 Frequentis   01/01/88 01:25

| PAGE | T | P | A | TRANS | HOLD | CONF | MON | PRIO |

			T18	T19	T20
1	2	3	T21	T22	T23
4	5	6	T24	T25	T26
7	8	9	T27	T28	T29	Q	Q	Q
*	0	#	T30	T31	T32	BUZZ	- VOL +
CLR	DEL	ENTER	T33	T34	T35	LIGHT OFF	END	END

Top 10
Busiest Airports in the World

International and domestic flights/passengers per annum

	Airport	Passengers
1	CHICAGO O'HARE (CHICAGO, USA)	65,091,000
2	DFW INTERNATIONAL (DALLAS/FORT WORTH, USA)	49,655,000
3	LA INTERNATIONAL (LOS ANGELES, USA)	47,845,000
4	HARTSFIELD ATLANTA INTERNATIONAL (ATLANTA, USA)	47,775,000
5	LONDON HEATHROW (LONDON, UK)	47,602,000
6	TOKYO-HANEDA INTERNATIONAL (TOKYO, JAPAN)	47,507,000
7	SAN FRANCISCO INTERNATIONAL (SAN FRANCISCO, USA)	32,769,000
8	STAPLETON INTERNATIONAL (DENVER, USA)	32,627,000
9	FRANKFURT (FRANKFURT, GERMANY)	31,945,000
10	MIAMI INTERNATIONAL (MIAMI, USA)	28,660,000

RUSSELL ASH, *THE TOP TEN OF EVERYTHING* (LONDON: DORLING KINDERSLEY LTD., 1996).

TECHNO

and

Working with Wetware:

DESIGN, LOGY THE BODY

During the past three decades, two technologies have developed in spectacular fashion and changed our lives: information technology, and biomedical engineering. But only information technology dominates the headlines; the new machines and systems which scan, probe, examine, and enhance our bodies seem barely to have registered. Yet, taken together, they raise questions about where 'human' ends and 'machine' begins; hence the expression 'wetware', coined by computer scientists to describe human beings on the same level as hardware or software.

These profound changes create little fuss because bio-engineering progresses by means of continuous, unspectacular modifications, rather than by dramatic leaps. Medical technologies provide an excellent case study of the nature of innovation — including radical innovation. No designer or company sets out consciously to redesign the human body; rather, thousands of people and enterprises strive continuously to fix, or improve, particular bits. It's when all those tiny enhancements are looked at together that the consequences for the body suddenly seem spectacular.

As often happens, artists and writers have spotted this bigger picture more clearly than those directly involved. Donna Haraway, for example, in her celebrated *Cyborg Manifesto,* writes that "late twentieth-century machines have made thoroughly ambiguous the difference between natural and artificial, mind and body, self-developing and externally designed. Our machines are disturbingly lively, and we are frighteningly inert". The profound ethical issues raised by the development of prosthetic extensions, or alternatives, to our bodies and minds is proof, too, that innovation is not a neutral process.

In addition to this ethical example, three other lessons may be learned about innovation and design from bio-engineering. One is the powerful potential of combining multiple skills. Biomedical engineering involves the convergence of knowledge from many branches of science and design, and multidisciplinary teams are the norm. A lesson can also be learned about usability design: when medical tools are used invasively, ergonomic considerations are, literally, vital. A third issue is adaptability: every human body is different, so medical devices cannot be standardised. And just as our bodies change with time, so, ideally, should any prosthetic devices, implants or additions to our bodies. And not just on a one-off basis when they are fitted or applied, but continuously, along with our own process of ageing.

Finally, the importance of social context and communication to innovation may also be clearly seen in this sector. Innovation in medical technology involves continuous communication between all parties: clinicians, patients, and technology suppliers need to stay in touch constantly. Medicine is as much a communication and service business, as a product business. Its products are better thought of as tools used by specialists in a knowledge-based service industry. Medical technology is becoming increasingly immaterial; more and more, the role of design is to organise the way that it is used, and how it behaves — not just what it looks like.

Bodily functions

The seven companies profiled in this chapter exemplify many of these trends. The state-of-the-art welding helmets made by the Swedish company **Hörnell** are a fascinating example of how medical knowledge about damage to the eyes caused by intense light has stimulated the transfer of high technology to an old industrial process. In this case, innovation has been better late than never; soldering and welding were first used more than 5,000 years ago, but it was not until the early 1990s that electro-optics were used to protect eyes from the dangers of arc light.

Invasive surgery, too, has ancient roots; it is perhaps the oldest form of medicine. Only in recent years has the design of tools proliferated. The practice of making holes in the skull — or trepanning — is prehistoric, while an early Egyptian papyrus lists several surgical techniques. But for centuries, surgeons remained a semiskilled class of medical practitioners; it was not until the 18th century that barber-surgeons were replaced by medical professionals. Since then, medical instruments have followed medical practice along its controversial path towards ever greater specialisation. The German company **Olympus**, for example, makes no fewer than 1,800 medical instruments.

Few of them are more psychologically disturbing than the urological devices which feature in the following pages. Olympus is one of the first companies to understand that design has an expressive and psychological role to play in medical technology, as well as a purely functional one. To compete in a crowded market, surgical devices must not only be precision implements and easy to use — but they must also look the part. Perceived precision and quality are therefore crucial to their competitiveness.

The protection afforded by Hörnell's helmets and the precision achieved by Olympus' instruments both involve hardware design. But the trend in medicine is also towards software solutions — the pre-emptive monitoring of the body's processes so that dysfunctions can be picked up early, and, ideally, be dealt with early, in order to avoid the need for high-risk operations or drug treatments.

Novacor's devices are leading-edge examples of this trend and are made as unobtrusive as possible. Novacor's miniature lightweight recorder — worn around the patient's neck rather like a medallion — listens to the heart and transmits data back to the clinician. The low psychological impact of the whole process is important to its efficacy. This patient-friendly form of examination takes the stress out of medical procedures and, because it does not involve hospitalisation, protects patients from the 'white coat effect' (i.e., the tendency for people to exhibit an irregular heart rhythm as a result of the anxiety caused by being in a hospital!). "Invisible and yet omnipresent," as the company puts it, Novacor's products seem to disappear physically, while, at the same time, the communication infrastructures that support them are growing at tremendous speed.

Health telematics is one of the three major markets for telecommunications (along with banking transactions, and education). The cost of services rendered by physicians in the United States grew from $13 billion in 1970 to $142 billion in 1990, so it is evident that any service which assists in the doctor/patient relationship by either saving the doctor or the patient time and money, stands to benefit handsomely.

The increased cost of drugs — and managing their disbursement — is another economic problem. Some computers can now recommend what kind of drug to prescribe, and the best dosage. Elimination of the paper prescription and the automation of medical insurance payments will reap the company which brings the enabling technology to market a vast share of the 48 billion ECU revenue of the pharmaceutical industry.

At the moment, the medical industries of both the United States and Europe have been much too busy grappling with reforming healthcare systems to devote much attention to telecommunications. "But the needs are potentially very large," says Mitch Ratcliffe, editor of Digital Media, an industry newsletter. "An electronic credit history or bank transaction is a minuscule amount of data compared to a 1,000-page patient record or a set of X-rays. The medical community will become a very large consumer of advanced telecommunications."

Bodies in the network
Health and medical telematics are expanding and interconnecting in the same unobtrusive — and unplanned — manner that characterises the way our body parts are being enhanced, or substituted. In one project, a vast database containing information about tens of millions of experiments and clinical trials is being centralised. In dozens of different experiments, patient records are being digitised and coded — which means that they can be accessed online from anywhere. In another sector, medical journals are migrating at high speed to online publishing environments, thereby shrinking the time lag between discoveries and their dissemination. The pharmaceutics industry is putting

performance data about thousands of drugs online. And bio-engineers have devised a multitude of non-invasive, digital patient monitoring systems that measure, record and evaluate our vital functions — continuously.

All this results in a vast, well-distributed, and — for the wired-up patient — immersive medical knowledge system in which the boundaries between 'me' and 'the system' are converging. Although it sounds fanciful when artists talk about "wetware", and "the recombinant body", it is undoubtedly hard to predict precisely where the convergence of all these subsystems within medicine will lead.

For example, the body itself will become a communication device if some engineers have their way. IBM's Thomas Zimmerman is one of the specialists in 'intra-body communications' who say that, before too long, the human body will be used as the wiring of a very small, but very useful, 'personal area network' — or PAN for short. 'Wearable' electronic devices will exchange data by passing low-voltage currents through the body and into hand-held appliances, head-mounted displays, shoes, watches, credit cards, etc. The hardware required to build such a novel interface seems to be quite inexpensive and could be implemented with cheap microcontroller chips which cost no more than a few dollars. Lorna Ross, a design researcher working at Interval Research in the United States, has already made prototypes of skin-tight gloves that function as a telephone when fingers are pressed onto the palm in different combinations.

All kinds of devices which monitor bodily functions have implicit networking capabilities. As Zimmerman explains, "the usefulness of each will be multiplied by the exchange of information with any other device we carry with us, and completely new devices will be invented to take advantage of this networking frenzy." PAN medical sensors could provide enhanced biological monitoring by transferring data to a cellular phone and thence to a nearby hospital. Arthur Kroker, an iconoclastic writer who has observed the convergence of technology and the body with glee, is enthusiastic: "Why be nostalgic? The old body type was always OK, but the wired body is infinitely better — a wired nervous system, embedded in living flesh."

Other engineers and designers are already busy creating medical sensors that monitor the human brain. The Finnish company **Neuromag** provides a spectacular example of the speed with which brain-scanning technology has advanced in recent years. The current design challenge for Neuromag has been to fashion a brain-scanning helmet that covers the whole head and which has 122 detectors to collect information conveyed by the brain's magnetic field.

Wilhelm Konrad Röntgen's discovery of X-rays was one of the wonders of the 20th century, but the new brain-imaging systems are not very far behind. The mapping of magnetic signals elicited by the human brain provides a modern means for functional imaging with millimetre and millisecond precision. A non-invasive method, magneto-encephalography (MEG), is becoming increasingly important in studies of both the healthy and the diseased brain. Cortical activity all over the brain can be accurately followed simultaneously; this results in increased throughput, more reliable data, and new experimental perspectives, thus opening a qualitatively new era in neuromagnetic studies. Neuromag's system has the potential to identify neurological and psychiatric disorders which are not the result of any evident structural change or damage. What happens when, through telematics, the helmet is able to communicate online with a doctor or brain specialist and the online monitoring of psychological states becomes possible? Nobody has yet confronted the ethical consequences of this imminent innovation.

Made-to-measure nose

Perhaps the greatest single advance in modern medical technology was the 13th-century discovery that glass lenses could be used to correct defective vision. Although the basic technology employed in the remedial amplification of sight — optics — has not changed dramatically since then, many small, incremental improvements have been made continuously: new diagnostic techniques; improved glass technology and better methods of making lenses; contact lenses, of course; and even a children's 'designer-nose' from **Optimom**, a French company frustrated by the difficulty faced by opticians trying to fit spectacles to the soft unformed noses of young children.

By comparison, technological aids to hearing have been slow to arrive. But, better late than never, hearing aids are now the most widely used sensory aids produced by biomedical engineering. The market is certainly huge: by the age of 65, one person in three suffers from some degree of hearing loss. But only ten percent of people who could benefit from an aid, actually use one, and the average customer suffers in some degree of silence for an average of seven years before seeking professional help. Statistically, if the marketing of this book has been successful, and it is being read by senior managers, then MORE THAN A QUARTER OF YOU READING THIS SENTENCE NEED A HEARING AID.

The singular achievement of the Danish company **Oticon** has been to recognise that the low take-up of hearing aids is just as much a psychological and cultural problem, as a technological one. We all either deny hearing problems or delay taking action about them — with often severe social consequences. The company's products are impressive enough: Oticon takes the kind of sound mixer found in recording studios, digitalises the operation, and puts it on a chip measuring less than half a square centimetre. But what makes Oticon unique in the medical technology field is its view of itself as a knowledge-based service organisation whose activities are based on the day-to-day needs — including the psychological needs — of the people who use its products.

Oticon consciously fosters interaction between all its business processes: basic audiology research, technological development, distribution, customer diagnosis, as well as the supply, fitting and monitoring of products. Oticon's service concept, which is articulated as 'The Human Link', has four elements: the 'Dispensing Wheel', a knowledge dissemination process which ensures that healthcare professionals have access to the latest information in their contacts with patients; a set of tools for auditory rehabilitation — COSI (Client Oriented Scale of Improvement); the Focus family of fully digital hearing instruments; and a programme of knowledge-sharing both within the company and between the company and its suppliers, distributors, and customers. This process exploits state-of-the-art 'groupware' communications technology, so that people in different locations can exchange knowledge and information online; but it is also based on the old adage that "face to face is best".

Hearing-impaired people have higher divorce rates than people whose hearing is good.

OTICON

What sets Oticon apart from most other companies in the medical technology sector is the fact that it recognises that the human body remains infinitely more complex than any technology. The company consequently uses design not just to determine what its products look like, but also to fashion an organisation, and a way of working, which is responsive to an infinite variety of users and open to continuous feedback from multiple sources.

What you hear is what you get

Twenty years ago, the Austrian company **AKG** could have been relied upon to generate many new customers for Oticon. At that time, the technologies of 'professional speech reinforcement', commonly known as PA systems, found mainly in theatres, small clubs and conference centres, were so crude that they could impair hearing if improperly used. Now, says AKG, without apparent irony, "the market is booming worldwide". AKG develops systems informed by basic research in psycho-acoustics that has led to a 'physiological loudness contour' — a specification and control system that allows the company to deliver excellent sound with minimum stress on the user's hearing.

Close to the user

No industry is closer to its user than biomedical technology; sometimes, as we have seen, its products end up inside us. Design plays an important role among the thousands of innovations that are constantly being implemented. Design enhances the functional and cognitive ergonomics of tools and systems; a different kind of design organises work processes so that multiple disciplines can work together. The fact that no individual or design team set out to redesign the human body — but that this is happening nonetheless — just goes to show what a mysterious and disturbing process innovation can be.

Late-twentieth century machines have made thoroughly ambiguous the difference between natural and artificial, mind and body, self-developing and externally designed. Our machines are disturbingly lively, and we are frighteningly inert.

DONNA HARAWAY, *CYBORG MANIFESTO.*

UNIVERSITY OF GLAMORGAN
PRIFYSGOL MORGANNWG

Learning Resources Centre

According to a study by the US Bureau of Labor Statistics, 67% of welding injuries are to the eyes. Half of these injuries occur when welding lenses are not worn.

Dale B. Pfriem, 'Technical Developments in Welding Eye and Face Protection', Svetsen, Special Issue 2E, 1993.

A BETTER VIEW ON WELDING

Winner '97!

Welding Helmets

Hörnell Welding is a dangerous business. Since its first uses in the early 1900s in industrial metal fabrication, welding technology and its many applications have continued to grow, but only recently has proper protection been developed for the eyes and respiratory system, allowing welders to do their work with safety, confidence, and precision.

Studies have shown that 67 percent of welding injuries are to the eyes, caused by UV radiation from the welding arc. This type of injury, known as 'arc eye' or 'weld flash', is often caused because conventional welding helmets, designed to protect the eyes while the welding arc is lit, inhibit vision while it is not. As a result, welders often 'nod down' the helmet visor at the last moment or take hazardous safety short-cuts like closing their eyes or looking away just before the arc is ignited. These injuries have resulted in lower productivity and millions of hours of lost working time.

To protect the welder's eyes from the light of a welding arc, an auto-darkening lens must have a switching time of less than 5 milliseconds.

Fifteen years ago, while Ake Hörnell, a Swedish engineer from Gothenburg, was working on the problem of eye injury caused by welding, liquid crystal technology was still in its infancy. Hörnell conceived the idea of using liquid crystals to develop a fast-switching filter that would automatically change from light to dark when the welder struck the arc. If a helmet incorporated this technology, it could be worn continuously, eliminating the problem of helmet nodding.

Hörnell Elektrooptik was founded in 1979, and after another two years of development, Ake Hörnell's idea was realised as the Speedglass, a helmet that incorporates automatically darkening welding filters. The construction of the filters is based on polarisers and liquid crystal cells in conjunction with photo-sensors that react to changes in light intensity. Since the early eighties, Speedglass filters have been sold worldwide and the company now has an extensive range of protective equipment that satisfies and exceeds the safety requirements of most welding methods.

Hörnell's latest welding helmet is the 'breathing' Speedglass 9000, which turns from light to dark in a tenth of a millisecond. It not only protects against IR and UV radiation in both the light and the dark state, but also contains a unique respiratory

system, offering protection against welding fumes and particles. The Speedglass 9000 is light, rugged, extremely comfortable to wear, and always contains fresh air, thus preventing fatigue and headaches. Side windows can be fitted to the helmet to improve the field of vision and reduce the feeling of claustrophobia. The front surface has a heat-reflecting silver coating, so that the helmet always feels cool, even under the most extreme circumstances.

Hörnell's experience with liquid crystal technology now extends over nearly two decades, and since 1986, seven fully-owned subsidiaries have been established, including five in Europe, one in the USA, and one in Singapore. There's no doubt that Hörnell has made the best of its technical lead — not so much through its own patents, which are costly and difficult for a small company to protect, but primarily through advanced manufacturing techniques, active product development, and by putting a lot of hard work into setting up an international marketing organisation. Although Hörnell can no longer compete as 'the only game in town', its hard-to-copy combination of technological leadership, production expertise, and continuous design development puts it ahead of the competition.

Lens ruggedness is very important to welders. A simple test for ruggedness: ask the lens salesperson to drop a lens installed in a helmet from at least table height (the higher, the better).

DALE B. PFRIEM, 'TECHNICAL DEVELOPMENTS IN WELDING EYE AND FACE PROTECTION', *SVETSEN*, SPECIAL ISSUE 2E, 1993.

The Safety Advantages of the Speedglass

1. Welders have increased protection from accidental arc flashes from nearby welders.

2. Helmet nodding and the resulting neck strain are eliminated.

3. Welders can chip and grind a weld without changing safety headgear.

4. Welders can visually inspect a new weld without fear that the molten metal pool will suddenly contract and pop in their faces.

5. Welders have a constant view of objects around them, including potential hazards.

6. Welders are not tempted to cut corners by neglecting to lower their welding helmets while doing very short welds.

A welder inhales, on average, 0.5 grams of dust particles per shift — over 100 grams, or 3 ounces, a year. This often causes symptoms such as dizziness, vision problems, and various forms of chronic and even lethal lung damage.

'A NEW FACE FOR THE WELDER, 10 YEARS OF THE AUTOMATIC WELDING HELMET'.

HEARING TECHNOLOGY AND PERCEPTION

Hearing Instruments

Winner '97!

Oticon

According to the Association of British Insurers, industrial deafness still represents the highest incidence of occupational disease claims, accounting for over 83% in 1993.

Look around at all the people wearing spectacles or contact lenses. We hardly think of these instruments as 'medical devices' — they're even fashion accessories. Why are hearing instruments, in comparison, so rarely used?

Although one in three people over the age of 65 is said to experience some degree of hearing loss, only ten percent of those with hearing difficulty actually use hearing aids. Some blame the fact that these instruments tend to distort sound, making it too sharp, too metallic, or too hollow; others complain of disturbance from cellular telephones; others simply find them indiscreet, unattractive, or inconvenient.

The mission of Oticon, a Danish company founded in 1904, is "to help people with hearing difficulty to live life as they wish, with the hearing they have." To do this, it must do more than produce a superior product; it must back it up with excellent service and communication, regular input from users, and constant integration of this 'real world' feedback with new technologies and design concepts.

Oticon's service philosophy, The Human Link, conceived to help find "the right balance between technology and human experience", defines the company's approach to developing and selling customised hearing aids. At one end of the chain, a programme for knowledge sharing helps transform audiological research into daily practice. Oticon's research centre, Eriksholm, brings together leading psychoacoustic experts, a worldwide network of researchers, and over 500 hearing-impaired people to test new principles for hearing instruments in a laboratory environment and in daily life. At the other end, The Human Link helps professionals to fit each client with the most suitable device, and to encourage continued feedback on the instrument's performance.

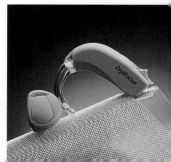

By applying the Human Link philosophy, Oticon became the first company to develop fully automatic

People with hearing difficulty wait an average of seven years before seeking help.

DigiFocus is the world's first fully digital compact hearing instrument.

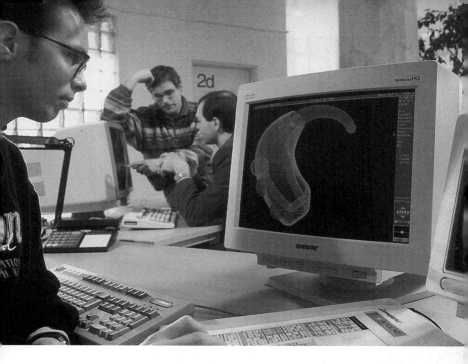

non-linear hearing instruments, where the amplification continually adjusts to changing sound environments. More recently, the Link has helped generate DigiFocus, the world's first fully digital compact hearing instrument, which applies the digital technology used for music CDs, digital video, mobile telephones, and other forms of advanced communication equipment. Weighing only four grams, the chip has the same power as a desktop computer. DigiFocus makes hearing as natural as possible for the hearing-impaired; sound never becomes uncomfortably loud thanks to seven frequency channels which automatically adjust to optimise the information content in speech and simultaneously reduce background noise.

Like Oticon's other hearing instruments, DigiFocus can be fine-tuned to each client's requirements with the company's PC-based fitting and programming software, Otiset. This user-friendly interface for programming takes the form of a 'belt' that is placed over the client's shoulder and uses infrared signals to communicate with a computer.

Innovations like these are evidence of Oticon's unique combination of 100 years of experience — it is the world's oldest hearing care company — with its dramatic rebirth as the 'ultimate flexible organisation', guided by company president Lars Kolind in 1991. "If you want people in your company to work like robots," says Kolind, "you design the company like a machine. If you want to develop and benefit from the knowledge of your people, you organise the company like a brain." Oticon's 'spaghetti organisation' — a tangle of relationships, interactions, and constantly changing project clusters — is ostensibly chaotic, "but in reality," says Kolind, "it is a fast-moving and flexible organisation, with short communication lines and decision chains. As opportunities emerge," he says, "we see them and we act."

Today, the company is characterised by its open-plan office landscapes, diversified jobs, paperless electronic offices, and interdisciplinary project organisation. Kolind's construction of 'freedom within a framework' has liberated the creative resources of his work force, helping this relatively small company to become an industry leader and compete with major multinationals.

One supplier now sells 'differently abled dolls' including dolls in wheelchairs and on crutches, a deaf ballerina who wears a hearing aid, and a blind doll with a white stick.

CHRISTINA HARDYMENT, 'TOYTOWN GONE MAD', *DAILY TELEGRAPH*, 13 APRIL 1996.

Oticon is a fast-moving and flexible organisation, with short communication lines and decision chains.

◄ *Electronic think-tank.*

▼ *The Human Link brings together experts, researchers, and hearing-impaired people to test new principles for hearing instruments.*

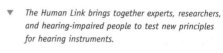

Of the estimated 19 million deaf and hard-of-hearing adults in the US, 33.7% report that their loss is due to some sort of noise. Another 28% report that their loss is due to age, while 17.1% report that it is due to infection or injury. Only 4.4% report the presence of hearing loss at birth.

OUTSMARTING THE BRAIN

Brain Scan Helmets

Neuromag

The brain is the last refuge of the self, and the thought that it may somehow be letting us down is uniquely disturbing. Fortunately, over the past century, medical science has learned a lot about brain activity thanks to various scanning techniques, most recent among them magnetoencephalography (MEG). One MEG system that constitutes a great improvement over earlier systems has been produced by Neuromag, a small Finnish company set up in 1989.

Unlike other MEG scanners on the market, which are made to look at one part of the brain at a time, the Neuromag system can examine the whole brain simultaneously and see how various parts of the brain interact at a given moment. The subject sits under a helmet-shaped magnetometer and may be given certain mental tasks to perform. The tiny electrical currents which accompany brain activity produce minute magnetic

Neuromag's helmet employs 122 detectors to collect all the information conveyed by the brain's magnetic field. Cortical activity all over the head can be followed simultaneously.

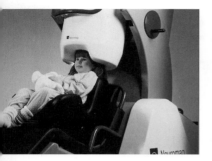

fields which are detected and measured by super-conducting sensors in the helmet. These measurements are then analysed by specially developed computer systems to locate where the brain activity is taking place, where it is not, and when. This information allows researchers to determine what may be wrong.

Neuromag's Antti Ahonen pays tribute to the effective knowledge transfer from the pure to the applied sciences which underlies the development of the new device. He believes that the firm benefited greatly from Helsinki University of Technology's long tradition of research into low temperature physics and basic brain studies, he says, and the software was the result of the combined experience of brain researchers, neurologists and computer experts.

Neuromag's whole-head magnetometer system first appeared on the market in 1992 and is currently used by brain research groups at universities, research institutes, and teaching hospitals. However, the company foresees clinical applications in the near future. In that context, ergonomic and psychological factors will become increasingly important. The equipment must not only be easy for medical staff to operate, but must also put the patient's mind at rest. "The fact that doctors are saying you need a brain scan is already worrying enough," says Ahonen. "It's therefore important that staff have the time to make you feel at ease, and that you, as the patient, find it comfortable and not off-putting. That's why we devoted a lot of thought to design and ergonomic considerations at a very early stage in the development of the whole-head scanner. When you're dealing with someone's brain, creating an atmosphere of trust and confidence is of paramount importance."

MAGNETOENCEPHALOGRAPHY

Magnetoencephalography (MEG) is a noninvasive method of determining brain activity by studying the magnetic fields associated with neuronal electrical activity. It is used diagnostically on epileptic patients, for example. Recent data has shown that MEG, carried out on an epileptic patient between fits, is effective in localising the irritative zone of the brain.

PROFESSOR J. ADAMS AND DR. M. DOBSON, UNIVERSITY OF MANCHESTER, DEPTARTMENT OF DIAGNOSTIC RADIOLOGY.

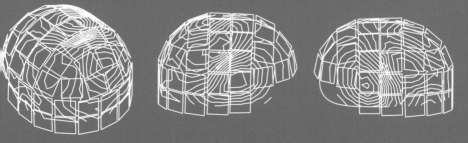

Neuromag's system generates maps, like these, which indicate the field patterns of the brain upon stimulation of the tibial nerve at the left ankle.

Children's Spectacle Frames

Optimom

MADE-TO-MEASURE NOSE

Optimom, a young French company, specialises in the design and distribution of spectacle frames for children and babies. When Joseph Sebban, the company's managing director and an optician by training, noticed that most spectacle makers had failed to give proper attention to children's glasses, he started to explore a number of solutions to meet the needs of this target group. To help him put his ideas into practice, he called on the design team of Cent Degrés.

The result of this fruitful collaboration is Optimom's Tropique range of eyeglass frames for children, which not only look great, but are also extremely comfortable to wear. They are used in combination with specially developed silicon nose-cushions available in six different sizes. These silicon 'made-to-measure noses' are stuck onto the frame to ensure a perfect fit. The frame itself is very lightweight and designed to follow the shape of the face naturally. The Tropique spectacles allow children to live their active lifestyles. Both the frames and the 'noses' come in many different bright colours.

Optimom also takes a proactive approach to the problem of identifying and treating children's eyesight problems. It has collaborated with centres of research, such as the French National Institute of Health and Medical Research (INSERM) and Oxford University to develop the Bébé Vision Tropique vision test which aids in the detection of eyesight problems in children of nine months. The success of this new test has led the French health authorities to include it in routine medical examinations of all babies in France.

Optimom's new products have increased sales by almost a quarter and have brought the company nationwide recognition, along with the promise of entering the international market.

Optimom's children's spectacle frames incorporate silicon nose cushions to ensure a perfect fit.

High blood pressure contributes to 75% of all strokes and heart attacks.

WWW.NOAH.CUNY.EDU/WELLCONN

With Novacor's interface, a doctor can receive a prerecorded or real-time ECG via the telephone line.

WHILE-U-WALK
Heart and Blood Pressure Monitors

Novacor People whose heart functioning or blood pressure needs to be checked regularly often find themselves inconvenienced by multiple visits to the doctor. To add to this frustration, examinations may not even be effective; they record only a momentary condition — missing past and future irregularities — and are often influenced by the 'white coat effect' — when stress associated with the hospital environment temporarily exacerbates the patient's condition. For a long time, the only alternative — both impractical and undesirable in most cases — was to hospitalise the patient for an extended period.

The French company Novacor, established in 1983, has developed a system that allows continuous monitoring away from the hospital, saving time, energy, and expense. Novacor produces two major lines incorporating this system. One is Diasys, for automatic blood-pressure monitoring; the other is R-Test, for ambulatory ECG monitoring. Both allow the operation of high technology close to the body without the need for the patient to get caught up in the technological jungle of today's hospital environment.

Following the success in the mid-1980s of their first generation of ambulatory devices, Novacor joined forces with Absolut Design, an agency specialising in the design of high-tech products. This collaboration has resulted in Integra and Evolution, the latest products in the Diasys and R-Test lines.

Integra, launched in 1996, is based on ten years of experience with the Diasys

200 systems. It allows simultaneous monitoring of blood pressure, heart rate, and arterial compliance. This compact device can be worn on a band around the upper arm. It is easy to operate and automatically takes into account the patient's activity — sitting, sleeping, standing, and so on — so that a more objective reading is given. The instrument can also be programmed to take measurements at fixed intervals and when the patient gets up in the morning.

The latest model in the R-Test series is Evolution, introduced in 1995. It is a revolutionary miniature lightweight recorder worn unobtrusively under clothing like a medallion around the patient's neck. The device can be activated by the patient to record cardiac activity at a particular moment — when a symptom is felt, for instance. But one of the main benefits of Evolution is that when set to automatic mode, its eco-friendly batteries will allow it to provide continuous monitoring for eight days on end, or periodic monitoring for up to six months.

Evolution calculates the heart rate and detects and stores the most significant pathological events. Deco-test, a multi-purpose interface, allows the doctor to connect the device to a computer and display the stored information on-screen. Numerical tables and histograms of all events can be produced according to criteria preprogrammed by the doctor. The software used is compatible with most computer systems (DOS, Windows, Mac). Using the interface, the doctor can even receive a pre-recorded or real-time ECG from the patient from anywhere in the world via the telephone line. Experts believe such health telematics applications are set to become every bit as important on the information superhighway as banking or video conferencing.

The R-Test Evolution is so simple and inexpensive to operate that it may well become used as a matter of course whenever a doctor has doubts about the condition of a patient's heart. The fact that it allows automatic monitoring over a relatively long period of time also opens up new possibilities both for physicians monitoring patients at risk and for researchers evaluating new therapies.

White-coat hypertension is a phenomenon whereby a patient's blood pressure rises in the presence of a physician and returns to normal at home. Some physicians believe that if a person's blood pressure shoots up under the stress of being with a doctor, it is also bound to increase in other stressful situations and therefore should be treated.

WWW.NOAH.CUNY.EDU/WELLCONN

Diasys, worn on a band around the upper arm, monitors blood pressure, heart rate, and arterial compliance.

The discreet R-Test Evolution can provide continuous cardiac monitoring for eight days, or periodic monitoring for up to six months.

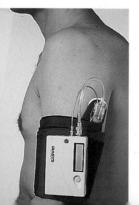

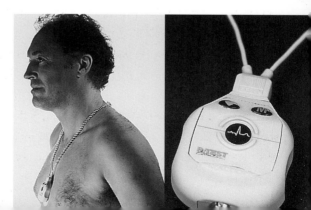

EXTENDING THE REACH OF SOUND

Acoustics Systems

AKG If Johann Sebastian Bach were alive today, he would leave his viola in its case. The great man preferred this rather shy instrument to the more prominent violin or cello because, as he put it, "I like to be at the heart of the music and to hear everything going on around me." Today we have one up on Bach. Most of the time we listen to music in recorded form, but new technologies allow us to experience it around us in a clear and natural way, at any time.

The Austrian firm AKG Acoustics, one of the world's leading specialist manufacturers of high-quality microphones and headphones, has taken pioneering steps to develop better ways of recording and reproducing sound to give the most natural result — using technology to extend the reach of our voices and ears.

Significant advances in this field have resulted from AKG's work on binaural processing and physiological loudness. When sounds or signals from a pair of headphones are processed binaurally, they are heard in such a way that the listener gains a three-dimensional aural impression. Not surprisingly, this is experienced as more realistic than the monaural processing which conventional headphones offer.

Sometimes sounds are clearer because they are louder. But while clarity is desirable, high volume often is not. AKG has therefore cleverly incorporated a physiological loudness contour into its headphones to ensure that each note can be heard clearly without increasing overall loudness. The result is superb sound, with minimum stress on the eardrum.

AKG is also a pioneer in the area of microphones. The highly acclaimed Tri-Power Series, with its newly designed Transducer Premium System provides a powerful, crisp sound, reducing ambient noise to a minimum. The company's Discreet line is specially designed to be inconspicuous: extremely slim gooseneck microphones for lecterns, boundary microphones (for floor, table, or wall mounting) smaller than the palm of your hand, and thumbnail-size lavalier microphones all provide essentially invisible amplification for the voice.

AKG supplies whole sound systems to a wide variety of customers, ranging from theatres, concert halls and conference centres to churches, schools, companies and local government. "We provide tailor-made solutions for all types of sound transmission, recording and reinforcement systems," says Hendrik Homan, the company's managing director. "We also make sure our products are easy to use since many of our non-professional target groups have little or no experience operating sound systems."

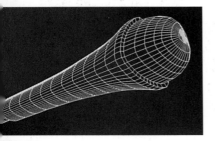

AKG's technical innovations have decisively influenced the entire audio industry. The company holds more than 1,400 patents and in 1995 received several awards for its entrepreneurial achievements, design, and technology.

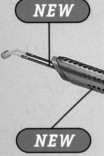

NEW

NEW

NEW

NEW

PRECISION ERGONOMICS: AN INSIDE STORY

Endoscopes

Olympus

NEW:

OPTICS
CE CERTIFICATION
WORKING ELEMENTS
MODULAR SHEATH DESIGN
THUMB RING
STOPCOCKS
TIP DESIGN
ATRAUMATIC MEATUS STOPPER

The resectoscope OES 4000: its lightweight and well-balanced construction enables more precision and less fatigue.

THEN

Even the earliest known practitioners of surgery made use of a wide range of tools. These included KNIVES (scalpels and lancets), AND DRILLING DEVICES, SCISSORS, SAWS, FORCEPS, CLAMPS, SYRINGES, MIRRORS (specula), TUBES for viewing or extracting fluids or foreign materials from body canals (catheters), NEEDLES, SUTURES, CASTS, SPLINTS, AND BANDAGES. Prosthetic devices such as simple ARTIFICIAL LIMBS made of wood and metal were also employed in ancient times, as were GLASS EYES and other simple cosmetic replacements of body parts.

In addition, early practitioners of surgery were well aware of the desirability of pain relief for patients, but few recourses were possible except the use of ALCOHOL or other STUPEFYING AGENTS. Variations of the tools of the early surgeon remain in use today.

COMPTON'S INTERACTIVE ENCYCLOPEDIA (COMPTON'S NEWMEDIA, INC., 1995).

ENDOSCOPES can be attached to powerful lights and multiple video cameras and effectively produce a three-dimensional image of a patient's anatomy. With a video endoscope in place, the surgeon can use a range of other miniaturized instruments, which can be passed through tiny apertures in the skin. An **INSUFFLATOR,** for example, can blow in carbon dioxide to dilate the abdomen, giving the surgeon more working space, while **SUCTION DEVICES** keep the area free of blood and fluid. There are **ULTRASONIC, HYDRAULIC, BALLOON AND LASER PROBES** for removing stones, clots, and other obstacles, and **CRUSHING FORCEPS** and shock wave generators for destroying stones. There are **HOOKS** for dissecting, **DIATHERM LOOPS** for burning and cutting, **CANNULAS** for injecting, and **GUN DEVICES** for stapling. The surgeon can manipulate all these instruments under video guidance with no direct view, inside the patient.

JOHN LAUNER, 'CUTTING EDGE...', *INTERNATIONAL MANAGEMENT*, VOL. 49, NO. 2, MARCH 1994.

NOW

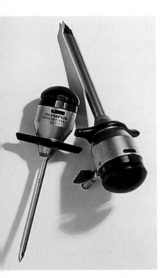

Minimally invasive, or keyhole surgery could be described as one of the most exciting developments in healthcare today. Safer and quicker than traditional surgery, and leaving only the tiniest of scars, it relies on the use of endoscopes, small telescope-like tools that can be inserted through a small incision to examine the inside of hollow organs. Attached to powerful lights and video cameras, they prepare the way for other devices, inserted through other small apertures in the skin, which help to carry out the operation itself. For such intimate and intricate work, both patient and doctor need to know — and see — that these tools are infinitely precise, totally hygienic, and of the highest possible quality.

German medical instrument maker Olympus Winter & Ibe has been applying new technologies and materials to make the confrontation between medical instruments and the body as 'painless' as possible. The company specialises in the design and manufacture of endoscopes and other tools for use in keyhole surgery. Due to the high degree of specialisation in this field, Olympus makes no fewer than 1,800 individual instruments, all of which have to meet the exacting standards demanded by this very sensitive area of the market.

A strategy that integrates design and technology has guided Olympus in rethinking and restructuring its complete range of products. The aims are to develop a consistent 'Olympus look', promoting brand identity, and to optimise the ergonomics of the instruments, with resulting benefits for both patient and doctor.

The success of this strategy is clearly demonstrated by the new OES 4000 series resectoscope, used for the removal of prostate tissue through the urethra. Because the surgeon needs to work with great precision and control over long periods of time, such an instrument must be comfortable to handle. It also has to be easy to clean and sterilise, to guarantee optimal hygiene.

The innovative design of the new resectoscope's handle allows a comfortable grip for precision tasks; and to make sure it fits every surgeon exactly, it comes with thumb rings in three sizes. The instrument is also lighter and better balanced than traditional resectoscopes because it incorporates titanium. Its tip is resistant to thermic stress, due to special ceramics — another first in the field.

The instruments in the 4000 series are designed as modular systems; and since they have to be taken apart during the course of an operation, Olympus has sensibly made sure that the pieces can be put together again easily and unambiguously. "Our guiding principle is that technological innovation should always be complemented by a continuous dialogue with those who will have to use it," says Hans-Joachim Winter, Olympus' managing director.

Important though it is, technology is not the whole story. With their clear and graceful contours and distinctive colour design, these instruments are unique in a field in which engineering qualities have hitherto reigned supreme. In this way, the company has succeeded in projecting a clear brand image.

Olympus specialises in the design and manufacture of
endoscopes and other tools for use in keyhole surgery.
It makes no fewer than 1,800 individual instruments.

Microchips and Smart Materials

THINGS T

We tend to think of products as lumps of dead matter: inert; passive; dumb. But products are becoming lively, active, and intelligent. Objects that are sensitive to their environment, act with some intelligence, and talk to each other, are changing the basic phenomenology of products — the way they exist in the world.

The result is to undermine long-standing design principles. "Form follows function" made sense when products were designed for a specific task — but not when responsive materials, that modify a product's behaviour, are available. Another nostrum, "truth to materials", was a moral imperative of the modern movement in design; it made sense when products were made of 'found' or natural materials whose properties were pre-determined. But 'truth' is less helpful as a design principle when the performance and behaviour of materials can be specified in advance, as is increasingly the case.

HAT THINK

Questioning received wisdom is tough: the idea that a 'product' is a discrete, hard, stand-alone *thing* is deeply rooted in traditional notions of design which developed to meet the needs of a system producing Model T Fords, domestic appliances, and a thousand other consumer products. They entail a linear design process that starts with an idea, develops that into a fixed specification, and is consummated at the end of the production line, when an object appears. But this model makes diminishing sense when products can be either physically adaptive, or networked together, or both.

I have a hammer, but I need a nail

Smartness, for now, remains more of a promise than a reality in most industries. Many of the more exotic smart materials are still at an experimental stage, and have yet to find widespread applications. "We have the hammer, but we're still looking for the nail," say researchers. And thousands of products are still produced that contain no microchips and remain dumb as dumb can be.

But the connectivity part of the equation is growing exponentially. Microchips are ubiquitous: 200 billion are in use already in all sorts of things, ranging from 747s to greetings cards. That's 35 microchips for every man, woman, and child on the planet. Each of those chips has the potential, using existing technology, to be connected to the others.

When that happens, products start to behave in economic terms, rather like gas meters. As more and more devices connect with each other, in the factory and in the home, and from there to telecommunication networks, value will be created by the supply and operation of networked devices — not in the sale of the hardware per se.

Formerly hardware-based industries will find themselves pushed remorselessly into the information business. Builders, who once built 'houses', will need to contend with issues of connectivity. Building suppliers, who once produced taps and doors and thermostats, will be forced to turn them into smart devices. Consumer electronics companies that now are happy to sell you a dumb stereo in a box, will have to teach it to talk to your television. Kitchen suppliers, accustomed to a world of chipboard cabinets and counter tops, must now contend with exotic materials and digital devices that change when heated, or spoken to.

These changes are already happening, but in a subtle way. None of the companies profiled in this chapter, whose products range from artificial legs to digital ticket systems, set out to make their products 'smart'. But in solving real-world challenges, the availability of microprocessors, or new materials, made their task easier.

Blatchford, for example, uses new materials and chips in its products — not for their own sake, but to help people walk. This British company, the first to develop an intelligent prosthetic limb, needed to make its products light, strong, and easily formed into complex shapes — so it sought out and applied advanced carbon fibre composite materials to the task. It also needed to control automatically the flexion and extension of the limb to make walking easier, so it incorporated sensors and microchips.

Another of our featured companies, **ScanView**, is engaged in how to deliver large amounts of processing power (for example, scanning 300,000 pixels of visual data per second) to a client group of graphic design offices without burdening them with physically large, or psychologically oppressive, hardware. An Irish computer storage company, **Eurologic**, which makes 'hot swappable device carriers', is motivated by a similar drive to reduce the physical and psychological footprint of its products.

The materials of invention

If companies have a problem at all in exploiting opportunities presented by chips and new materials, it is that they are spoilt for choice. For the first million years or so after his appearance, man used essentially five materials to make tools and objects: wood, rock, bone, horn, and leather. For 9000 years following the Neolithic revolution, there was a significant enrichment: clay, wool, plant fibres, and — in relatively recent times — metals. But it still took at least a generation for information about smelting to cross a single continent in the iron age.

Today, novel substances are being cooked up in academic and corporate laboratories faster than industry can find uses for them. Designers and manufacturers are faced with an enormous and expanding field of possibilities — in the selection of materials, and of industrial processes to transform them. An important book by Ezio Manzini, *The Material of Invention,* puts into perspective the revolutionary implications for product development and design of new materials. Known and trusted physical limits, that are deeply embedded in the skills and cultures of craftsmen and production engineers, are suddenly disappearing.

As well as choosing among a myriad alternatives to meet existing needs, designers also confront the problem of what a product should look like. What form should it take? New materials have no absolute form. Neither do they have 'natural properties' to determine a product's shape. A material of invention is no longer a found material; rather, it is calculated and engineered to achieve a specific, desired performance.

The problem for companies and designers is that inventors categorise their materials according to what they are — rather than what they do, or how they behave. Grouping materials by type does not help the product designer confronted by databases and directories bulging with thousands of plastics, ceramics, fibres, composites, rubber and foam, glass, wood, and metals. What's needed are information systems that direct designers first to *properties*, and thence to the different materials that possess them.

Dematerialisation
Ironically, the most interesting property of new materials is their capacity to promote the dematerialisation of products — the use of less matter to accomplish a given task. SRI, an American think-tank, evaluates new materials and processes against just this benchmark (see box on p. 288). Researchers at Domus Academy, a design think-tank in Milan, concur that smart materials can make their products lighter, simpler, and better connected to each other.

Lightness: A range of composites, laminates, and what are known as 'structurally gradient' materials is being used to replace heavier materials such as steel or concrete. Some new materials are so light and ethereal that we have not yet worked out how to exploit them: silica aerogel, for example, is an ultralight material, comprising 99.9 percent air, developed at the Livermore National Laboratories in California. One entranced reviewer of the substance, Julie Wosk, said it "had the translucency of clouds and the eerie, phantasmagoric look of a hologram." Aerogel is used as an insulating material, and as a filter, but has not yet been exploited by product designers.

Simplicity: Simplicity delivers quality — a consumer need which dominated the business agenda of the 1980s — when complex and therefore failure-prone assemblies of sub-components are minimised. New materials that behave as if they are devices — but are not — enable the substitution of mechanical with membrane keyboards, or of lightbulbs with electro-luminescent surfaces.

Smart stuff: SRI's list of materials, information, and process technology to watch

- Advanced Silicon Micro-electronics/ULSI (M), (I), (P)
- Biocatalysis (P)
- Biopolymers (M)
- Biosensors (I), (P)
- Computer-Aided Software Engineering (I)
- Conductive Polymers (M)
- Diamond Thin Films (M), (I)
- Engineering Polymers (M)
- Fibre-Optic Communications (M), (I)
- Fibre-Optic Sensors (I), (P)
- Flat Panel Displays (I)
- Fuel Cells (P)
- Fuzzy Logic (I), (P)
- Groupware (I)
- High-Definition Imaging Systems (I)
- Knowledge-Based Systems (I)
- Machine-Vision Systems (I)
- Membrane Separation (M), (P)
- Metal/Intermetallic Matrix Composites (M)
- Micromachining (P)
- Natural Language Processing (I)
- Neural Networks (I)
- Nondestructive Testing and Evaluation (M), (P)
- Object-Oriented Technology (I)
- Optical Storage Technologies (I)
- Optoelectronic Systems and Circuits (M), (I)
- Parallel Computing (I)
- Photovoltaics (M), (P)
- Polymer Matrix Composites (M)
- Portable Batteries (M)
- Portable Intelligence (I)
- Quantum GaAs Micro-electronics (M), (I)
- Rapid Prototyping (M), (I), (P)
- Robotics (I), (P)
- Smart Materials (M), (I),
- Solid-State Microsensors (I), (P)
- Speech Recognition (I)
- Structural Adhesives (M)
- Structural Ceramics/Ceramic Matrix Composites (M)
- Superconductivity (M)
- Virtual Environments (I)

SRI.

Hardness: Modern ceramics and advanced composites can be nearly as hard as diamonds and are equally resistant to heat and corrosion — but cheaper. They are being made into turbines, dental braces, prosthetic body implants, even bullet-proof face masks.

Transparency: Dematerialisation does not just mean less matter in a product — it also means less physical presence. Architects, who are leading the way in a search for 'de-massified' buildings, have stimulated the development of new strong but lightweight glazing systems, translucent panels, and light-reflective finishes that make objects disappear.

Environmental sensitivity: Fibre-optic sensors, which have been used for many years to deliver information, are now being combined with sensing technologies such as piezo-electric materials — shape memory alloys which change their shape according to temperature — so that distant environments may be monitored remotely. Applications range from security to medicine.

Nice to meet you
We are accustomed to conversing with a computer, or interacting with a cash dispenser. But if they have chips, and most of them do, our microwaves, fax machines, CD players, washing machines, light switches, thermostats, burglar alarms, and door locks also have the capacity to *communicate with each other*.

The growing use of 'mechatronics' does not mean that dumb toasters will suddenly become philosophers. But it does mean that the borders between 'products' and 'information' are starting to dissolve.

This is clear enough in the case of **SkiData**. Ostensibly in the business of dispensing millions of electronic tickets to people attending trade fairs, joining toll-roads, parking in garages, or heading for ski slopes, the Austrian company is in fact in the business of information network services; its hardware, and in particular its wrist-worn devices developed with Swatch, are what you notice; but in value terms they are simply interfaces to the system — a bit like mobile telephones.

Most of us probably assume that microchips are small things that sit inside desktop computers — but 90 percent of all microprocessors are in automobiles and domestic appliances. (Or in the case of the Icelandic company **Vaki**, in boxes under water counting fish!). It famously takes more computing power to run a BMW motor car today than it took to send early astronauts round the moon. The average value of electronic components in cars today is already 750 ECU; according to the Economist Intelligence Unit, that will soar to over 1,350 ECU per car within a decade. "The world market for automotive electronics will be a staggering 66 billion ECU by 2005," says the EIU; "electronics will become the driving force behind vehicle design."

Where cars lead, other consumer products invariably follow. Computer company Novell estimates that there are about 145 microprocessor-controlled devices in every (presumably American) home. Novell is developing home-based systems, which it calls NEST (NetWare Embedded Systems), that permit any device to communicate with any other. When such systems are in place, a central computer can do everything from turning off lights to turning on sprinklers.

The potential for energy savings alone, when such networks combine smart sensors with an intelligent controller, are immense. Buildings consume some 50 percent of the world's energy — and by some estimates, at least half that could be saved if heating (and cooling) systems were more sensitive to the minute-by-minute needs of users. Even the most advanced buildings still consume vast amounts of energy to sustain average temperatures even when rooms or buildings are empty. **Holmhed**, a Swedish company that makes small demolition robots, may be part of the answer: its 'jackhammers on tracks' now have programmable remote controls — so presumably they could be instructed to go forth and tear down energy-inefficient buildings.

But microchips will not just enhance practical aspects of running a house. Affective and aesthetical qualities can also be enriched. **Artemide**, the Italian lighting company profiled in this chapter, is legendary in design circles for totemic lighting fixtures, such as the Tizio desktop lamp that graces designer desktops in films and advertisements, and sells several hundred thousand units a year. But even Artemide, once a byword for object fetishism, is going digital with its remarkable *Metamorfosi,* which affords the householder up to 12 million different lighting combinations. So far, Metamorfosi is microprocessor controlled but stand-alone; but for how long? Potentially it can talk to the other lighting systems now — so sooner or later it will.

Hundreds of manufacturers are developing system infastructures for the control of a houseful of gadgets — the software, transceivers, routers, and other networking equipment that link the microprocessors in discrete products together. This technology takes the decentralisation of computing — which has its roots in the transition from mainframes to PCs—one step further. Once these smart sensors and microprocessors are joined together, you get yet another network — and a context in which hardware and software become the infrastructure for a new kind of service.

Embedded, but not asleep
A world in which products and appliances talk to each other sounds fantastic, but it's not so long since the advent of electricity was greeted with similar amazement: then, objects which once had to be worked by hand, began to power themelves. Now, objects which we expect

to have to control ourselves, will tell themselves what to do.

If the rapid electrification of everyday life just two or three generations ago is any guide, embedded computing may not be so hard to get used to for consumers. But the task for product developers and designers is harder. How can a radically new technology (or rather, family of technologies) be introduced to a public that is either ignorant of the benefits, or downright hostile to the whole idea?

When electricity was first introduced into the home, there was a tendency in industry to portray its aims, its technological prowess, and its dynamic power in mythological terms. AEG, for example, used the Goddess of Light as its trademark. But once electricity's magical novelty wore off, and everyday products began to be 'electrified', designers had to find new ways to make products such as electric irons, kettles, lightbulbs, and cookers interesting to consumers. Reasoning that "even an electric motor must look like a birthday present," artists like AEG's Peter Behrens turned themselves into industrial designers to accomplish just that.

Today, electric motor technology has disappeared from view almost entirely. It's there, humming away inside a swarm of everyday household products. Today's Network visionaries anticipate a future in which products are transformed from discrete lumps of matter into components of an integrated consumer appliance and office automation 'medium'.

Flaky? It's a bewitching vision of the future — but James Woudhuysen, who manages long-term market research for Philips Sound and Vision, thinks these scenarios are further away than we think: "The consumer of digital media and appliances meets convergence only in the same way that, in a blizzard, the snow seems to 'converge' upon you. We all may hope that everything will one day be controlled by a single, submissive black box below the stairs — but in new technology, systems are more prone to being incompatible than to matching up with each other."

In contrast to the heady days when electricity arrived, the main task of design in connection with embedded intelligence is systems integration. The creation of new design languages to articulate the wonders of domestic smartness will be less of a priority for the time being.

Nonetheless, the nature of innovation and design will have to change. In 1903, AEG's Paul Westheim observed of design at the dawn of the electrical age, "in order to make a lucid, logical and clearly articulated entity out of an arc lamp, a complete transformation of our aesthetic notions was necessary." The same could be said today of information technology. A new presence has come into our lives, yet it lacks visible form or expression. As with electricity in 1900, so with embedded information systems now, design is faced with an aesthetic as well as a practical challenge: how to represent something essentially abstract in such a way that it can be used and appreciated by us all.

Ezio Manzini observes that we are living in the 'twilight of mechanics', an age of boundless possibility in which anything thinkable becomes possible. But what happens when we do not know what 'needs' this explosion of material creativity is supposed to meet? "The uncontrolled increase of performances and forms, made possible by technique, takes place beyond adequate cultural control," says Manzini, "thus producing noise and trash."

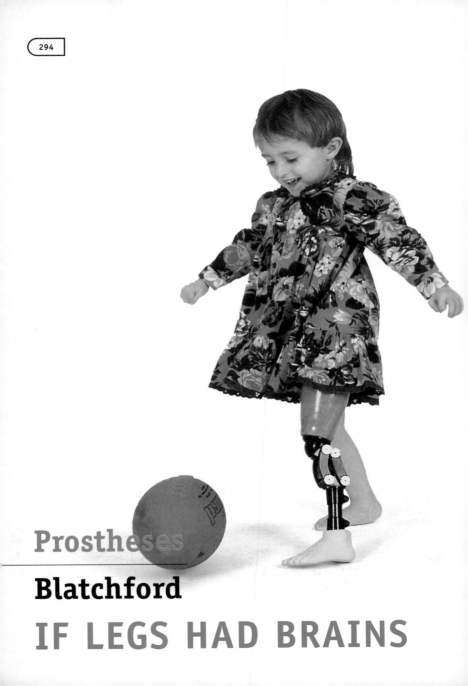

Prostheses

Blatchford

IF LEGS HAD BRAINS

Researchers are trying to develop artificial limbs that can transmit sensations to the brain. The first step has been the development of a neural implant that will be capable of connecting a person to an artificial neural impulse system. Next, researchers must develop a neural interface that can simulate natural sensations like texture and temperature.

TECHNOLOGY REVIEW, VOL. 97, NO. 7, OCTOBER 1994.

"One moment, captain," says the new crew-member, taking from his pocket what looks like a TV remote control device; "I just need to reprogram my legs to compensate for the Enterprise's change of gravity warp." Even Jean-Luc Picard of the Starship Enterprise would raise an eyebrow in admiration at where modern science is going. The leg with a brain is here right now — a remarkable achievement by the British manufacturer of artificial limbs, Charles A. Blatchford and Sons.

The concept of a computer-controlled prosthesis, first proposed in Japan in the mid 1980s, was taken up by Blatchford, who introduced the first commercial computer-controlled prosthesis in 1995. This new prosthesis, known as the Endolite Intelligent Prosthesis Plus (or IP+, for short), contains a tiny microprocessor to control the speed and precise movements of the limb.

The great advance that the IP+ represents can probably only be fully appreciated by those who have undergone amputation above the knee and tried earlier prostheses. The IP+ allows them to experience natural walking again at a wide range of speeds. The intelligent limb incorporates a sensor that detects any variation in the wearer's gait through changes in the angle of the knee joint. This information is relayed to a microprocessor that controls a miniature stepper motor. With most artificial legs, the wearer has to exert a considerable amount of muscular effort to restrain the swing or, conversely, to kick through. Now, the flexion and extension of the limb are automatically controlled, making the experience of walking more effortless. During fitting, the microprocessor is programmed to correspond to the customer's individual patterns of walking. Later, the wearer can use a remote control to reprogram it in a matter of minutes. The comfort, convenience, more natural gait, and increased

range that the IP+ provides speed up amputees' rehabilitation considerably.

Since it was founded in 1890, Blatchford has been at the forefront of artificial limb technology. In the late 1970s, the company solved a long-standing problem in prosthetics — the seeming incompatibility of lightness, strength, and malleability — by introducing carbon fibre composites. These lightweight materials are stiff and strong and can be easily formed into the complex shapes required. The first flexible prosthesis made of this material was introduced in the late 1980s.

All Blatchford's products are designed and developed in conjunction with its marketing, quality, and manufacturing departments. "This multidisciplinary team carries the project from start to finish — and beyond," says Saeed Zahedi, senior research engineer at Blatchford. "We continue to provide customers with support after sales, and take that opportunity to collect vital feedback." In the case of the IP+, the company entered into a joint venture with an electronic design firm and carried out systematic evaluations with users and professionals to ensure that adjusting the product would be as easy as possible for both groups. "The IP+ was going to be such a revolutionary product," says Zahedi, "that we had to prepare people for it."

Today, innovation is, as it has always been, Blatchford's 'secret weapon'. "We've found it to be key to successful product development," says Stephen Blatchford, the company's managing director. "And we see our fluid approach to design as instrumental in helping us to continue that tradition."

Since it was founded in 1890, Blatchford has been at the forefront of artificial limb technology.

The IP+ contains a tiny microprocessor to
control the speed and precise movements
of the limb.

An above-knee artificial limb can cost as much as $12,000. Others, used by mountaineers and skiers who have lost a leg, can cost $16,000 to $20,000. Braces for the legs can range in price from $150 for an 'ankle-foot orthotic' to $2,500 for a 'long-leg' type with springs that lift the toes and locks that shut automatically to keep the leg straight. Standard manual wheelchairs cost $2,000 to $3,000. Power-driven chairs cost about twice that amount, and more high-tech models start roughly at $10,000. A 'sip and puff' wheelchair made for those with no ability to move their arms or legs can cost $15,000 to $20,000.

ETHNIC NEWSWATCH/SOFTLINE INFORMATION, INC., STAMFORD, CT.

The Tizio desk lamp, designed by Richard Sapper,
is just one of Artemide's famous 'classics'.

BRINGING NATURE INDOORS: THE METAMORPHOSIS OF LIGHT

Winner '97!

Lighting Fixtures

Artemide Age-old associations with the spirit of life, with mystery and magic, with quiet reflection or stimulating activity have long made light a powerful creator of atmosphere. While theatre and film have always used lighting for dramatic effect, the application of such techniques in the everyday world has remained relatively limited. Artemide, a well-established Italian manufacturer of lighting fixtures, is changing all that.

Artemide is a design-oriented company whose now classic objects have graced the pages of the foremost design magazines for decades. But its new Metamorfosi lighting system marks a radical shift in its approach to interior lighting, away from the fixture or luminaire towards the intangible qualities of light itself and the infinite variety of atmospheres it can create.

Metamorfosi is nothing less than a technical revolution in interior lighting. It allows people to create and design their own lighting, varying its colour and intensity simply by pressing a button on a remote control device. Each variation suffuses the room with a different atmosphere to suit a particular situation.

The system works like this: three parabolic reflectors project light from three 100-watt halogen bulbs through three separate filters in red, green, and blue. Each filter creates a single-coloured beam of light surrounded by several haloes, which are also coloured. Together, the three-coloured beams produce white light. A fourth projector with a 150-watt halogen bulb provides additional white light. The light emitted from each of the lamps can be controlled separately and simultaneously by a patented microchip. Twelve different lighting 'atmospheres' have been preprogrammed into the chip, but people can also create and store their own combinations for later use, reprogramming them as often as they like; of the 12 million possible subtle variations, 54 can be stored at any one time. Using the remote control, it is possible to switch from one to another and to vary the intensity of the light.

"Because it lacks colour variation, interior lighting has never really been able to convey the full meaning of natural light," says Ernesto Gismondi, Artemide's managing director. "Natural light has a whole range of symbolic and emotional associations for us: just think of how sunsets, moonlight, or dappled light filtered through trees can affect our mood. Metamorfosi gives people the resources to use light to create their own ideal atmosphere indoors, to fit the mood of the moment."

Artemide has an advanced research and development centre which re-examines individual product components on a continuous basis to see where improvements can be made and to ensure that appliances conform to European standards. Relevant technologies, such as new light sources, dimmers, fibre optics, microprocessors and remote control systems are continually reviewed and exploited where appropriate. The company's design and product engineering departments make use of CAD systems, and its laboratory ensures that Artemide products and services are automatically certified to the highest standards of quality.

By shifting its focus from fixtures to the infinite potential of light itself, Artemide has taken interior lighting an important step forward, moving it beyond the mere aesthetic, towards the truly timeless.

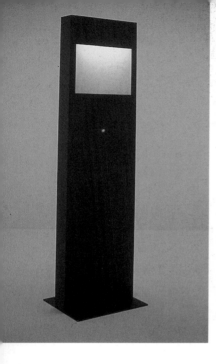

Metamorfosi allows people to create and design their own lighting, varying its colour and intensity simply by pressing a button on a remote control device.

The alternation of day and night leads to a complex relationship with light, giving rise to intimate connections with our biological rhythm and our moods.

PAOLO INGHILLERI, *LIGHT FIELDS*, ARTEMIDE/GRAFICHE MAZZUCCHELLI, 1996.

CAISSE AUTOMATIQUE

SKIDATA

*SkiData's recent APT 450 car park system is probably
the world's most advanced system of its kind.*

OPEN SESAME

cket Systems

kiData

"Tickets, please!" will soon sound as antiquated as the ic town crier's "Three o'clock and all's well", if the Austrian company SkiData ts way. SkiData develops, produces, and markets electronic ticket and entry ms for ski-lift units, garages, motorway toll stations and trade fairs. All the any's products are based on the principle that tickets should be hands-free and argeable, not only for convenience, but also to minimise the problem of litter ed by paper tickets.

The key role of design at SkiData is reflected in the perfect functionality and the striking forms its products take. "Our aim is to meet the needs of our immediate customers — those who install our systems — and of the actual end-users," says W. Kocznar of SkiData.

One of the company's principal innovative systems is its KeyWatch technology, developed in collaboration with the Swiss watchmaker Swatch. This technology is used in the colourful Swatch Access watch, which incorporates a ski-pass. The skier 'loads' the watch at a cash point with a ski-pass of the desired type. Then, as he or she passes the Swatch Access scanner, the watch is 'read', and — Open Sesame! — the turnstile opens automatically. Once the validity of the pass expires, the watch can be recharged.

KeyWatch forms an integral part of all SkiData ticket systems, including KeyDetector, the company's new hands-free trade fair admission system. It is being further developed as the company's core competence.

SkiData's recent APT 450 car park system is probably the world's most advanced admission and payment system of its kind. A sophisticated combination of four ticket technologies, it allows 'one-slot shopping'. All types of cards fit into a single slot: it can process barcodes (for short-term parking tickets), magnetic data (for credit cards, etc.), chip-cards (for 'cash' payments), as well as SkiData's KeyWatch technology (for season tickets), in the form of a KeyCard or KeyZip (a watch-like device). Season ticket-holders can also equip their cars with a special device which is recognised by a detector in the ground and opens the barrier as the car approaches.

More than a million SkiData hands-free data carriers are now in use throughout Europe. Setting new standards of convenience, flexibility, and environmental care, these rechargeable electronic tickets are fast showing the traditional paper ticket to the nearest exit.

SkiData's modern access terminal Ski System 330 was first put into operation in 1993 and is now used in many large and well-known ski areas, such as Zell am See and Gstaad.

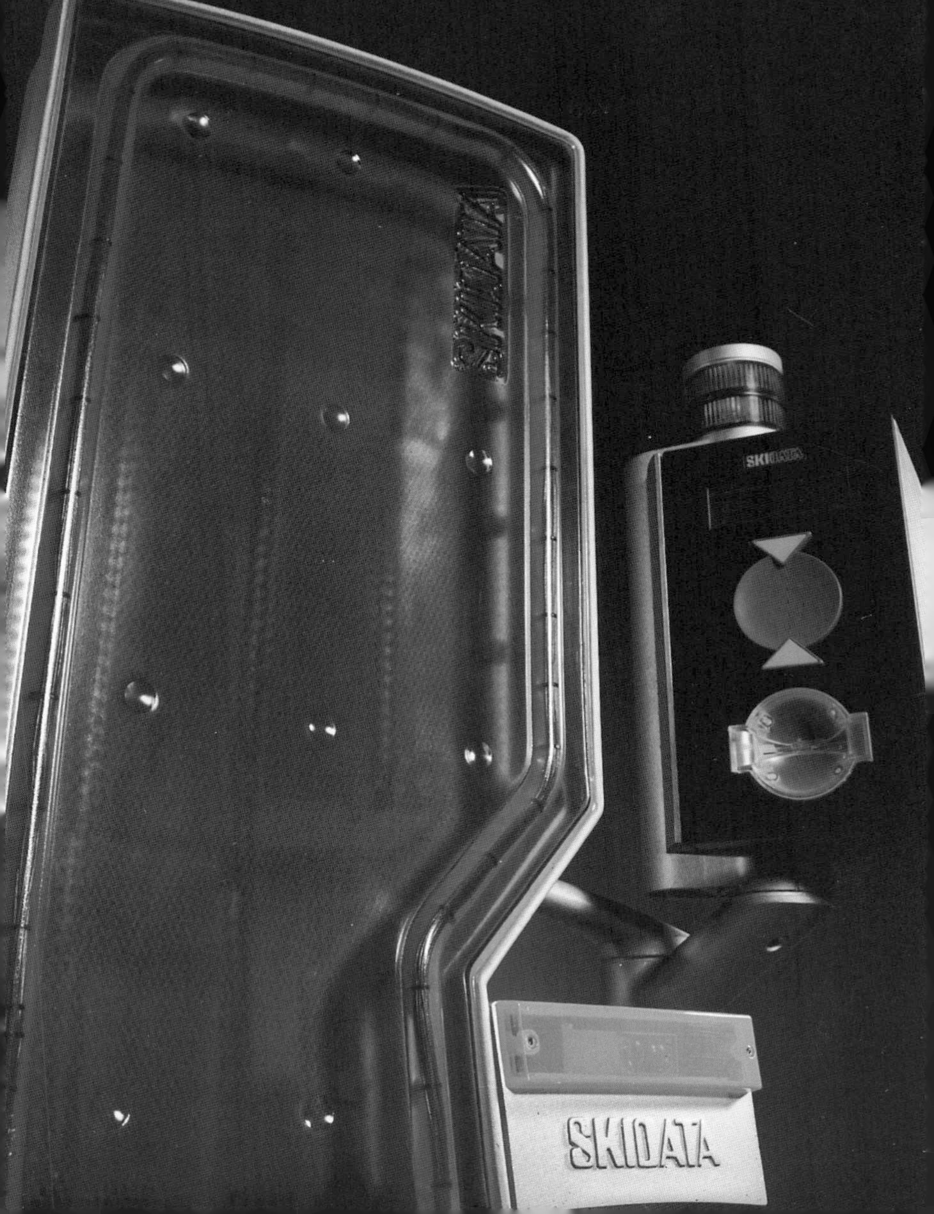

If each adult pu
each week, the t
1,200,0
per year in

hases two tickets
ket market totals
0,000
rope alone.

DIGITAL
COLOUR QUARTET

Colour Scanners

ScanView The human eye can perceive many more colours than any machine can reproduce, but the pre-press industry is constantly on the look-out for new ways of analysing and processing images that will maintain and enhance colour quality through the various stages of reproduction.

One of the primary tools used in this industry is the scanner. Until recently, only two types of colour scanners were available: large, expensive drum scanners, which provided excellent quality but could only be used by trained professionals, and small, more affordable, flatbed devices, whose comparative ease-of-use was offset by the lower quality of their scans. Bridging this gap between quality and ease-of-use was the challenge ScanView took on when it was founded in 1990. The aim of this young Danish company was to bring professional scanning quality within the reach of new markets by making drum scanners smaller and selling them for a fraction of the price of traditional models.

ScanView's first product, the ScanMate compact drum scanner, came out in 1991 and was awarded the prestigious Danish ID Prize for its outstanding industrial design. During the next few years, the company produced several other high-quality compact drum scanners and expanded its range to include digital cameras and image setters.

ScanView also developed an innovative software package for automatic colour correction, ColorQuartet, whose flexible, modular structure makes it sophisticated enough for professionals and simple enough for amateurs. Colour correction is always necessary when an image has to undergo several colour mappings on different devices, which may interpret colours on the basis of inconsistent standards. ScanView's system is based on the 'colour space' standard of the *Commission Internationale de l'Eclairage* (CIE) — a mathematical model of the human eye's response to colour which allows any perceivable colour to be defined precisely. "Using the CIE model not only makes colour more measurable and easier to compare," says Ib Drachmann, ScanView's managing director, "it also provides a way for us to make machines adapt to human needs, instead of the other way around."

Recently, ScanView has further broadened its product range to incorporate the latest advances in flatbed scanning technology. The company's first high-quality flatbed, the ScanMate F8, has a scanning speed of up to 300,000 pixels per second, making it up to twice as fast as standard flatbeds. Its unique built-in light table makes it possible to compare the digitalised image on the screen with the original in the scanner, without interrupting the process.

From the outset, ScanView's products have attracted international acclaim for both their internal technology and their external design. Says Drachmann, "We've taken great pains to design our products to fit gracefully and efficiently into all sorts of environments."

In its short lifetime, ScanView has evolved into one of the world's most versatile suppliers of open systems for colour handling, with two wholly-owned subsidiaries, major market shares in Europe, and a growing presence in North America and the Far East. In 1990, ScanView was a company of three with a turnover of one million ECU. Six years later, it employs 140 people and has increased its turnover twentyfold.

The ScanMate F8 is an unusually attractive and compact flatbed scanner that fits easily into any working environment.

DATA STORAGE COMES OUT OF THE CLOSET

Data Storage Systems

Eurologic Storage of data is increasingly becoming storage of computer data. But as computer files take the place of paper ones, traditional attitudes toward archives as purely functional areas seem to have changed little. Many of today's electronic data storage systems are relegated to separate computer rooms where they look as austerely functional as the shelves and boxes that preceded them. But the role and nature of data storage has changed radically. Our lives are becoming increasingly computerised and our interaction with new archives is much more intensive than it was with the old ones. At the same time, miniaturisation and

more efficient technologies have reduced the need for a separate physical space. So why must data storage systems remain so unattractive? The Irish company, Eurologic Systems, has set out to prove that they don't — that data storage systems can emerge from the backroom proudly to take their place in the front office, or even in the home.

Eurologic designs, manu-factures, and markets a range of high-availability, high-perfor-mance data storage systems for computers. Its XL 400 series for the fileserver and mid-range markets is innovative in terms of both its technology and its styling. "We've broken with convention in designing an eye-catching and attractive product in an area which has traditionally been very conservative," says John Maybury, Eurologic's managing director.

The heart of the series is what is known as a 'hot swappable device carrier', a drawer-like unit that can accommodate a wide variety of storage devices — hard disks, CD units, tape-streamers, power supplies, controller and display units, etc., in both narrow and wide formats. Up to nine of these 'drawers' can be stored in a tower array in flexible combinations. The carriers can be easily taken out and replaced by others, thanks to the array's single internal backplane, which can be configured to comprise one or two separate SCSI buses (small computer system interfaces). The system can be expanded indefinitely simply by adding more tower arrays.

The XL 400 series incorporates leading-edge technology: it conforms to the latest Ultra SCSI specifications (one of the first products in its class to do so); its cooling mechanism can cope with drives as fast as 10,200 RPM; and a patented controlled release mechanism ensures the easy insertion and removal of the carrier.

Eurologic has utilised both in-house and European-based external resources to develop its innovative design concepts. "To be successful in the rapidly changing hardware market, you've got to be better than the competition," says Maybury, "and that means delivering better functionality, performance, pricing, support, and value than your competitors. We believe that our innovations and superior design will allow us to achieve all that."

Eurologic's XL 400 data storage system not only incorporates leading-edge technology but is also an eye-catching and attractive product.

A SENSITIVE HOME-WRECKER

Demolition Equipment

Holmhed "It was love at first sight," says Mikael Holm about MiniCut, the world's smallest demolition robot. Holm was one of the first to work with the machine during a recent renovation project in Karlsstad, Sweden. The building in Karlsstad — a historic structure with a number of fine, interior architectural features — required something more versatile and precise than the typical demolition equipment. "The beams in the building couldn't take more than 450 kilograms, so we weren't able to use our heavy wrecking machines," says Holm. Weighing in at a mere 380 kilograms, the MiniCut is a bantamweight in comparison.

Renovating a house or building complex usually involves hours of tedious, physically strenuous, and potentially dangerous demolition work, which must be carried out in confined spaces, often by hand. To help make demolition work more efficient and more economical, the Swedish company Holmhed came up with MiniCut,

The MiniCut is the world's smallest demolition robot.

an agile, lightweight, compact demolition robot that can access hard-to-reach spots, move effortlessly over heaps of rubble, and complete each job with safety, speed, and precision.

MiniCut is essentially a powerful, remote-controlled jackhammer on tracks. Its programmable digital remote control eliminates the risk of workers suffering muscle strain or being injured by falling debris. A special new hydraulic breaker, developed especially for use with the MiniCut, is three to four times more effective than a conventional hand-held jackhammer.

Martin Johansson, managing director of Holmhed, readily acknowledges the important role design has played in the success of the robot. "We engaged a product designer from the very beginning of the development project," he says. "For us, designing the MiniCut meant stepping into a whole new world of possibilities." The machine, known affectionately as 'The Cat', was designed using three-dimensional computer graphics systems and animations. These techniques meant that various technical and design solutions could be easily tested, refined, and retested until the best result was obtained — all without the need for costly preliminary engineering work.

With the MiniCut, Holmhed offers contractors a safer way to carry out demolition work that would otherwise be time-consuming and expensive — a 'home-wrecker' that is a milestone not only for the company, but for the whole demolition industry.

The lightweight, versatile, and remotely-controlled MiniCut can safely access the most hard-to-reach spots.

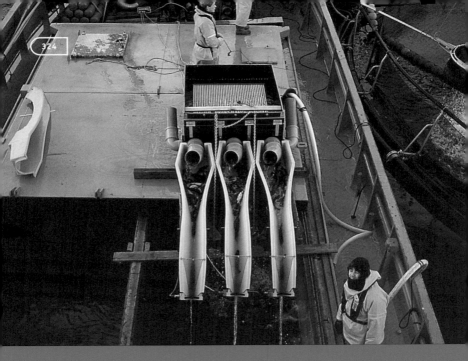

In 1948 the total world fish catch
was about 19 million metric tons.
With the introduction of advanced
harvesting technologies,
the total catch rose to
over 60 million metric tons by 1970.
Although there have been major
fluctuations, the trend since
1970 has been upward:
almost 77 million metric tons
in 1982, to more than 97 million
metric tons in 1990.

GROLLIER MULTIMEDIA ENCYCLOPEDIA, 1995.

COUNTING FISH

Aquaculture Systems

Vaki Fish farmers need precise information about numbers in order to manage their stocks properly. Vaki Aquaculture Systems, a small Icelandic company established in 1986, produces the world's first automatic devices for counting and estimating the size of live fish. Not surprisingly, Vaki's Bioscanner has quickly established itself all over the world as an essential tool in the handling, transfer, and sale of live fish. It uses infrared imaging technology to count up to 60,000 fish per hour — from three-gram babies to sturdy, six-kilogram adults — with an accuracy of virtually 100 percent.

The Bioscanner works in three stages. First, the fish are directed through a V-shaped channel, which regulates the flow of fish and water and separates the fish so that they can be counted. Up to four scanners then 'see' the fish as they pass through and count them. Finally, a control unit gathers and displays the data. If two fish pass the scanner simultaneously, advanced software analyses the data, images, and silhouettes from the scanners, to distinguish between them. The Bioscanner, which is available in several models to meet varying needs, is used by over 700 fish farms around the world.

The same basic technology is used in the submersible Biomass Counter, which performs the same task with respect to fish in underwater sea cages. Farmers need accurate information on biomass to be able to plan harvesting and sales schedules, to decide which cages to harvest and how much food or medication to give.

The Biomass Counter consists of a scanner frame and a display unit. The frame is submerged and placed between two cages. As each fish swims from one cage to the other, its number and size are recorded by the display unit. This is linked to a PC which analyses the data, using software developed by Vaki with two Norwegian companies. The software not only displays distribution curves and average weight but can also review historic and current data to give a reliable forecast of future biomass and size distribution. Installed in fish ladders, the device has proven particularly useful for counting and estimating the size of migrating salmon.

Design was unheard of in the fish farming industry before Vaki came along. Of the company's eight employees, two are full-time designers, and external design consultants are called in when needed. "Design plays a big part in our efforts to find and implement solutions to meet customers' needs," says Hermann Kristjansson, Vaki's managing director. Turnover has doubled over the past five years and the success of the company's new technology has led to initiatives to extend it to new areas — Vaki is currently developing similar equipment to count chickens.

Vaki's River Stock Monitor for counting and
weighing migrating fish in rivers.

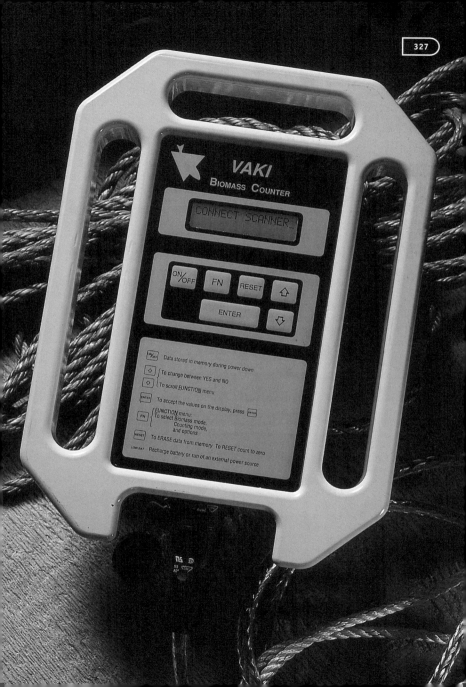

The annual per capita consumption of fish and shellfish in the years 1986 to 1988 averaged 20.5 kg in the US, 50.9 kg in Hong Kong, 71.2 kg in Japan, and 92.4 kg in Iceland.

COMPTON'S INTERACTIVE ENCYCLOPEDIA (COMPTON'S NEW MEDIA, INC., 1995).

Forecasts show a worldwide shortage of 30 million metric tons of fish by the year 2000.

THE EUROPEAN, APRIL 14, 1995.

Fish, mostly cod, accounts for about 80% of Iceland's merchandise exports.

INTERNATIONAL MANAGEMENT, VOL. 49, NO. 2, MARCH 1994.

ECO
LIMITS

LOGICAL

A Business Opportunity?

Most companies experience 'the environment' as a great weight of pressures and limits — not as a positive business opportunity. For 30 years, a stream of ghastly projections about the dire fate of the planet has left many people demotivated. As a business issue the environment seems all pain and no gain; environmental campaigners like Greenpeace use modern media techniques skilfully to get their message across, but the result is that many people feel guilty, rather than motivated to act. But without business, we will never tackle the environmental problem.

Pieter Winsemius, Director of McKinsey and Co. in the Netherlands, has discussed environmental issues with many managers. "When you listen to people, they always make the right sounds about the changes necessary for sustainable development," he says. "Everyone agrees that we cannot go on polluting the environment and destroying ecosystems. The interesting thing is that nothing — or at least not enough — is actually changing."

Is there business to be had in getting these graphs to turn downwards?

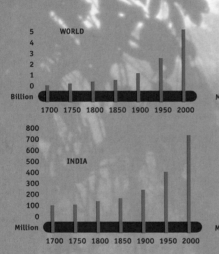

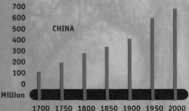
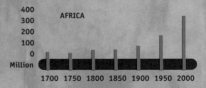

World population 1700 - 2000 AD
CLIVE PONTING, *A GREEN HISTORY OF THE WORLD*, (NEW YORK: PENGUIN, 1991).

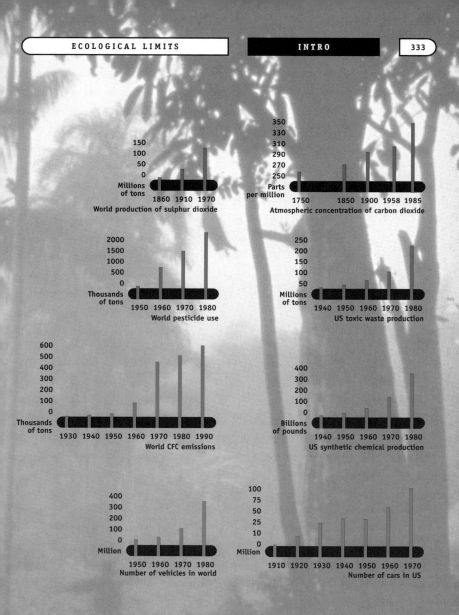

World production of sulphur dioxide

Atmospheric concentration of carbon dioxide

World pesticide use

US toxic waste production

World CFC emissions

US synthetic chemical production

Number of vehicles in world

Number of cars in US

Pollution

CLIVE PONTING, *A GREEN HISTORY OF THE WORLD*, (NEW YORK: PENGUIN, 1991).

Dr. Winsemius has identified the following five barriers to change confronting business managers:

- 'Issue overload': many managers are preoccupied by operational issues and quite understandably find it difficult to develop a long-term perspective on something as abstract as the environment.
- There is a tendency to overestimate what has been done, and to underestimate what remains to be done; this diminishes any sense of urgency.
- There is a shared lack of understanding — the result of too little communication — among business, government, experts, NGOs, and eco-campaigners.
- Company structures and systems, especially of larger companies, are too slow to change.
- People in key jobs are simply apprehensive about the scale and pace of change that they are being asked to embrace.

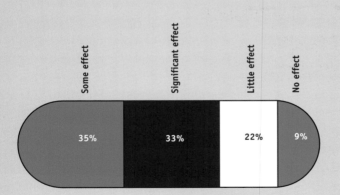

SME perception of the impact of environmental concerns on their businesses over the next five years
GALLUP SME ATTITUDE SURVEY, 1995.

56%	Site condition/appearance
66%	
83%	Waste management
63%	
72%	Energy consumption
62%	
64%	Use of raw materials
59%	
90%	Water pollution
51%	
71%	Recycling
50%	
89%	Air pollution
48%	
64%	Noise pollution
48%	
45%	Product life cycle
48%	
68%	Traffic congestion
43%	
79%	Land contamination
40%	
56%	Water usage
38%	
57%	Odour pollution
37%	

■ SMEs
■ Environment in general

Issues considered important to SMEs and the environment in general

Helping the environment	31%
Improved image	28%
Higher employee morale	21%
Cost savings	21%
Compliance with legislation	19%
Increased sales	17%
New markets and opportunities	12%
Attainment of environmental standards	12%
Improved management systems/practice	11%
Competitive advantage	11%
Better standing in the community	5%
Customer satisfaction	5%
Other	12%
Don't know	4%
None	24%

SME perception of the actual and potential benefits of pursuing positive action

GALLUP SME ATTITUDE SURVEY, 1995.

Cost savings	73%
Legislation and regulatory pressure	64%
Directors' liability	62%
Market opportunity	61%
Positive company image	60%
Customer pressure	59%
Employees' concerns	42%
Local community concerns	33%
Feel-good factor	30%
Investors/shareholders	28%
Banks and insurance companies	28%

Factors effective in motivating SMEs to adopt an environmental policy

GALLUP SME ATTITUDE SURVEY, 1995.

Issue overload is real enough. Seventy percent of respondents to a Gallup SME Attitude Survey in the UK ("Small Firms and the Environment: A Groundwork Report", Birmingham, UK; November 1995) stated that they were 'fairly' or 'very' concerned about their companies' environmental performance; no fewer than 41 percent had been asked by their customers about their environmental performance; 68 percent of the firms surveyed recognised that environmental issues will have 'some' or a 'significant' impact on their business over the next five years. However, the British survey also detected a general indifference to taking positive environmental action: "All too often, managers are unaware of how to deal with the environmental pressures facing their businesses," the report concludes; "yet their survival may depend on their ability to grasp the relevance of such issues and respond effectively."

Green as Gold

Once again the language is accusatory, as if managers are in some way to blame for their failure to take action on this complex and seemingly distant problem. But more interesting than casting blame, is recognition of companies like those profiled in this chapter that have embraced the concept of 'green design'. They have done so not just in a defensive sense — in response to regulations — but pro-actively, as a competitive weapon.

Plustech, from Finland, a small engineering concern, uses advanced 'walking technology' to reduce environmental damage within an industrial system — forestry — that remains otherwise unchanged. **Bates**, a Danish company whose core business is paper refuse bags (they make 130 million a year), takes a whole systems approach to the process of domestic waste disposal, and has rethought every stage.

Long before modern technologies like bionics became important, creative people have exploited and adapted the lessons of nature. In pre-historic times, natural biological materials — animal hides and furs, wood, plant matter for building — were the only option. The medical devices and wound dressings made by the British firm **ITG** are spectacular examples of technology and nature working together, which is surely where our future lies.

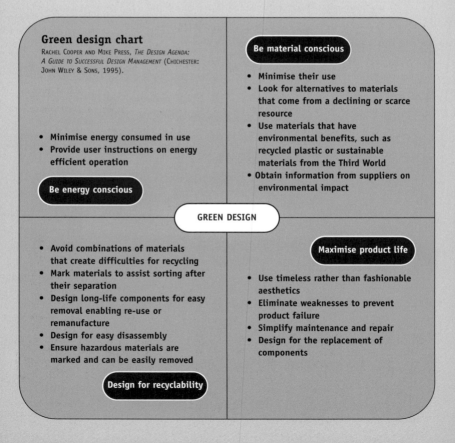

Green design chart
RACHEL COOPER AND MIKE PRESS, *THE DESIGN AGENDA: A GUIDE TO SUCCESSFUL DESIGN MANAGEMENT* (CHICHESTER: JOHN WILEY & SONS, 1995).

Be material conscious

- Minimise their use
- Look for alternatives to materials that come from a declining or scarce resource
- Use materials that have environmental benefits, such as recycled plastic or sustainable materials from the Third World
- Obtain information from suppliers on environmental impact

- Minimise energy consumed in use
- Provide user instructions on energy efficient operation

Be energy conscious

GREEN DESIGN

- Avoid combinations of materials that create difficulties for recycling
- Mark materials to assist sorting after their separation
- Design long-life components for easy removal enabling re-use or remanufacture
- Design for easy disassembly
- Ensure hazardous materials are marked and can be easily removed

Design for recyclability

Maximise product life

- Use timeless rather than fashionable aesthetics
- Eliminate weaknesses to prevent product failure
- Simplify maintenance and repair
- Design for the replacement of components

Green tape and green consumers

The efforts of such innovative small companies are seldom reported in the media. Most coverage is about the difficulties SMEs face in complying with eco-regulations. And as our chart shows, the enactment of new laws is indeed rising rapidly — with 300 new EU Directives and Regulations being introduced on top of existing national ones. The European Union's Fifth Environmental Action Programme, adopted in 1992 for the period 1993-2000, sets the EU on a path of economic sustainability that is bound to accelerate the supply of legislation. Green tape will abound.

The ISO 14000 series of standards being developed in the US will provide a worldwide focus on environmental management and sustainable development. The standards also promote a voluntary consensus approach to controlling environmental aspects, in which industry becomes more self-regulating and less dependent on the command-and-control approach of the current regulatory framework.

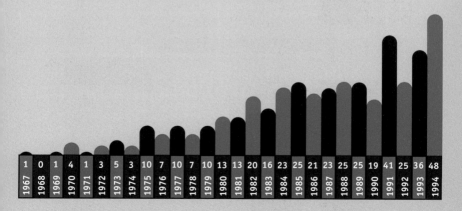

1	0	1	4	1	3	5	3	10	7	10	7	10	13	13	20	16	23	25	21	23	25	25	19	41	25	36	48
1967	1968	1969	1970	1971	1972	1973	1974	1975	1976	1977	1978	1979	1980	1981	1982	1983	1984	1985	1986	1987	1988	1989	1990	1991	1992	1993	1994

Environmental laws adopted by the EU since 1967

IEEP, ENVIRONMENT BUSINESS MAGAZINE, *EU ENVIRONMENTAL POLICY GUIDE*, 1995.

Delivering what consumers want is another powerful driver of innovation. According to Lidewij Edelkoort, an influential trend forecaster based in Paris, who carried out a major survey for the Dutch government in 1995, what companies already know about consumer demand for green products is the tip of an attitudinal iceberg. Anyone who thinks consumers will be fobbed off for long by eco-friendly bubble baths, or non-polluting ice-cream, is in for a surprise. Another indicator of a major shift in consumer values is the strong growth in membership of environmental organisations. Curtis Moore, in his book *Green Gold,* quotes a Golin/Haris poll in the US which reported that 87 percent of respondents would boycott a company that is careless about the environment. Mintel, a market research company in the UK, found consumers willing to pay 13 percent more for green products. "The greenest of green consumers are also the richest," according to Frances Cairncross of *The Economist*. In her book *Green Inc.,* she quotes a 1993 MORI opinion poll which showed that more than half of consumers earning over 15,000 ECU a year are classified as 'environmental activists'.

Environmental regulators*	37%
Customers	24%
Employees	18%
Shareholders or investors	18%
Local community	17%
Environmental/conservationist groups	13%
The media	13%
Banks and insurance companies	12%
The general public	12%

Groups exerting pressure on SMEs
*e.g. the NRA or local authority
GALLUP SME ATTITUDE SURVEY, 1995.

Big companies are slow to appreciate the significance of this change in consumer values; their sales figures only tell them that 'the recession' is taking a long time to lift, and that 'consumer spending' is strangely reluctant to recover. But they are totally missing the point: in the words of Curtis Moore, "these [attitude survey] results barely scratch the surface of a consumer commitment to environmental protection so deep and enduring that it reconfigures global business."

Shades of green

The 'eco-problem', in other words, is not going to go away. On the contrary, environmental limits form the overriding context for all the other issues and drivers confronting small (and large) businesses. So what kinds of innovation strategies can companies adopt?

One of Europe's experts in the new field of environmental management, Professor Han Brezet of Delft University in the Netherlands, has identified four ways companies can respond:

- step-by-step improvement of present products
- radical redesign based on existing concepts
- development of alternative product and service concepts
- redesign of whole systems with the goal of full sustainability.

In an attempt to emphasise that these four strategies are not mutually exclusive, Professor Brezet has devised an 'eco-wheel' diagram (page 343) on which the relative impact of these different strategies may be plotted.

These varieties of green design are a radical reordering of priorities within product development processes. Not so long ago (in 1971) Victor Papanek, the celebrated American writer, wrote: "There are professions more harmful [to the environment]

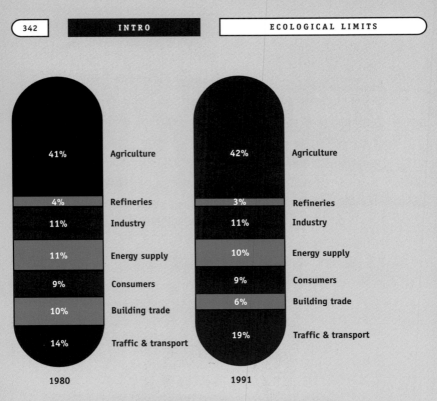

1980		1991	
41%	Agriculture	42%	Agriculture
4%	Refineries	3%	Refineries
11%	Industry	11%	Industry
11%	Energy supply	10%	Energy supply
9%	Consumers	9%	Consumers
10%	Building trade	6%	Building trade
14%	Traffic & transport	19%	Traffic & transport

Environmental pressure by target groups, relative proportions, weighted by sustainability levels

ALBERT ADRIAANZE, *ENVIRONMENTAL POLICY PERFORMANCE INDICATORS* (THE HAGUE: SDU, 1993).

than industrial design, but only a very few of them." With sustainable product design strategies, the contribution made by design is reversed.

In its 1987 report 'Our Common Future', the World Commission on Sustainable Development — also referred to as the Brundtland Commission — introduced the concept of 'sustainable development' as the guiding principle for international policy on global resource use. The commission defined sustainable development as "development that meets the needs of the present without compromising the ability of future generations to meet their own needs."

Martin Charter, who runs the Centre for Sustainable Design in Farnham, England, describes sustainable product design as "a design management practice which aims to balance the triple bottom line — environmental, social, and economic needs. The process acknowledges the need to develop innovative product and service concepts which minimise environmental and social impact through the life cycle."

The beauty of sustainable design is that it can be a 'win-win' strategy. When limits set by regulators, or by consumer pressure, are embraced, the quality and

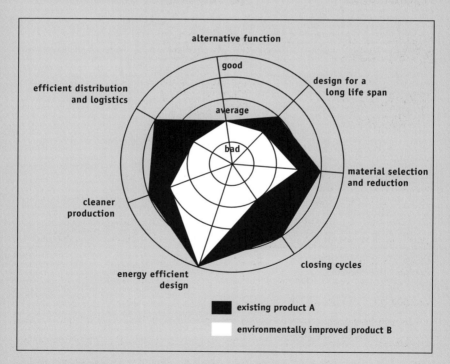

Eco-wheel diagram
C.G. VAN HEMEL, DELFT UNIVERSITY, THE NETHERLANDS, 1995.

profitability of products is often found to improve. The reasons are not complicated: to waste materials is to waste money; to pay a clean-up bill for pollution costs more than designing pollution out of the system. Inefficient production is poor-quality production — and quality is what consumers want. In the words of Jeffrey Leonard, who runs the Global Environment Fund, green design delivers "better, cleaner, faster, and cheaper" products and services.

Eternally Yours?

Many consumers believe that product life spans have been getting shorter. Independent research bears them out: according to the New Economics Foundation, today's cookers, vacuum cleaners, kettles, and irons are less durable than their predecessors.

Telephones	3 years
Washing machines	7-10 years
Microwaves	8-10 years
Televisions	10 years
Radio cassette players	10 years
Refrigerators	10-12 years
Cars	11-12 years
Cookers	10-15 years

Product life spans
NEW ECONOMICS FOUNDATION, 1994.

Durability is only partly a function of the product's physical specification: modern products also have a psychological life span. In Amsterdam, a group of design researchers called Eternally Yours has studied our psychological desire for novelty and is developing design strategies to counter our short-termism.

Green Packaging

If they are suspicious of short-life products, many consumers are downright hostile to wasteful, misleading, or hard-to-use packaging. For companies, the question is not whether or not to use packaging — it will always be necessary to protect foods and products in some way — but how to

3000 BC	Glass containers in Egypt
1500 BC	Paper, casks, baskets produced
300 AD	Glass containers common in Rome
1700	Paperboard boxes first produced
1809	Appert discovers preservation of food by heat
1810	Durand uses metal cans (soldered tin plate)
1846-95	Mechanisation of tin can-making up to first automatic machinery
1871, 79	Albert Jones and Oliver Long issued patents for corrugated board
1892	Mechanised glass bottle-making
1895	Wells Fargo accepts 'cellular board boxes'
1914	Pridham decision
1925	Plastic era begins
1925-30	Cellophane, PVC, PE, PS, and Bakelite introduced in packaging
1935	First beer cans on the market
1936	Thermoforming used in France
1937	First extrusion blow-moulding
1946	PVdC (Saran) used as moisture barrier
1959	Aluminium used for cans
1964	Two-piece Al impact extruded can developed in USA
1965	First tin-free steel can
1966-68	Two-piece drawn and wall-ironed cans
1973	PVC and Acrylonitrile used for beverage bottles
1977	Retort pouches introduced
1977-	Aseptics in flexible packaging
1977-	Modified-atmosphere packaging, controlled-atmosphere packaging
1977-	Bag-in-box systems
1977-	Vacuum packaging

Important moments in packaging history

Frans Lox, *Packaging and Ecology* (Surrey, UK: Pira International, 1992).

Leather
> wrapping, bags, sacks, bottles

Cloth
> wrapping, bags, sacks

Wood
> boxes, casks, kegs

Grasses and split round wood
> baskets and mats

Stoneware
> small pots and jars

Earthenware
> pots, pitchers, jugs, urns, bowls

Metals
> containers, bowls, pitchers

Glass
> amphorae, jars, pitchers, beakers

Summary of ancient packaging materials and wares

FRANS LOX, *PACKAGING AND ECOLOGY* (SURREY, UK: PIRA INTERNATIONAL, 1992).

reduce its 'environmental impact'; preferably to zero. After all, packaging has always been with us: coconut shells and gourds were used during the Palaeolithic age; Egyptians started using glass containers in 3000 BC. But today, with almost six, soon-to-be-ten, billion people on the planet, a combination of rising environmental pressure, and far-reaching changes in patterns of production, storage, and distribution, herald a major transformation in the packaging process worldwide.

In his book *Packaging and Ecology,* the Belgian scientist Frans Lox calculates that the consumption of packaging materials in Europe has increased faster than the population ever since the introduction of supermarkets during the 1950s. He puts packaging's share of Europe's GDP at a hefty five percent. Packaging costs can range from two percent to 25 percent of a product's selling price; it's a huge business in which big money and lots of jobs are at stake.

But sooner or later, says Professor Lox, voluntarily or by decree, environmental costs will be added to packaging: costs to the environment during raw materials production, during the cleaning of multi-trip packages, when packaging becomes litter, during the treatment of household refuse, during the generation and

Boxes and trays

card, corrugated fibreboard, wood, tin plate, plastic

Wrappers, foils, films

paper, metal, plastic

Bottles and jars

glass, ceramic, plastic

Ampoules

glass

Tubs

glass, paper, plastic

Sleeves and pipes

metal, paperboard, plastic

Containers

metal, plastic

Tubes

metal, plastic

Thermoforms

plastic

Bags and sacks

paper, plastic, natural and synthetic yarns

Cases, drums, casks

wood, metal, plastic

Space filling

paper, wood shavings, cotton wool, plastic

Bowls

paper, paperboard, plastic

Main groups of packaging forms and materials

Frans Lox, *Packaging and Ecology* (Surrey, UK: Pira International, 1992).

distribution of mechanical and electrical power, and costs for the resources and raw materials consumed during packaging production. It is extremely difficult to isolate the environmental impact of packaging from other production and distribution factors — but the pressure to reduce it is inexorable and will grow exponentially.

Experiments with bio-engineered gourds, and the ubiquity of palm leaves at eco-conferences, are signs that 'green packaging' is rapidly moving up the agenda. The packaging industry is developing software tools to measure the eco-profile of different systems, and the relationship between those systems and the overall environmental impact of the product concerned.

From 'end-of-pipe' to 'whole-of-life' Green design has started to achieve a critical mass mainly because it addresses the short-term needs and problems of companies: it looks at ways to make today's or tomorrow's products less wasteful of materials, less polluting, easier to recycle. If traditional 'green design' has a limitation, it is that it intervenes at the 'end-of-pipe' — modifying individual aspects of the process, but not transforming the industrial process as a whole.

In many big companies — which tend to think more about big processes — a specialisation called environmental management has developed which takes a whole systems approach. Environmental management stresses the importance of 'metrics' — measures of success — so that its strategies can be justified to shareholders and investors. It also encompasses the whole business framework and thinks in terms of product life cycles.

Life Cycle Assesment (LCA) is one of the environmental manager's most effective tools. The actual use of a product tends to receive minimal attention when the product's environmental impact is evaluated, but in many cases it makes a bigger impact than its manufacture and disposal combined. Even something as innocuous as a pair of jeans, which is relatively eco-friendly to make, has a serious impact when the number of times it is washed and dried are factored in. Dr. Conny Bakker, an eco-design specialist at the Netherlands Design Institute in Amsterdam, gives the example of a coffee machine: "Its dominant environmental impact does not come from the production of the machine or the choice of materials, but the use of ingredients — coffee; plastic coffee cups; the standby energy consumption; and the emissions caused by servicing the machine. This is true of tens of thousands of products."

Although life cycle assessment is complicated, a variety of software programs has been developed to help managers interpret and act upon the complex and dynamic data involved.

Production	4,7%
Distribution	1,2%
Use	93,6%
Disposal	1,7%

Cradle-to-grave assessment of environmental impacts of washing machines
PAUL BURALL, *PRODUCT DEVELOPMENT AND THE ENVIRONMENT* (LONDON: GOWER, 1996).

LCA Design Checklist

- Consider from the outset what the ideal life might be for the proposed product: calculate data cradle-to-grave.
- Ensure that the product will be easy to use and repair, and that product manuals encourage repair.
- Increase the 'service intensity' of the product.
- Avoid trendy designs that encourage early product replacement.
- Design to facilitate upgrading (e.g. modular components).
- Consider from the outset how the product is to be disassembled.
- Check that any fixing methods and finishes do not inhibit recycling.
- Ensure that plastic components carry permanent identification of materials.
- Optimise high-turnover goods (e.g. food) for low transport intensity.
- Investigate setting up a destination for recycled elements in advance.
- Ensure that materials do not create a hazard on disposal.

ADAPTED FROM PAUL BURALL, *PRODUCT DEVELOPMENT AND THE ENVIRONMENT* (LONDON: GOWER PUBLISHING, 1996), PP. 113-114, AND SACHA KRANENDONK, WUPPERTAL INSTITUTE, GERMANY.

The Ten Percent Solution

Software programs to plot the life cycle of a toothbrush may not be enough on their own to save the planet, but they are a start. And the fact that we have started is important psychologically: too much environmentalist propaganda ignores the fact that profound change is already underway. In business, if not in the headquarters of Greenpeace, a new economy, in which eco-friendly criteria such as lightness, speed, and dematerialisation are a pre-condition for success, has become a reality.

In *The Solid Side,* Ezio Manzini, one of Europe's leading experts on long-term strategies for sustainable design, puts it this way: "We can look forward to a society whose metabolism — its capacity to transform environmental resources into the satisfaction of needs — will be very different from that of the present one. To be precise, it will be a society that meets our demand for well-being while consuming less than ten percent of the resources that it consumes today."

Ten percent? Is it realistic to insist that companies increase their efficiency by a factor of ten? A growing number of sober experts insists this is how it has to be. Paul Hawken, in his powerful book *The Ecology of Commerce,* quotes a 1993 study by the US National Academy of Engineers which showed that of the materials we use 93 percent is thrown away before final production — and 80 percent of what we do use is thrown away within six weeks. Hawken is no green fundamentalist; his first book was called *Growing a Business,* and among many of the new 'industrial ecologists', his explicit aim is to discover ways that living systems, human systems, and industrial systems can coexist in an environmentally positive way.

We need a new design strategy for nature. We have to use nature, not just preserve it, save it, conserve it; "use it," as Hawken puts it, "as our design template, our model, our mentor for re-imagining everything that we do and make and provide as a service to another human being." And those principles are very simple. As opposed to industrial systems, natural systems have exquisite metabolic efficiencies — so much so that we're still deciphering them. But we know one important principle that underlies them: there's no waste. Waste is re-metabolised, re-used, and provides life again. Hawken again: "If we throw away 98 percent of our stuff, which we do in the USA within six weeks, we're saying that the next industrial revolution will be about the elimination of inefficiency."

Dematerialisation
At Germany's Wuppertal Institute, these rather abstract principles inform the analysis of quite mundane design problems, such as the packaging and distribution of strawberry yoghurt, whose different ingredients travel some 8,000 kilometres within Europe before reaching someone's mouth: the strawberries from Poland, the aluminium lid from Australia, the cultures from Hamburg, and so on. Without changing anything about the product itself, but simply by reconfiguring material sources and logistics, Wuppertal researchers were able to reduce the yoghurt's eco-impact by a factor of four. Their teams have applied the same technique to dozens of products.

Whole systems redesign, of even the simplest products, is therefore a form of information science. Along with materials scientists, production experts, marketing, logistics and database experts, designers are thinking more and more in terms of services and systems — and less about the formal qualities of individual products.

Sustainability via dematerialisation is as much about money as about ethics. Matter costs more than energy; energy costs more than information. An everyday example of this trend towards economic dematerialisation is paper. It will physically disappear, or at least diminish, for economic as well as environmental reasons. Environmentally, some cultures waste paper to an abominable degree: the average

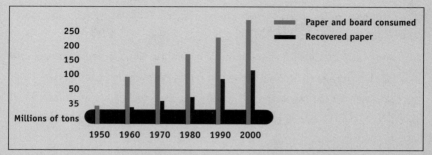

World consumption of paper and board
COMPRINT.

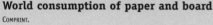

Printer/copier data transfer rates (speed and resolution)
COMPRINT.

American consumes 47 kilograms of paper each year, compared with 15 for the average Indian. But the economic argument is stronger: since 1970, the ratio between speed and cost for the delivery of information by paper — its basic function — has remained broadly the same. But the same information delivered by digital means is 100,000 times faster and 1,000 times cheaper today than it was in 1970. In ten years, add another one or two zeros to both those figures and it will be obvious: paper doesn't stand a chance, except in niche sectors. The immaterial way of transmitting information will get steadily faster and cheaper.

The German company **Authentics**, by comparison, takes a more pragmatic approach to dematerialisation. It has greatly reduced the amount of plastics used in its products — domestic containers of all kinds — and it also makes these plastics fully recyclable. So the materials they do use remain within the system, so to speak. In theory, most of the materials are never fully 'consumed'.

Dematerialisation does not mean that we will all don high-tech helmets and migrate into cyberspace. On the contrary: our aggregate need for real things — food, clothes, products, and homes — will increase as the world's population grows and gets richer. What dematerialisation means is that the most valuable and profitable business opportunities are in organising the production and delivery of those real products and services. And as eco-limits bear down, the optimisation of these information design skills can only increase.

Recycling and Resource Substitution

Pollution Control

Environmental Services

Ecologically Tailored Energy Supply

Biotechnology

Information Technology

Energy Efficiency

Industries with a golden future
HERBERT BRYANT MAYNARD AND SUSAN E. MEHRTENS, *THE FOURTH WAVE* (SAN FRANSISCO: BENNET-KOEHLER, 1993).

In developing countries

In Germany

	In Germany	In developing countries
Energy consumption (TJ)	158	22
Greenhouse gasses (t)	13,700	1,300
CFC (kg)	450	16
Roads (km)	8	0.7
Transport (Goods) (tkm)	4,391,000	776,000
Transport (People) (Pkm)	9,126,000	904,000
Passenger cars	443	6
Aluminium consumption (t)	28	2
Cement consumption (t)	413	56
Steel consumption (t)	655	5
Waste (t)	400	ca. 120
Toxic waste (t)	100	ca. 2

GERMAN FOOTPRINTS ON THE GLOBAL ENVIRONMENT
Annual environmental impact of 1,000 people:
Gemany vs. developing countries

WUPPERTAL INSTITUTE (STATISTISCHES BUNDESAMT, OECD, UNEP, WRI).

Act like ants? Behave like bees?

We may not experience them as an immediate crisis, and the experts disagree vehemently about how bad things are, but nobody really disputes that the environmental problems of the planet are profound, structural, and threatening society. Fine-tuning is not the answer. So what is?

It would be absurd to suggest that design can save the planet, but it can indeed be a powerful tool. We have seen throughout this book that although some people use 'design' as a noun — to refer to the physical qualities of an object, a building, or a document — design can also describe the processes by which such things are produced, or the way systems are organised. Design in this sense is as much about people, infrastructures, materials, energy, matter, and information, as it is about things. The accepted principles of sustainability — minimising the waste of materials and energy; reducing the movement and distribution of goods; using more people and less matter — entail redesigning systems to make them more efficient and less damaging to the environment.

This goes beyond 'green design' or 'eco-design', which tend to be concerned with redesigning existing products to make them recyclable or less wasteful. Those tasks are important, but 'end-of-pipe' is only half the story. To achieve sustainability, we have to design completely new ways of living — new products, new services, and new systems for producing and distributing them. For business — eco-minded or not — imagining and realising new products, services, and systems are what competition is all about. So the essence of competition through innovation does not need to change. But the criteria do.

The radical decrease in our absolute consumption of matter and energy that is necessary to achieve a sustainable world can only be accomplished if a cultural shift of great magnitude takes place. No amount of legislation, no tax regime, and no technological fix, on its own, will save us. Of course, breakthroughs may be made possible by technology — for example, in delivering new protein sources, or ultra-efficient engines. But true dematerialisation will only be achieved through intense, bottom-up, economic and cultural creativity — stimulated by, but not relying on, new technologies, and involving a dynamic collaboration between businesses, experts, and the creative input of untold individuals.

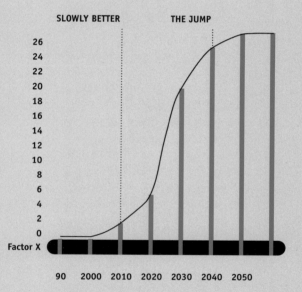

Factor 10-20 chart
True sustainability means improving the efficiency with which we use matter and energy by a factor of 10-20. Incremental change has started, but sooner or later a jump in the efficiency of products and services will be needed.
DTO.

REFUSE BAGS AS A CUSTOMER SERVICE

Bates makes more than 130 million paper bags each year in more than 1,000 different shapes and sizes.

KUN TIL MADAFFALD

A recent survey found that for more than half of the responding families, the male head of the household takes the trash to the curb for pick-up. Women are second, at 28%, and children are third, at 11%.

THE PLASTIC BAG ASSOCIATION: HTTP://WWW.PLASTICBAG.COM.

Winner '97!

Waste Disposal Systems

Bates Environmental awareness offers not only the promise of a healthier future, but also — for those companies ready to take up the challenge — immense business opportunities. The Danish paper bag producer, Bates Emballage, is one such firm. Growing concern about the environment, health hazards, working conditions, and limited resources have led the firm to rethink the whole process of household waste collection and to come up with a new system to meet today's — and tomorrow's — tougher standards. "What we're doing," says Bates' managing director, Arne Juul, "is taking the paper sack into the 21st century."

Bates manufactures industrial sacks and sack-handling machines, dunnage bags for freight protection, and paper refuse sacks and waste systems. The company, employing 350 people, was formed in 1995 through the merger of two long-established firms, Bates Ventil Saekke Co. and DAC Emballage. Since the 1950s, Bates had been producing sacks using paper produced from the highest quality

Scandinavian timber — carefully checked for weight, tensile strength, wet strength, etc. Now making more than 130 million paper sacks each year, in more than 1,000 different shapes and sizes, Bates places great emphasis on paper's compatibility with nature: "Paper is not just something to be used," says Juul, "it can also be reused. After recycling, composting, or incineration, paper once again becomes a natural part of the ecological cycle."

The new Combi System, which consists of paper sacks, a console with sack-holders, a vehicle with an automatic sack-changing function, and a trolley, offers a number of benefits. The design of the console and the sacks allows organic waste to dry out, drastically reducing its weight and making it easier to process; walking and lifting are minimised; and hygiene is improved — the console remains clean, no dangerous micro-organisms can develop, and the collector never comes into direct contact with the refuse itself.

Designers played a key role in the project from the start, working as part of a multidisciplinary team which consulted regularly with labour unions, local authorities, industry, and environmental agencies. With turnover up by 5 million ECU since the introduction of the Combi System, the value of design has been proven. "Naturally, the process was not without its flaws," says Juul. "You need to work to create common ground between the various partners. But by establishing a clear-cut plan at an early stage, we found that we could go a long way towards playing what Buckminster Fuller appropriately called 'the world game'."

The average American throws away 4 pounds of garbage each day.

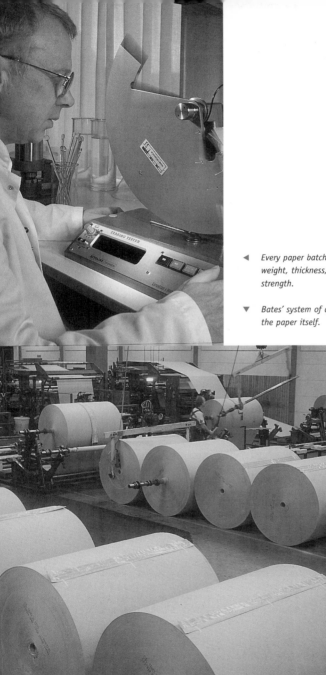

◀ *Every paper batch is carefully checked for weight, thickness, tensile strength, and wet strength.*

▼ *Bates' system of quality control begins with the paper itself.*

Top 10
Rubbish Producers
of the World

Domestic waste produced per head per annum (kg)

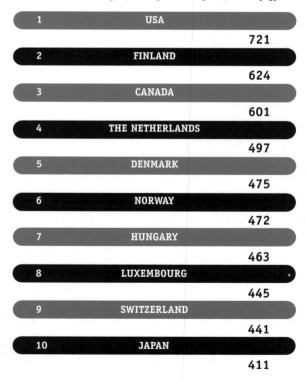

1	USA	721
2	FINLAND	624
3	CANADA	601
4	THE NETHERLANDS	497
5	DENMARK	475
6	NORWAY	472
7	HUNGARY	463
8	LUXEMBOURG	445
9	SWITZERLAND	441
10	JAPAN	411

Russell Ash, *The Top Ten of Everything* (London: Dorling Kindersley, 1996).

A state-of-the-art incinerator consuming **2,250** tons of household garbage daily would emit annually **5** tons of lead, **17** tons of mercury, **580** pounds of cadmium, **2,248** tons of nitrous oxide, **853** tons of sulphur dioxide, **777** tons of hydrogen chloride, **87** tons of sulphuric acid, **18** tons of fluorides, **98** tons of particulate matter small enough to lodge permanently in the lungs, and **210** different dioxin compounds.

PAUL HAWKEN, *THE ECOLOGY OF COMMERCE* (LONDON: WEIDENFELD AND NICHOLSON, 1993).

HOW THE BATES EMBALLAGE "COMBI 2+2" SYSTEM WORKS

- Householders sort waste into four categories: glass, paper, organic waste, and 'other'.
- They take glass and paper waste to centrally located containers (bottle and paper banks)
- Organic and 'other' waste are stored in separate sacks in the console until collection.
- Each type of waste is collected every two weeks.
- The refuse collector wheels a sack-holder with an empty sack to the console.
- The sack-holder is slid into the empty position in the console.
- One of the full sacks (in its holder) is slid onto the trolley and wheeled back to the truck in the street.
- This sack (still in its holder) is slid onto one of the truck's two lifts and tipped into the container.
- Without waiting, the collector takes another sack-holder (with a fresh sack) from the other lift and wheels it to the next household.

More than a substance,

plastic is the very idea

of its infinite transformation.

It is, as its common name indicates,

ubiquity rendered visible...

It is less an object

than the trace of a movement."

Roland Barthes, *Mythologies* (Paris: Editions du Seuil, 1957).

MORE THAN SIMPLE: PLASTIC AS A NATURAL MATERIAL

Winner '97!

Home Accessories

Authentics Plastic is not the first material that springs to mind when considering eco-friendly products. Yet Authentics, a young German company that designs, manufactures, and markets plastic articles for household use, is exploiting plastic's 'natural' qualities to show that we can use synthetic materials and be environmentally friendly if we consider from the outset the energy and materials a product uses throughout its life.

Authentics was established in 1980 as a subsidiary of the import company Artipresent. Led by designer Hans Maier-Aichen, its aim was to create affordable everyday objects that were distinctive in their understated, functional qualities. "We're not interested in creating expensive cult objects," Maier-Aichen explains, "we want to reach people who are looking for products whose uniqueness lies in their inherent clarity and their ingenious simplicity."

Authentics sees plastic not as a cheap alternative to finer materials, but as a substance with its own unique beauty. Since launching its first collection of plastic products ten years ago with its 'push can' waste bin with a domed lid, adapted from the American model in metal, Authentics has produced a range of products — bowls, pitchers, vases, and containers of all shapes and sizes — made of polypropylene, a recyclable thermoplastic. These objects are striking in their translucency, their thinness, their texture, and their subtle colour effects, all achieved through a minimal use of materials.

In its latest products, the company abandons the bright colours of previous years to explore a more neutral range of 'non-colours'— white, beige, and ecru. With their translucent, matt surfaces, these objects have the discreet elegance of sandblasted glass.

Authentics has successfully set out to restore the dignity of plastic. "We want to create the 'perfect' article for the modern market by combining an intensive awareness of materials and an economical use of resources," says Maier-Aichen. "We strive to pare objects down to their essentials, practising the 'art of making more with less'. Thanks to our design in plastic and our use of plastic in new materials, it has become both a highly valued and an ecologically responsible material."

Authentics' minimal use of materials helps to achieve ▶
translucency, thinness, and subtle colour effects.

The 'push can', adapted from the American model
in metal, has become an Authentics classic.

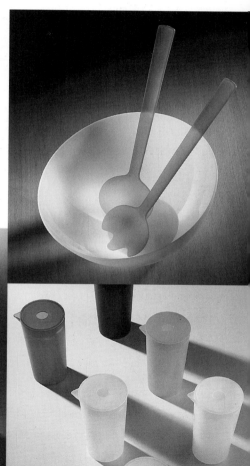

*Plustech's timber-harvesting machine adjusts to
rough ground, mountainous terrain, and steep slopes.*

THE SOUL
OF A WALKING
MACHINE

Walking Technology Applications

Plustech Imagine a timber-harvesting machine, not bulldozing its way through the forest but tip-toeing gently, leaving little trace of where it has been. It may sound like science fiction, but the Walking Forest Machine developed by the young Finnish company Plustech, demonstrates that it isn't.

Walking technology is not new (a mechanical horse was designed and patented as early as 1893), but only recently has it been applied to the problems of forestry. Plustech, established in 1992 and employing 18 people, is a versatile research and development company specialising in mobile machinery. By combining advanced

Of the virgin forests that once covered the United States, less than 5% remain today.

THE 1995 GROLIER MULTIMEDIA ENCYCLOPEDIA (GROLIER INC., 1995).

mechanics, high-performance power transmission, and high-level control systems, the company has developed walking technology so that it can be used in various applications.

Plustech's Walking Forest Machine — used for harvesting timber, felling, de-limbing, and measuring trees — is the first off-road machine application of walking technology in the world. Because each of its six 'legs' moves independently, the machine goes not only forwards and backwards, but also sideways and diagonally. It can even turn around on the spot!

The 'soul' of the walking machine is an intelligent control system in charge of the leg functions. Since 'stepping' is regulated automatically, the operator can simply steer the machine with a single control lever that simultaneously regulates speed.

Unlike tracked vehicles, which compact the ground, making it difficult for new generations of trees to grow, this machine carefully steps over obstacles, easily adjusting to rough ground, mountainous terrain, and steep slopes. It can thus cover areas that are unreachable for conventional machines.

The machine's adjustable ground clearance feature means that it can also be used for thinning out young tree plantations, reducing the need for chemical methods. It uses only biodegradable hydraulic oil and consists almost exclusively of recyclable materials. With sustainable wood production and the preservation of forest biodiversity as key goals in Finland's proposed new forestry legislation, and with other countries bound to follow suit, the Walking Forest Machine represents an important ecological and economic development.

The harvester has significant market potential in mountainous forest regions, like those in Central Europe, North America, and Japan. According to Swiss studies, this machine could halve the current logging costs associated with mountainous forests.

The Walking Forest Machine is the first off-road machine application of walking technology in the world.

Development of hybrid superurethanes.

Automated dipping process
for condoms.

The world market for medical devices,
including diagnostic and therapeutic
equipment, is in the region of $100
billion. Within this industry is an
implantable and extracorporeal device
sector with a world market for
biomaterials in the region of $12 billion.
Global growth in this sector is predicted
at between 7% and 12% per annum.

THE USE OF MATERIALS IN THE UK, 1995.

ITG uses natural materials, like seaweed
to make wound dressings which are highly
absorbent and biodegradable.

LEARNING FROM LIVING SYSTEMS

Biomaterials/Medical Devices

ITG When some businesses hear the word 'environment', they think of an endless stream of costly restrictions and regulations. Others, like Innovative Technologies Group (ITG), think of the opportunities it gives them to produce better products. This young British firm, which started only five years ago with six scientists working in a garage, sees the environment as a rich source of ideas for new materials that are not only biodegradable, but also more in tune with our own human tissues. It uses design to bring together technologies, natural materials, and people's needs. ITG's main field of application is healthcare. It produces a complete range of

The market for woundcare products is approximately 5 billion ECU, with a high-tech segment close to 1.6 billion ECU that is growing by more than 20% per annum.

THE UK INSTITUTE OF MATERIALS, 1995.

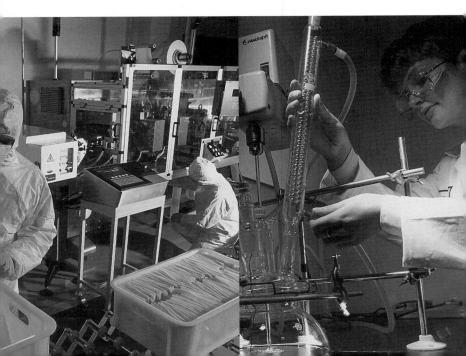

'intelligent' wound dressings and woundcare products made from natural materials, such as seaweed and chitin, a sugar extracted from prawns and seashells. "The seaweed dressing can absorb extremely high levels of wound exudates," says Diane Mitchell, director of ITG, "much more than ordinary dressings. And because it comes away from the wound as a gel, it doesn't pull off any tissue which is healing." The dressing is biodegradable, unlike more familiar synthetic polymer dressings, which are difficult to dispose of in an environmentally friendly manner.

ITG has found ways to incorporate fruit pectin into alginate or chitin dressings, helping to remove dead tissue in a natural way, and it has also come up with bioactive adhesives for sticking plasters, which solve the problem of allergic reactions and even promote the healing of the wound.

But ITG's work extends far beyond the area of wound dressings. Polyurethanes are being used to make a new generation of synthetic heart valves, a heart-assist device, and other artificial body parts. The new heart valves are not subject to rejection and last longer than traditional artificial valves. The heart-assist device processes blood for critically ill patients awaiting transplant operations.

"Living systems function by design," says Diane Mitchell, one of ITG's directors. "We've taken that principle and applied it to all facets of our business. That's probably the key to our success. We even use design at the molecular level. We build up our polymers in a highly systematic way — a unique approach. This allows us to hand-pick a particular material with the properties most closely matched to the intended application."

◄◄ *Quality testing in the product packaging department.*

◄ *Lab scale polymer production.*

To exploit the commercial opportunities offered by its polymer and dipping technologies, ITG also produces products such as medical and clean-room gloves, contamination protection gloves, waterproof ski gloves, and condoms. The Group has established an alliance to develop fully automated dipping plants and a prototype robot has been operating in-house for several months to develop the process conditions which are directly scalable to a full-size plant.

From its modest beginnings, ITG has grown enormously, now employing 129 people and supplying its products to the EU, North America, and Japan. Since 1991, its turnover has increased by over 4,000 percent to over six million ECU. "Our aim," says managing director, Keith Gilding, "is to be the 'one-stop-shop' for biomaterials and medical fabrication technology."

Dipping technologies applied to medical and clean-room glove production.

It was estimated in 1988
that US hospitals generated
2.2 million metric tons of waste,
80% of which was incinerated.

AGENCY FOR TOXIC SUBSTANCES AND DISEASES REGISTRY, USA.

The Western European market
for waterproof breathable textiles
in 1992 was estimated to be worth
1.4 billion ECU, and is predicted
to approach 2 billion ECU in 1996.

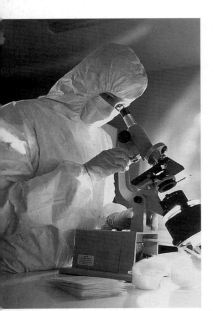

◀ *Biomaterials design: ITG's approach is to mimic living systems.*

▶ *Many of ITG's dressings incorporate bioadhesives, which minimise allergic reactions and promote healing.*

▼ *ITG aims to be a 'one-stop-shop' for biomaterials and medical fabrication technology.*

Approximately 30% of US medical waste consists of plastic and plastic products.

AGENCY FOR TOXIC SUBSTANCES AND DISEASES REGISTRY, USA.

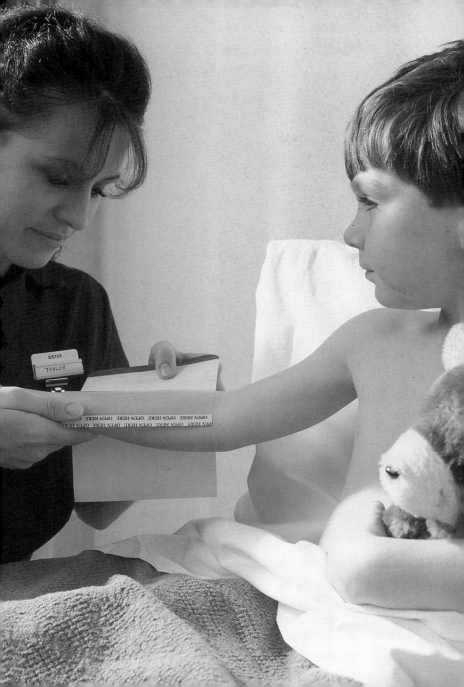

ONE

The Internet and Business
Connectivity

"Only connect," said the novelist E. M. Forster. "Everything is in connection with something else," echoed Goethe. "That which separates, is sin," thundered Nietzsche. Europeans are natural networkers, so we should not be surprised that they gave us the World Wide Web, which they did at CERN, the particle physics lab in Switzerland.

But Europeans have always been less good at exploiting their own inventions. Americans tend to be quicker on the uptake when they encounter new ideas. So when the first issue of a new magazine called *Wired* described the Internet as "the most important invention since the discovery of fire," Europe scoffed — and Americans went immediately to work.

Three years on, the Internet continues to burn brightly in the imagination of business, young people, and the media. But between the myth — whose power is undeniable — and the reality, uncertainty reigns. Something big is supposed to be happening — but it's by no means clear what it is, and the world feels much the same.

TO ONE

We're awash in startling 'facts'. All Internet charts point upwards. Telecoms are six percent of the total world economy. Half the population of the world has access to a telephone. One-in-ten has a line. 20 million people acquired mobile phones last year. We spent 53 billion minutes making international calls in 1995. Telecommunications infrastructure costs 56 billion ECU a year. Between now and 2000, more money will be spent on the infrastructure than in the 115 years since Alexander Graham Bell invented the telephone. 110,000 personal computers are sold every 24 hours. There are 180 million of them in the world... Wow! Yippee! It's amazing. But what does it mean?

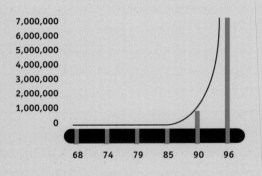

Internet Host Growth, 1968 to 1996
NETWORK WIZARDS.

It's not about size If you ask a simple question — like "how big is the Internet?"— you get wildly conflicting answers. Internet Surveys, a respected online research group (www.nua.ie/choice/Surveys/state.html#intro/) estimates that in November 1996 there were some 25-30 million people online in the United States and Canada, and another 5-10 million in the rest of the world. That gives a worldwide total of some 30-40 million. By 2000, says Internet Surveys, something like 200 million people will be online. Others say a billion. The number of people using the Internet doubles every 54 days, or every year, depending on which survey you believe.

The impressive size and velocity of these numbers makes many people anxious that they have missed an important boat. They see 'SS Internet' steaming out to sea without them. But let's put things into perspective. The number of people connected to the Internet, in comparison to telephone users, is rather small; and many of them, particularly in Europe, are business people or researchers. Few Internet users in Europe, for example, are 'consumers' in the traditional sense; a British market research company, Romtec, surveyed 2,000 UK households in 1996 and found that although 27 percent had PCs, only 2.7 percent of them also had modems.

Besides, it has never been clear why one is not deemed to be 'online' when one has a telephone. Even if one billion people *are* online, in the sense of being connected to the Internet, by 2000, it will still only be about 15 percent of the world's population.

	1995	1996	1997	1998	1999	2000
Users of PCs	144	167	184	203	217	225
E-Mail	35	60	80	130	180	200
Net/Web	9	23	46	81	122	152
Online/Hybrid	8	13	18	23	27	30

Worldwide Connectivity Market 1995-2000E (millions of users)
MORGAN STANLEY RESEARCH ESTIMATES.

Now if you sell software for online applications, or own some bit of the telecommunications infrastructure, then the total number of people going online in the world is important. But if you are in some other business, along with 99 percent of the companies in the world, the absolute figures don't really matter. It's like knowing how many people in Albania have telephones: it's mildly interesting, but not momentously important if you run a café in Paris, or manufacture bathroom taps in New Jersey.

Finland	
United States	
New Zealand	
Australia	
Sweden	
Norway	
Switzerland	
Canada	
Holland	
Denmark	
Britain	
Austria	
Israel	
Germany	
Hong Kong	
Belgium	
France	
Japan	
Czech Republic	
South Africa	
Spain	
Taiwan	
Italy	
South Korea	
Poland	

percentage of population   2   4   6   8   10   12   14

Connectivity: who's wired

INTERNET SOCIETY/THE ECONOMIST.

What most people *actually* do right now is use e-mail — a 25-year-old system that doesn't even need the World Wide Web; there's no significant business mileage to be had in that. The conceptual difference is not yet clear between the Internet revolution now, and earlier technological revolutions — the telegraph, electricity, telephones, television, networked personal computers, or CD-Roms. We were told that those technologies, too, would change the world out of all recognition; and yet now, not much later, they seem commonplace. And at least they had an obvious function; with the Internet, it's far from clear what, apart from e-mail, it's actually *for*.

Some Europeans would like it to be for learning. In 1995 a report from the inelegantly named 'High Level Expert Group on the Social and Societal Aspects of the Information Society' under the chairmanship of Luc Soete (meritbbs.rulimburg.nl

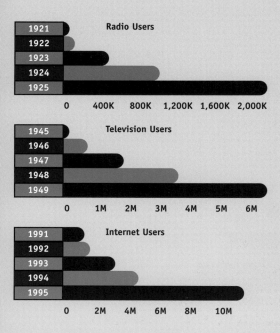

If radio and TV are any predictors, we're nearing the end of the typical gestation period when a new mass media technology suddenly flourishes.
APPLE COMPUTER.

/hleg.html) argued that it is neither possible nor desirable to separate the social and societal aspects of the information society from the technical, industrial, and economic aspects. "It is essential to view the information society as a learning society," says Professor Soete, "based on the know-how and wisdom of people, not on information in machines."

Nobody really knows how the Internet will transform business. The future is not something ahead of us, waiting to be discovered behind a curtain at the end of a yellow brick road. 'The future' will be the result of what we do *now,* and in the coming few years. Yet relatively few of the people, companies, and organisations who will make the future are even online yet. And the one thing we know about past technological revolutions is that their consequences are always different from those anticipated at the time.

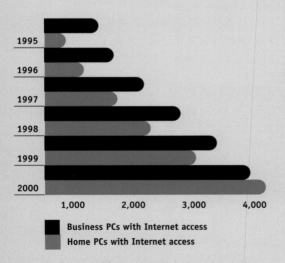

Business PCs with Internet access
Home PCs with Internet access

Business drives Internet boom in Europe (thousands of users)

IDC, *INFORMATION STRATEGY MAGAZINE.*

That will surely be the case with the Internet, too: we can't predict what will happen. What we can do is look at different scenarios, and consider what the consequences of each might be.

Missing: a business model

Various ways to exploit the Internet for business have been proposed. "The best way to think of the Internet is a direct-to-customer distribution channel, whether it's for information or for commerce," says Steve Jobs, creator of the Apple Computer (*Wired*, February 1996); "it bypasses all middlemen... who tend to slow things down, muck things up, and make things more expensive."

It does make sense that producers, suppliers, and customers, by communicating better with each other, will squeeze out cost inefficiencies; or that new customers will gain easy access to information about products and services; or that tiny companies with near-zero overheads will be able to compete head-on with bloated multinationals.

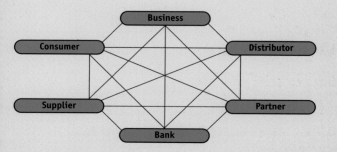

The electronic value net. With connectivity, all commercial relationships can be re-configured — and will be.
NETHERLANDS DESIGN INSTITUTE, 1996.

Three business models which seem to make sense are:

- communication model: a company gives away free information to build relationships with customers
- publishing model: subscriptions or fees are charged for content
- transaction model, or 'electronic commerce': people buy and sell things.

Although it is still tiny, electronic commerce does seem to be gathering momentum. Forrester Research estimates that online retail sales will grow from 240 million ECU in 1995 to 4.8 billion ECU in 2000. But most entrepreneurs are less impressed by data than by engaging success stories. Like that of 1-800 Flowers, a very popular online enterprise. Customers give the company a list of important anniversaries concerning friends, family members, and loved ones. A week or so in advance of each date, 1-800 Flowers e-mails customers a message like, "Do you want to send your mother flowers for her birthday?" Can you guess how they answer? The florist already e-mails 200,000 reminders to clients in a single year, and reckons its online customers spend three times as much on flowers as others; they also spend about 9 ECU more per transaction. The whole operation is sublime.

In Great Britain, the supermarket chain Tesco has put 20,000 products into an online catalogue whose contents people can order by phone, fax, or through the Internet — "even specifying" (reports the *Sunday Times*) "whether they would like their bananas yellow or green, and tomatos firm or soft". Initial scepticism has been confounded by the popularity of the service among consumers; the company now expects between ten and thirty percent of such supermarket shopping to be done from home within five years. The British seem to be comfortable in cyberspace; the worldwide success of **Psion**, which helped invent the PDA (personal digital assistant) market, is testament to the Brits' inventiveness and enthusiasm for all things online.

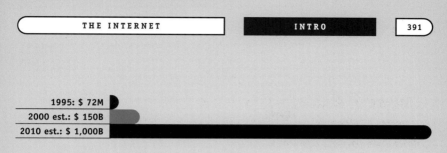

1995: $ 72M	
2000 est.: $ 150B	
2010 est.: $ 1,000B	

Value of goods & services sold via the Web
GIGA INFORMATION GROUP.

"Eventually, every type of product and/or service I would ever purchase will be available through online computer services"

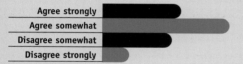

Agree strongly	
Agree somewhat	
Disagree somewhat	
Disagree strongly	

Key distribution mechanism
CYBER DIALOGUE, BUSINESS WIRE POLL.

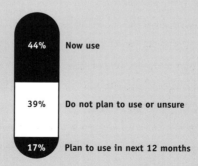

44% Now use

39% Do not plan to use or unsure

17% Plan to use in next 12 months

Six out of ten companies use the Internet (44%) or plan to use the Internet (17%) in the next 12 months.
INTERNATIONAL RESEARCH INSTITUTE, 1996.

Research and development of electronic commerce infrastrucure and software is also gathering pace. Microsoft alone is developing a whole family of software and systems that connect customers, suppliers, and producers together. The company's so-called 'merchant services' include 'store-building' and operations software; merchandising tools; ordering and payment-capture capability; order-processing and order-routing capability; web server access security; secure payment transactions; reporting and system-management tools; interfaces to current information systems; supply-chain integration tools; and so on.

At the same time, goods that were traditionally distributed through far-flung centres are becoming increasingly available via the networks. The taxing of the distribution of these goods, which has traditionally formed one of the essential bases for national, state, or even local government's tax revenues is, as a result, eroding rapidly. According to Professor Soete, the EU's expert on these things (www.ispo.cec.be/hleg/bittax.html), the use of the Internet by individual American consumers accessing mail order companies, exempt from sales taxes, meant a reduction in state sales taxes revenues of over $3 billion in 1995.

Soete ran into heavy flak for floating the idea of a 'bit tax' to compensate for this erosion on sales tax revenues. The argument prompted him to recall the story about Faraday's response to a sceptical politician who, following Faraday's discovery of the basic principle of electricity (electromagnetic induction) in 1831, asked what it was good for: "Sir, I do not know what it is good for. But of one thing I am quite certain, some day you will tax it."

Communication: or contamination? Businesses

around the world have already put millions of pages online. Most of them are less to do with substantive communication than annual reports or sales brochures being 'poured into websites' without much thought about the reasons for doing so.

A systematic study of all this material was recently published by Professor James K. Ho of the University of Illinois at Chicago (www.uic.edu/~jimho/www1000.html). When Ho began his study, 29,236 commercial websites were listed on the Commercial Sites Index — and the number of new listings was growing by over 500 a week; today, the rate of increase is even faster. Ho evaluated 1,000 of these commercial websites from the perspective of what their value might be to a potential customer. His findings were not encouraging. Online visitors could not, for the most part, actually purchase what they saw; order processing was limited to e-mail of forms; and there were few truly interactive transactions.

The devil's new machine When the printing press was

invented in the 15th century, the church called it 'the devil's machine'. Book and magazine publishers must have the same opinion of the Internet; they have been among the most scornful critics of brochurisation — but, try as they might, and spend as they might, they have not managed so far to make online work well as a business.

This must be frustrating, because economic logic favours online over print every time. Although it sounds like an information business, paper-based publishing is in fact an old-style manufacturing activity. Capital is invested in a 'product' — a book — which then wends its way through the distribution and retail system, waiting for someone to buy it, for months — sometimes for years. The publisher's capital is locked up in the product — which is basically a lump of dead matter — throughout this time. The US Library of Congress contains 27 million different products that have been processed in this archaic fashion. And every year, 60,000 new titles in English alone crawl their way into the publishing system. It's hardly surprising that most publishers make such modest profits.

In scientific and professional publishing, pressure to digitise the process is stronger. Every day of the year, some 5,500 papers are published in academic and specialist journals — that's two million a year. Rumour has it that fewer than 20 percent of these papers are read by anyone — including the editor of the journal concerned. Either way, the economics of printing and distributing these highly specialised pieces of information — to users who are scattered in micron-thin layers around the world — are horrendous. Functionally, the system is absurd: in extreme cases, the time lag between a researcher submitting a paper and its publication can be five years; two years or more is normal. Compare that to the few seconds it takes to e-mail a text document from one side of the world to the other, and the only wonder is that any publisher still prints journals at all. It's even less comprehensible that the bigger American universities should agree to spend $20 million a year or more on journals produced in so cumbersome a manner.

Publishers have tried various subscription models to make money from online publishing, but most have not lived up to expectations. Many web users expect to get information for free; a majority of the Internet's 'early adopters' were (and still are) attached to academic institutions. A combination of well-endowed libraries, and the expertise of 'cybrarians' in tracking down toll-free information, has accustomed a big proportion of publishers' potential customers to getting information for nothing. The prospect of 'metering', or 'micro-transactions', in which visitors to a website would pay fractions of a cent per page, and painlessly — in much the same way that we clock up phone bills today — may change the online publishing economy. But we're not there yet.

Many publishers of information have therefore given up the struggle to sell content direct and have reverted to old-fashioned advertising. Frost & Sullivan discovered that Internet advertising accounted for 3.4 percent or $0.85 billion of all ad dollars spent in 1996 in North America — and that the market is expected to grow to 22.2 percent or $5.48 billion by 2002. Internet Surveys quotes another estimate, by brokerage firm Hambrecht & Quist, that yearly advertising revenue will rise to $3.8 billion by the year 2000 — far above projections for 1996 of $300 million. In 1995 the total was just $12 million.

Old business, new bottle
The lesson so far seems to be that the Internet is not a new business in itself, but a new way to do old business. Mitch Ratcliffe, editor of *Digital Media*, an industry newsletter, considers it a mistake to look for blue-sky business concepts on the Internet. Keep an eye on household connectivity, he says, because the information superhighway will be dominated by recombined versions of tried and true business, and in particular by financial transactions, remote medical care, and education. While there were no ATM transactions at all in 1980, Americans made purchases or got cash out of a wall *seven and a half billion times* in 1992; that figure has continued to grow steeply. And the volume of credit card purchases will have quadrupled in 20 years — from $201 billion in 1980 to an estimated $882 billion by 2000. This explains why the prospects of **Trintech**, an Irish finalist for the European Design Prize, which makes the hardware and software that support these transactions, are so good.

Remote medical care is a more low-profile but still immense market, thanks to a combination of demographics — more older people — and escalating treatment costs. Between 1970 and 1990 the cost of physician services grew from $13 billion to $142 billion in the United States; the drug business turns over $60 billion on top of that.

Education

Similar escalating costs for the delivery of education, combined with a demand for 'lifetime learning' — by people who are nonetheless too busy to take time out of the office to go to school — explain why the market for educational online services is also set to grow sharply.

The use of information technology in college courses — including e-mail, multimedia, CD-Rom, commercial 'courseware', and simulations — is growing dramatically — as is the number of students and faculty staff routinely using the Internet and the World Wide Web. According to the 1995 Campus Computing Survey (a US survey) more than seven million college students and staff routinely use the Internet and World Wide Web as part of their daily and weekly activities. More than half of the institutions participating in the survey reported a WWW home page. Commercial and consumer market studies may miss the huge numbers of academics who use, indeed depend on, the Net, says Mr Green, who organised the survey. "At growing numbers of colleges and universities across the country, Internet access is viewed by faculty and students as a core resource and a basic right, similar to a library card."

Digtal Media's Ratcliffe estimates that these three services — banking transactions, healthcare, and education — grind through $1.6 trillion a year. "If interactive networks take just three percent of these markets," he says, "they will have earned $50 billion a year. That's more than the video game industry, Hollywood, cable television, and book publishing, combined."

Make me one of those

But even the big users of online communications may eventually be dwarfed by the scale of activity achieved by small businesses when they begin to use the Internet seriously. There are nearly 16 million companies in the 15 countries of the European Union. 99 percent of these companies have fewer than 50 employees; but although small, these companies account for over two thirds of all jobs in Europe, and create the bulk of national wealth.

And they do so locally. The vast majority of small and medium-sized companies operate within a radius of 50 km (30 miles). Most of the early hype and rhetoric surrounding the Internet stressed its miraculous conquest of distance — "wow, you can look at someone's home page in Australia" — but the likelihood is that the Internet will actually be *useful* at a local level.

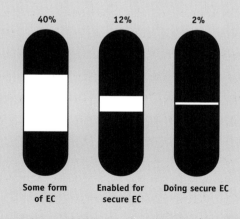

40%	12%	2%
Some form of EC	Enabled for secure EC	Doing secure EC

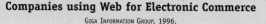

Companies using Web for Electronic Commerce

GIGA INFORMATION GROUP, 1996.

Until just 150 years ago, when someone wanted a product, they said to a maker: "Please make me one". 100 years ago, small boys on bicycles were a common sight delivering bags of groceries to people's doorsteps. Even 30 years ago a 'French Onion Seller' on a black bicycle would come regularly to our house in the North of England. Since then, the march of the Walmarts and Tesco SuperStores has seemed invincible, and buying direct seemed to have gone forever. But now, if you believe the signs, one-to-one commerce is on the way back, thanks to the wonders of the Internet.

LETS disintermediate
It's early days to predict that some kind of online 'farm-to-market' economy is emerging. But there are interesting hints of what may indeed be a startling change. One of these is the rapid but so far little publicised growth of local exchange and trading systems, or LETS. An amazing array of sole traders and local businesses are discovering that it makes sense to receive payment in local barter currencies, which get called things like 'bobbins', 'acorns', or 'beaks'. What happens is that local people form a club to trade among themselves, using their own system of accounts. They compile a membership directory containing offers and requests — goods, services, or items for hire; these are priced in local credits. Members use the directory to contact one another whenever they wish. They pay for any service or goods by writing a LETS credit note for the agreed amount of local credit. The credit note is sent to the local LETS accountant, who adjusts both members' accounts. Each member receives a personal account statement, directory updates, and a newsletter.

From humble beginnings in the small town of Courtenay, Vancouver, LETS systems have spread to the United States, New Zealand, Australia, and Europe. By 1995 an estimated 30,000 people were participating in some 400 local LETS around the UK alone; similar networks have been established in 16 European countries. And this despite the fact that LETS is overwhelmingly a completely manual system. People sit for hours in each other's kitchens filling out ledgers and sorting little bits of paper. If something so unwieldy, cumbersome, and slow can grow so quickly, its potential once online and speeded up must be fantastic.

Internet academics have coined a ghastly word — 'disintermediation' — to describe the potential of the Internet electronic commerce to cut out the middle man. So far, Internet connectivity among small businesses remains relatively low — and,

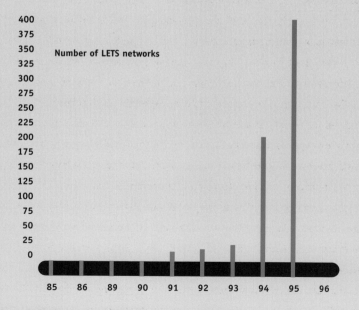

Number of LETS networks

Growth of LETS in the UK (1985-1995)
LETSLINK UK.

in Europe at least, it's even lower among consumers. But this has to be a temporary lag. A report by the International Research Institute in 1996 found that six out of ten companies, including European ones, either use the Internet, or plan to use it shortly. And the experience of other new technologies, such as satellite dishes, suggests that consumers are capable of getting connected very quickly once they decide that the online world has something valuable to offer them. But the quality has to be right or — very sensibly — they won't bother.

Context deprivation

The quality of human-to-human communication — which is what the Internet supports — is determined only partly by technology. Far more important than bits and bytes is the social and cultural context — all those tiny but important cues and prompts, in which communication takes place. Nicholas Negroponte, head of MIT's MediaLab, famously uses the example of a wink of an eye as a 'low-bandwidth, high-meaning' act of communication. There's even a buzzword — 'context deprivation' — to describe the miscommunication that occurs when online exchanges are too bland. This may explain why entrepreneurs are loading themselves down with so many communication gadgets. None, on its own, is able to satisfy their insatiable demand for connectivity.

So what is this 'context', and how do we add it to the *infobahnen?* A variety of experts discussed this question at a Doors of Perception conference in 1994 (www.design-inst.nl/). They were asked what would happen when a new communication technology comes into the home. Now 'home' is simultaneously a space, a place, an idea, an experience, and a memory. It is both a material construction — a thing — and, at the same time, a powerful generator of meaning. So depending on who you are, 'home' represents a market for information services; a laboratory to test the social consequences of a network culture; a metaphor for certain mental states; and somewhere private and intimate. 'Home', in other words, is a complex and perplexing thing — exactly the messy kind of subject that confronts the multimedia developer and interaction designer who is serious about making online environments inhabitable for ordinary people.

The three-dimensional space of a physical home, for example, can strongly influence communication between people. Designing this kind of space is by convention the domain of architects — so why should architects not get involved in the design of electronic 'homes' as well? But home is also a social reality; it represents community, togetherness. Designing 'community' into the technology is a priority for those who believe we should prioritise many-to-many interactions on the network — not just the one-to-many transactions that today's content providers seem to favour.

Above all, the home of the imagination is crucial to the design of communication contexts. The power of home as an idea is tremendous: consider how relatively small amounts of homely information can trigger powerful mental responses: a grainy photograph; the smell of cooking; a few words whispered down the phone. For all of

Percentage of North American small business CEOs using	1991	1995
Laptops	25%	86%
Network PCs	34%	96%
Pagers	24%	67%
Cellular phones	39%	88%
The Internet	3%	70%

Managers go online.
INC. MAGAZINE (INC. 500, 1996).

us, 'home' is a lifetime's accumulation of experiences and feelings, of mental and physical interactions, that does not lend itself to being described in binary code.

Designing online
So far, wit and imagination have been in short supply in the design of commercial websites. A 'village street' metaphor is prevalent in which you leave your cutesy little home to visit cutesy little shops, quaint libraries, and folksy cinemas arrayed on your screen. Such banal concepts are the results of an Olympian disdain for ordinary people that runs deep in online circles. Typical of this condescending approach are these words from Michael Schrage, an influential American journalist writing in *HotWired*: "Let me put this in the harshest possible way: the rising success of simple and easy Internet bundles will inevitably mean a rise in netizens who are only capable of dealing with sites that are easier and simpler."

Happily, the patronising assumption that ordinary people are "only capable of dealing with sites that are easier and simpler" is not shared by all designers. Many are keen to explore radically different ways of travelling, metaphorically, 'through the window' of their computers .

Nico Macdonald (www.spy.co.uk/), an English expert who monitors developments in online design, observes that the user's experience on the web depends upon the speed of their computer, modem, and Internet connection, their software, and the size and colour richness of their monitor. A website, however designed, will therefore behave differently for each user. "Designers have to learn to deal with and exploit this uncertainty," says Macdonald. "They need to get used to a certain loss of control, and concentrate on the essence, not the detail, of communication."

Online design today is rather like early film making before it found its own 'language'. On the one hand, the first film makers were 'realists', who exploited the capacity of the medium to make 'photographs that move', but not much more; on the other hand, there was a 'formative' tendency, determined to give free reign to artistic imagination. Luis Buñuel demanded, "I ask that a film discover something for me." But no Eisenstein or Buñuel of the Internet has emerged yet. Richard Lanham, Professor of English at the University of California, spoke for many when he wrote in his book *The Electronic Word* that we have not yet exploited the Internet as a radically new medium of expression.

But things are starting to move. A new generation of hybrid design, software, and production companies is beginning to 'stretch the envelope' of online and multimedia development.

One of the most dynamic is Art Technology Group (ATG) in Boston, which is run by two graduates of MIT's MediaLab, Jeet Singh and Jo Chung. ATG is a one-stop-shop for ambitious clients, who range from airlines to business schools, united by a desire to be online and to be there now. ATG provides design and development services that span a whole range of disciplines — from business strategy to software, from user interface design to quality assurance. The company's young staff design network architectures, integrate systems, set up databases, design templates and typographical styles, and train the client's personnel. And they do all this at breakneck speed. It is not unusual for ATG to deliver a fully-functioning website with commercial transaction capability in 100 days or less from the first meeting. "What people used to come to us for was a look-and-feel design effort," says ATG's Singh; "what they now get is a fast development that integrates their business processes in the medium of a customised software environment."

If ATG is an embryonic MGM of the Internet, doubling in size every few months, other online pioneers prefer to stay small and fleet-of-foot. Kristi van Riet (www.vanriet.com), who works out of Amsterdam (where she is responsible for the Netherlands Design Institute's website), describes herself as an 'online producer': she puts together teams of specialists to create websites and online environments in much the same way that a film producer assembles one-off teams to make a film. Van Riet prefers to keep her company as small as possible because every project requires a different mix of skills. "Many web-design companies are either run by graphic designers, who don't understand online business models; or by technical people, who don't appreciate the value of design," she says. "It's nobody's fault: we just don't have a stable model yet of who should do what, and how." In Van Riet's case, this means that if sophisticated database programming is required, or expertise in a new form of electronic transaction, she finds the most competent specialists when she needs them. And she emphasises to clients that "a website is for life — or at least for a long time. Failure to invest in people to run a website after it's built is one of the main reasons they fail; ideally, companies should put staff members onto a project who will stick around."

Willem Velthoven, director of European Design Prize winner **Mediamatic**, is another pioneer of the Amsterdam Internet scene. He, too, is sensitive to a big difference between European and American approaches to design for online. Part publisher, part management consultancy, part training centre, part production company, Mediamatic's fluidity of mission is highly characteristic of companies in the vanguard of this dynamic sector. One constant is shared by all projects: a conceptual approach in which design is not only about the shape of things, but also about the 'shape' of processes, organisations, and relationships. Content is never separate from design.

Launch and learn

Is it book? A magazine? A CD-Rom? A radio? A telephone? A library? An opinion poll? A park bench? A frontier town? The Internet is all of these — and none of these. Researchers at Apple Computer, who came up with this list of metaphors in an intelligent little book called *Thinking It Through* (www.apple.com), are among a minority of realists who acknowledge that although the Internet can be explored on many levels, nobody really knows where things are going.

They don't even know how to get there, wherever 'there' is. Different experts talk about scenarios, screenplays, storyboards, recipes, blueprints, authoring. They describe online in terms of literature, theatre, film, everyday life, comics strips, shopping malls, corner shops. They see online as a place to tell people things, to ask them things, to discuss with them, to meet them, to sell them stuff, to buy. They talk about 'content', topics, chunks, nodes, modules, units, pieces, fragments, links, chains, blocks, and sections. They ask if you want feedback, interaction, access, privacy, text, sound, indexes, search engines, directories, animation, keywords, passwords, graphics, movies, or applets.

The proliferation of buzzwords and private languages says more about the Internet's technical complexity than it does about its future as a medium. The good thing is that everything is still up for grabs: there are no stable business models; nobody has a monopoly of wisdom. Most people are making it up as they go. This is why the best strategy, even for the smallest company, is probably to 'launch and learn'.

IN THE PALM OF YOUR HAND

Palmtop Computers

Psion "I recently caught the train to work and took out my Psion Series 3a organiser. Nobody batted an eyelid. In fact, three other people, two men and a woman, were also hammering away on their Psions. I took out my mobile phone, connected it to the Psion, and dialled the office to pick up my e-mail. The two men sitting opposite me ceased their hammering and stared across. 'What are you doing?' one asked. 'Picking up my e-mail from the office,' I replied. Next thing, both men were standing beside me peering at the screen. The woman, too, on her way to the dining car I assume, had paused briefly and was peeping over one of the men's shoulders. A

few seconds later, connection made, I had downloaded the latest sales figures and the agenda for our next international conference. 'Wow,' they said, 'wow.'"

David Potter, founder and chairman of the British company Psion, relates this incident to illustrate how familiar we've become with miniaturised computing, and at the same time, how much more than we realise is already possible. E-mail is just one example. More and more providers of Internet or modem-based services are making them compatible with Psion's palmtop computers (or 'organisers' as they are also known). Through Compuserve, for instance, Psion users can now 'surf the Net'; telecommunications companies allow short messages to be sent and received via mobile phones; banks, such as Lloyds Bank and Citibank in the UK, offer Psion-compatible banking services; and through Reuters, share prices can be tracked in real time.

David Potter was a university lecturer when he founded Psion in 1980. He had become excited by the early signs of what microprocessors and chips could do and used some capital gained in the stock market to set up the company. Its Greek-sounding name is in fact an acronym for Potter Scientific Investments Or Nothing. The company's first success was a computer game called Flight Simulation. Though rather primitive by today's standards, it proved a runaway success. By the time rival computer games began to appear, Potter had moved on to the next opportunity.

In 1984, when he launched the world's first handheld computer for information management, the Organiser, the company became — almost overnight — one of

Britain's most successful computer exporters. The Organiser's technology used surface-mount assembly and introduced the idea of a solid-state disk or data card. By 1988, the company was listed on the London Stock Exchange, and in 1993, it introduced the Series 3a organiser, Psion's most successful palmtop computer to date.

The Series 3a works for about 50 hours on two inexpensive AA batteries, giving it an immediate advantage over larger, and more expensive, 'notebook' computers. Its small size is achieved through the use of miniaturised multilayer printed circuit boards. It comes with a powerful range of built-in applications software, up to two megabytes of built-in memory and 16 megabytes of optional plug-in memory. Its word processor and spreadsheet files are compatible with Microsoft Word and Excel applications. Data can easily be transferred between the organiser and a PC using special Windows-based communications software.

It has been estimated that the market for portable computing will grow at an annual rate of forty percent a year until the year 2000. "We've only just started to scratch the surface of all the things people will be able to do on the move with their organisers," says Potter, "so the markets beyond that horizon are likely to be even larger." He is confident that "Psion will be there, continuing to 'wow' consumers well into the next millennium."

It has been estimated that the market for portable computing will grow at an annual rate of forty percent a year until the year 2000.

Mediamatic

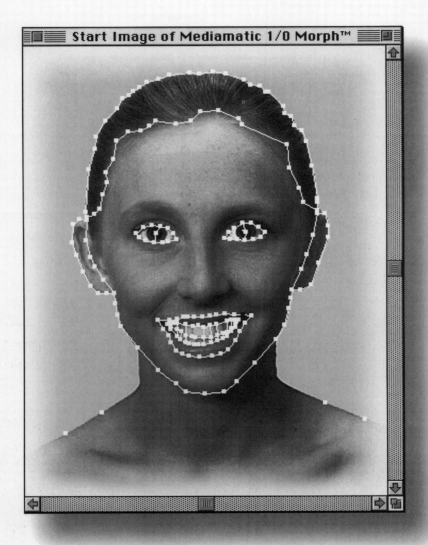

Start Image of Mediamatic 1/0 Morph™

Vol 7#1 The 1/0 Issue

THE THIRD CULTURE

Winner!

Online Services

Mediamatic Interactive multimedia is rapidly becoming the most dynamic field of business and artistic activity of the late 1990s. The accelerating convergence of modern media has created a maelstrom in which hype and relevance are difficult to distinguish. Locating itself in the eye of this maelstrom, the Dutch company Mediamatic is an active participant in this digital 'third culture', where art and technology merge. Part publisher, part management consultancy, part training centre, part production company, Mediamatic's fluidity of mission is highly characteristic of companies at the vanguard of this dynamic sector.

In 1985, the Amsterdam-based company started a magazine — called Mediamatic — to provide a much-needed vehicle for the ideas of video artists and TV dissidents. It evolved into a sophisticated international quarterly, which is now published in print, on CD-Rom, and online. Having established a profile for its ideas, Mediamatic went on to work in consulting and production for a wide variety of clients, ranging from small cultural institutions to government and multinational companies. The projects range from book design to corporate communications, from virtual banking to organistional advice and training. One constant is shared by all projects: a conceptual approach in which design is not only about the shape of things, but also about the 'shape' of processes, organisations, and relationships. Content is never separate from design.

In other services — editiorial work, design, training, and production — Mediamatic deliberately remains a node in a network of cooperators, so that projects can take any direction. "When a client comes in for a website, it may be the case that their goal is better met by something quite different," says Willem Velthoven, Mediamatic's director and editor-in-chief. "And then we have to be able to help them by finding out for them exactly what they want, and do it for them. We need that flexibility."

Mediamatic's magazine takes a theoretical approach to the new media; it publishes analyses, polemics, experimental theory, speculations, and even fiction. Authors from Europe, Japan, and North America examine all kinds of themes through the filter of Mediamatic's viewpoint that "the new media are changing every facet of human endeavour more rapidly and more deeply than anyone can guess".

"We provide considered reflection on 'computopia' from within," says Velthoven."The magazine is for anyone interested in the cultural impact the computer revolution is having on people and society. Marshall McLuhan once said our information-processing capacities are greater than we think they are and that information overload leads to pattern recognition. It's the patterns of the media society that Mediamatic writes about."

Mediamatic Online, an easy-to-use bulletin board, provides information about forthcoming issues of the magazine, complete texts of articles, a forum for debating hot topics, a regularly updated calendar, and a database of useful addresses. The full version of the magazine is also published online and is accessible free of charge.

M e d i a m a t i c   V o l u m e   8 # 2 / 3

the Home Issue

**Six out of ten
companies use
the Internet(44%)
or plan to use the
Internet(17%) in
the next 12 months.**

"Publishing online has actually boosted sales of the printed version," says Velthoven. "Some people still prefer reading from paper."

Mediamatic has production facilities for graphic, CD-Rom, and Internet projects. By producing a limited number of projects in-house every year, it is able to refresh its know-how constantly and do rapid prototyping. In this way, the performance of technical and design subcontractors can be optimised.

The company also publishes a series of books on new media screen design, Multimedia Graphics, and, jointly with the Netherlands Design Institute, organised an international conference, Doors of Perception, on the design challenges posed by communication networks and the new media. The proceedings of the first conference, published on CD-Rom, have won major awards in Europe and the USA. Mediamatic also runs World Wide Web courses for designers, editors, writers, and illustrators. The courses are attended by the staff of Mediamatic's clients, but also by major Dutch design consultancies, advertising agencies, and publishers.

"Design is one of the driving forces in project development: it affects form, structure, usability, and communication," says Velthoven. "By integrating old and new media — print and digital — in a fluid way, we provide people with a fresh look at ways of coping with our 'virtual' future."

One of Mediamatic's activities is the design of websites.

PAYWARE

Trintech

Electronic Payment Systems

The Compact 9000 in combination with the PIN-Pad can easily deal with PIN-based debit card transactions.

Few products are as inconspicuous but so economically important as credit card payment terminals. These small devices connect the virtual world of global electronic commerce to businesses selling products to real customers — and needing to be paid. Credit card acceptance equipment and PIN-pads are the physical manifestation of vast communication networks that allow us to make financial transactions at the swipe of a card, all over the world. Payment terminals represent a huge investment for banks and credit card companies who provide them as a service to hundreds of thousands of shops, restaurants, taxis, and other outlets.

Competition in this fast-changing, high-tech market is intense. Prices are dropping at between five and ten percent a year, and customers — mainly banks — are big and expert enough to shop around internationally for the best deal. Which makes all the more remarkable the success of Trintech, a small Irish company, in being one of the technological leaders in Europe. Trintech's hardware and software — which it calls 'payware' — are used by the Bank of Ireland, Bank of Scotland, SE-Banken in Sweden, and the Berliner Bank. Trintech even has an 18 percent share of the tough German market.

The Dublin company recently teamed up with Microsoft and the Bank of Ireland to provide Ireland's first secure Internet shopping mall. "We work to a 70 percent innovation ration," says Trintech's managing director, Cyril McGuire. "That means that, three years from now, 70 percent of our revenue will be based on products that do not exist in the market today."

Extremely rapid software development is the norm in these markets, but Trintech is quick with hardware development, too. The company's designers exploit advanced 3D modelling techniques and stereo-lithography for rapid prototyping and vacuum casting. Prototypes of new devices are put into the marketplace to assess customer and user reactions — and that input feeds directly and quickly back into the product designs. In the case of Trintech's Compact 9000, a small physical 'footprint' and an easier-to-use graphical user interface are both due to this rapid field-testing. The jewel-like 'compact mouse' is particularly arresting in its appearance.

"We like to surprise our markets with what we can deliver from a small team," says McGuire. Trintech nearly doubled in size from 60 to 115 people during the time we wrote this story. One suspects it will be bigger again by the time you read it. Certainly, few competitors expected Trintech to bring Internet software (the product is called PayGate) to the market so quickly. The Bank of Ireland is one of the first banks in Europe to offer Internet payment, and already some familar companies are jumping onto the virtual bandwagon — Guinness among them. Trintech's systems provide the Bank of Ireland with an open, platform-independent payment application which is secure for all parties — consumer, retailer, and bank.

While there were no ATM transactions at all in 1980, Americans made purchases or got cash out of a wall seven and a half billion times in 1992; that figure has continued to grow steeply.

And the volume of credit card purchases will have quadrupled in 20 years — from $201 billion in 1980 to an estimated $882 billion by 2000.

HOW TO DO IT

Innovation by Design

From a spoon to a city   "Everything flows," said Heraclitus — an early advocate of innovation as a continuous process. "The old game was results, the new game is process," repeated *The Harvard Business Review*, a while later. Innovation never stops: it's what happens when you always believe things can be improved, and constantly try to organise things better.

So how does design contribute to innovation? Well, in different ways. Design involves the way concepts are developed, the way products are made, the way they look, the way they behave, and the way they are used. In Italy, they say design can be applied "from a spoon to a city" — only nowadays you have to add "in cyberspace, too". So it's hard to define design. But does it matter? Can you define 'creativity', or 'organisation', or 'communication'? Probably not. But you need them in your business, and the same goes for design.

Design scenarios   Companies use design for different ends. One of these ends is thinking about the future. Design scenarios, in which a hypothetical product or service is simulated or envisioned, can be a catalyst for change within an organisation and help change its mind-set. Design scenarios are basically stories about how things might be organised differently. At the Netherlands Design Institute, we often use a technique called 'back-casting', in which we start by describing a hypothetical destination — such as "we now use twenty times less matter and energy in the company," or "90 percent of food is eaten within 50 kilometres (30 miles) of where it is produced". We then put these rather fantastical statements into multi-disciplinary workshops — with the brief to describe, retrospectively, the steps by which we could have got there. Designers play a key role in these workshops: their planning skills to make the story coherent and their presentational skills to make it

persuasive are extremely useful. The end result is not a product; it's not even a business plan. When a workshop goes well, it's something more valuable: ideas, awareness, enthusiasm, new ways of working.

The idea of collaborative innovation and shared creativity — with users, designers, and producers creating new products together — is the most exciting feature of the new economy.

One-sided relationships between a company and its clients (users react, they do not propose) are being superseded by 'envisioning laboratories', environments in which users can play with new technologies before an application has been packaged as a finished product.

Pre-prototyping user needs has obvious benefits even in traditional hard product development, where design decisions tend to be irrevocable once tooling and production investments have been specified. When the whole technological environment is novel, as in the case of interactive computers and communications, the ability to involve users in the design and simulation of new applications is even more valuable.

So where are ideas for new needs to come from? However well envisioning labs engage with groups of users, someone has to provide an aesthetic stimulus — to throw ideas into the ring — in order to provoke genuinely fresh thinking. Design can be a useful mediator in breaking down the isolation from each other of artists, computer scientists, and users and in promoting the fruitful interaction between them that may just yield the new concepts and applications needed to fulfil the promise of the new technologies.

Buy early and save

Designers can also play an important role in reconfiguring production and distribution systems. Industrial or product designers in particular, even though they are brought up to think about 'things', are also rather good at process and system design. In the advanced research group of the Dutch telecom company KPN, whose job it is to think about advanced network applications, eight of the 50-strong team are industrial designers. Could it be because they think in three dimensions, are committed to making things work, and think constantly about the user, that industrial designers make good network designers, too?

Of course, most designers still think about discrete products and how to make them better. And better again. (Designers are not good at leaving things alone.) How to make a product stand out in a crowded department store. How to make it cheaper and more energy-efficient to produce. How to reduce its packaging. How to make it recyclable. Designers work towards these goals in many different ways, but one lesson

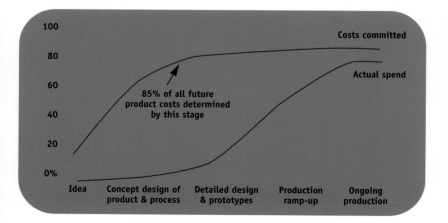

The design of a product dictates its costs: the impact of early work has far-reaching financial effects.
DESIGN COUNCIL (UK).

is universal: the earlier a designer is involved, the better. Dr. Colin Mynott, a former industry director at the Design Council in Great Britain, estimates that, by the end of the design and development process, 80 percent of a product's costs have been ordained; beyond that stage, production can typically create only 15 percent of additional value (see chart above). Andrew Bradley, a design management consultant in Dublin, agrees: "It pays to spend money on design, but it's important to spend early and carefully. The design phase of new product development typically absorbs 15 percent of its budget, but commits at least 80 percent of its costs."

It's not what you make, it's the way that you say it

For good or ill, there are ten times more graphic designers than product designers. The reasons for this state of affairs boil down to a simple proposition: it's easier to make a product look different, than be different. Or at least, that has been the case during the age of mass communications; it made sense to pour millions into building up a brand when consumers could be sprayed with high-value imagery *en masse*. The amount of money spent on presentation and communications can be 100 times more than is spent on the product itself. The way a product is advertised; its packaging; the way it is displayed in the shop; the way the shop is designed — this is where the big money has been spent for the last 20 years. This included design, which enjoyed a spectacular boom when it became a subset of marketing services, alongside sales promotions, incentive marketing, media advertising, corporate identity, packaging, exhibitions, merchandising, public relations, direct mail, and so on. A plethora of communication-producing semiotic trash. No wonder design got a bad name during the 1980s.

Today, with the media fragmenting and consumers getting wise to the way branding works, the rules of the game are changing. To be fair, designers have been sensitive to the fragmentation of audiences for some time. In *Corporate Image and Reality*, David Bernstein lists nine ways in which a company communicates with the outside world: "product, correspondence, public relations, personal presentation, impersonal presentation, literature, point of sale, permanent media, advertising". (An obvious tenth — the Internet — was not known in the design world when Bernstein wrote his excellent book in 1984.) However product-focused a company may be, no product can be marketed without communication. To the extent that it 'speaks' to a customer ("Buy me! Buy me now!") a product itself is a form of communication. The question is not "Communication: yes or no?" — but "What sort?" and "How?".

The nine publics of a company image
D. BERNSTEIN, *CORPORATE IMAGE AND REALITY*.

Kuilman's core competencies
Dingeman Kuilman, who heads a large graphic design group within Philips, has thought a lot about design's evolving role in a world of multidisciplinary teams; Kuilman's job is to

Why there are more graphic designers than product designers

Stationery and forms letterheadings, continuation sheets, compliment slips, visiting cards, invoices, statements, delivery notes, credit notes, order forms, memos, quotations, estimates, address labels, cheques, computer forms, application forms, report covers **Transport & equipment** logos, telephone numbers and slogans on trucks, vans & tankers, truck sheets, containers, cars, the Gulfstream, ships, cranes, fork-lift trucks, earth movers, rail trucks, warehouse vehicles and lifts **Signs** door signs, gate signs, identification signs, office signs, shop fascias, factory signs, depot signs, projecting signs, window signs **Advertising** more signs, bumper stickers, permanent and temporary hoardings, roof signs, signs at sports grounds, display ads in magazines and newspapers, flags, stickers, crap giveaways **Information signs** car park signs, store signs, interior directional signs, signs in the lift, offices and factories, external factory signs **Products** yes, but don't forget they too have graphics, instructions, labels, product identification and technical signs, not to mention **Packaging** crates and transit packs, outer packaging, unit packaging, inner packaging, instruction leaflets, guarantees, point-of-sale material, tickets, labels, tapes, warehouse identification, customs and shipment documentation **Corporate print** annual reports, IPO brochures, (very expensive) brochures for trade fairs, recruitment booklets, financial literature, house magazines and newspapers, employee information booklets **Publicity** leaflets, direct mailshots, their envelopes, their reply cards, institutional and product leaflets, more booklets, more brochures, price lists, TV and radio advertisement graphics, film titles, sponsorship material, technical literature, posters, press releases, leaflet dispensers **Interiors** need designing, e.g. reception areas, corridors, communal areas, boardroom, staff restaurants, shop interiors, office interiors, factory interiors and then you can still fill them with book matches, ashtrays, cups and saucers, menucards **Exhibitions** exhibition stands, folders full of documents, slides for the press, shipping cases, dreadful videos **Occupational garments** uniforms, factory clothing, laboratory clothing, donkey jackets, security guard uniforms, safety helmets, charming corporate ties.

integrate graphic design within the broader design and communication processes of a large multinational enterprise. His approach is to look at graphic design as a set of 'core competencies', and to deploy those competencies tactically, in different combinations, as a project demands. 'Kuilman's competencies', as we may call them, are:

- process knowledge: the overall process of graphic design and of its production in various media
- medium or genre knowledge: skill and expertise within a particular medium: print (mainly two-dimensional); packaging (three-dimensional); product graphics; graphic user interface (on a screen); exhibition graphic design (in a space)
- transversal expertise: a set of skills that transcends individual media or genres: identity design (creating, maintaining, and protecting a company's identity); information design (the development of symbols, graphs, charts, and diagrams and the design of navigation through information structures); typography (communication composed in type); colour study; and applied semiotics (the study of the meaning of graphic communication).

It's all in the source

Kuilman's schema of design competencies could usefully be developed for other areas of design, too, such as product design. Competency filters make a lot of sense in the task of sourcing and organising design.

Design comes from three sources: from in-house designers; from design consultants; and from 'non-designers', when people design things themselves, sometimes without realising it. Until recently, there was a trend in larger companies to replace in-house design departments with contracted-out services; but a growing realisation that design is a core competency has reversed that trend; in-house design departments have stopped shrinking and designers are moving closer to the centre of thinking and doing in many big companies.

Europe's Top 500 companies have enormous design purchasing-power between them. It's difficult to determine how much they spend on design because so many departments purchase design independently, but the biggest companies must spend more than 20 million ECU ($24 million) on design each year; some probably spend even more.

Small and medium-sized enterprises (SMEs), of which there are an estimated nine million in Europe alone, can also be active users of design. The winners of the European Design Prize are not a typical group, of course, but it's significant that with an average size of 233 employees, their average design spend is 364,000 ECU ($440,000), that is 1,562 ECU ($1,875) per employee.

The public sector is another growing user of design services. Government ministries and institutions use design a lot. Policies are being more actively communicated. State-owned postal and telecommunications services have turned to design amid increasing competition. A pattern of privatisation of state utilities has also stimulated demand.

> **With an average size of 233 employees, the average design spend of the winners of the European Design Prize is 364,000 ECU ($440,000), that is 1,562 ECU ($1,875) per employee.**

Cities are a booming market for design, too. An estimated 300 different cities and regions within Europe are competing against each other for inward investment with unprecedented vigour, using the design of social amenities, multiple forms of communication, and urban renewal programmes as competitive weapons. From Groningen to Glasgow, Bremen, Lyon, Nîmes, Barcelona, and Valencia, design infrastructures and policies have been created. A similar process has been taking place at regional level.

An awfully big cottage

Although commonly perceived to be a cottage industry, design is a big and successful service industry. There are nearly 10,000 design companies in the European Union (although they tend to be small; most have fewer than 25 staff, many have only two or three); alongside these agencies are at least 150,000 staff designers employed by companies. At any one time, 180,000 students are enrolled in design courses somewhere in Europe; 30,000 students graduate each year, and most of them get jobs. By the year 2000, expenditure on design by governments, cities, multinationals, small firms, and agencies is forecast to rise to more than 12 billion ECU ($14.4 billion).

Most of this money appears to be well spent. According to industrial research in Europe, 85 percent of design projects recover their costs through improved sales, higher profit margins, or lower manufacturing costs. Of these profitable design-related projects, 47 percent paid back their total investment within a year or less, with the average being 15 months from the launch of the design project.

How to find, select, and appoint designers

Research among European and North American clients shows that, in commissioning a designer, they rely overwhelmingly on past experience or on direct word-of-mouth recommendation. Fewer than five percent of them select designers solely on the basis of pictures in a catalogue or directory. Of course, even experienced design-buyers use yearbooks as a starting point when they are in search of new talent, or when — like the designers themselves — they want to see what the competition is up to. But creative, innovative, and effective design is usually the result of a process which involves more players and more factors than just the input of a designer. Without a good client and a good team, good design is rare.

The passage of time is an important success factor, too. For communication or product development to succeed, a client and the designer need ideally to develop a relationship based on mutual understanding, even when the people concerned may well be very different from each other. Most design projects involve both technical ("Can they do it?") and cultural requirements ("Can we work together?"), so it is important that a client starting to look for a designer be clear in advance about the technical skills and personal attributes being sought. The tighter the brief, the easier the selection will be.

When economic times were easy, the myth of the designer as a kind of 'flying doctor' was sustainable. Designers would justify a learning period — for which the client paid — as a neccessary price for a 'fresh point of view'. Clients, too, were content to hire designers for a single task — such as a piece of packaging or a visual identity for the company — because, even when inefficiently used, design still made a contribution to competitiveness. Now, when clients are focusing more intently on value, longer-term relationships with designers make better sense. For this reason, some clients are opting to assemble rosters of designers and agencies with whom they intend to work over a period of time. The biggest clients — those spending, say, more than 20 million ECU a year on design fees — work increasingly with limited groups of perhaps four to six design agencies — as against dozens a few years ago for some multinationals. Rosters cut out the waste and the uncertainty of continually recruiting new designers; project management is generally much more efficient when designers already know the system; and designers themselves do a better job when they have the opportunity to develop an understanding of the policies and direction of the company or organisation they are working for. Despite the benefits of long-term relationships, of course, there is the danger that young designers will find it even harder to get started in business, and that rostered designers will become complacent.

But it is hard to measure success. The Judge Institute in Cambridge, England, has embarked on a project to benchmark aspects of the design process — the first such in Europe. Project researcher Nick Oliver has looked at 18 design projects, assessing their productivity, quality, and duration. In quality, for example, his chosen metrics were the number of specification changes made during development, the proportion of scrap material, and so on. Hugh Aldersey Williams, a British writer on design issues, says the common factor for all companies that are managing creativity is the need to assess the risk involved — even if they then decide, on reflection, to take it. "There's always the danger that semi-quantitative procedures will so impress some managers that the unquantifiable side of innovation will be neglected or disparaged," he says. "There are aspects of the creative process that are beyond the reach of benchmarking techniques, and will remain so."

Technology and design

Although design manifests itself in many ways throughout industry, a feature common to all varieties is rapid technological (and therefore capital) intensification. Not so long ago, a designer could get by with a Number Two pencil and a yellow pad. A designer doesn't need much more today — but the range of machines and software available is extraordinary (see box overleaf).

Design tools yesterday

Number 2 pencil   yellow pad

Design tools today

ACT
ALIAS
Animation software
   Director
   Premiere
   Video Fusion
Apple
AST
asynchronous transfer
   mode line
Authorware 3.5
AutoCAD/ProE
Avid editing suite
CAD/CAM programs
   Strata/Studio/3D
   Studio/Form-Z
CD-Rom burner
CD-Rom drives
colour copier
colour plotter
colour printer
Database software
   FileMaker
   Access
   Excel
DAT drive

dedicated phone line
Dell
digital camera
disk array
DTP software
   QuarkXpress
   Pagemaker
   Framemaker
Drawing programs
   Photoshop
   Freehand
   Illustrator
   Corel Draw
dye sublimation device
E-size plotter
Ethernet hub
external disk drives
flatbed cutter
Flexisign & Casmate
Hewlett Packard
IBM
ink jet plotter
Internet software
ISDN line
Jaz
laser printer

Linotronic printer
local area network
machine plotter
Maclink
Microsoft Mail
milling machine
modem
Netpower
network server
PC
pen plotter
Photo CD
plotter
Pro-designer
(rendering)
Pro Engineer software
router
Silicon Graphics
Soundedit 16
Syquest
tablets
teleport
video hardware
writable optical
Zeos (Pentium)
Zip

NETHERLANDS DESIGN INSTITUTE.

Carel Kuitenbrouwer, who runs the 2D programme at the Netherlands Design Institute, recently completed a comparative study of technology trends among design companies in Holland, Germany, and the United States. He discovered that the proliferation of software technologies into every aspect of the innovation process is mirrored in design. "The average European or North American design office — and remember, most contain fewer than 25 people — spends 24,000 ECU ($29,000) a year on computer hardware, software, and training," says Kuitenbrouwer.

Technology works in unexpected ways — and what boosts designers' productivity today may undermine their business tomorrow. So-called 'rules-based' design programs, for example, may well end up eroding a sizeable chunk of design's economic base. In Europe and North America there are about 20,000 practising graphic designers. But there are already more than three million desk-top publishing programs in circulation, and sophisticated 'Be your own designer' programs are increasingly being bundled in with new computers' operating software or with office-in-a-box products. There are 180 million personal computers in the world — most of which can run these designer-software programs — and another 100,000 personal computers are sold every 24 hours; so the indicators do suggest that the profitable underbelly of design consultancy may be dangerously exposed.

How to manage design
During the European Design Prize process, all the nominated companies were asked to make a chart showing where and how design fitted into their business processes. Every single chart was different! The companies all used design in different ways and in different combinations in relation to customers, technology, research, finance, marketing, distribution and logistics, information technology, and so on. Their design projects involved hardware, software,

people, processes, purpose, organisation, and behaviour. The message from the experts was unanimous: managing design is hard to systematise.

Design management is a complex and multi-faceted activity that goes right to the heart of what a company is and does — especially in the case of a small manufacturing company. It is not something susceptible to pat formulas, a few bullet points, or a manual. Every company's strategy, management structure, and internal culture is different; design management is no exception. But the fact that every firm is different does not diminish the importance of managing design tightly and effectively.

It may seem obvious, but it is worth reassuring potential clients that once they have selected a designer, the client should drive the design process — not the designer. Only rarely should a designer be expected to develop business or organisational objectives. On their own, most designers lack the training and experience to develop the complex synthesis of product, production, markets, communications, and consumers that running a business and defining a design project involves. Some companies exist that are genuinely 'design driven'; for example, companies making office furniture or building products that are specified or purchased by other designers. But in the 1980s, particularly in the corporate identity field, some designers came to believe that the identity of a company was the company, and that they, the designers, could be relied upon to 'redesign the enterprise'. Disbelieve such talk. In the new economy, organisations will suceed only if they deliver real value to their customers at every level of their operations. A prettily painted face is no substitute.

As well as stating the nature of the task rather clearly, clients should also be precise about the time and money they are prepared to invest in a project. In a commercial transaction, this sounds like a statement of the obvious; but many clients are strangely reluctant — perhaps because they believe designers to be 'artists' — to specify the deliverables they expect from a design project. Such reticence only encourages professional sloppiness about deadlines and budget limits which are in the interests of neither party.

Stringent performance criteria are in the best interests of both designers and clients in the longer term. Defining —and sticking to — precise targets for time, costs, and quality should be the automatic basis for relationships between designers and clients. If they are not adhered to strictly, clients will rightly focus only on failures to meet targets, rather than on the other qualities added to a project by the designer. Many designers will be indignant at this idea. "You can't measure quality," they will say. "Such calculations produce the lowest common denominator of design." These are the arguments of the intelligent ostrich. Of course, evaluation can stifle innovation. But in today's harsh conditions, with the exception of marginalised design on the fringes of society, the pressure to explain the value of design — and even to measure it — cannot be avoided. The challenge is to demonstrate how, and by how much, creative, innovative design works better than indifferent design. If designers do not develop their own criteria, others will do it for them.

How, then, are we to reconcile the external pressures on design to improve its functionality and cost-effectiveness, with an 'internal' tradition, deeply rooted in its culture and education, which places a high value on formal innovation, technique, and expressiveness? The answer is that designers and clients should resolve to invent the future together, propose new relationships, anticipate limits, and accelerate trends.

THE
EUROPEAN
DESIGN
PRIZE

The EU's Innovation Programme

If European industry is to make the most of the single market, it has to be competitive. Innovation is a key element, perhaps the key element, in a company's ability to compete in a world where technological changes are happening at an ever faster pace. Companies that do not innovate wither and die — and with today's global markets, the competition is getting tougher by the minute.

This has been recognised at national and European Community levels; as a consequence, the Fourth Community Framework Programme of Community activities in Research and Technological Development (R&TD) and Demonstration (1995-1998) now provides for a specific programme for the dissemination and optimisation of the results of research activities. This third activity of the Fourth Framework Programme is known as the Innovation Programme.

The overall aim of the Innovation Programme is simple to understand but complex to achieve. It is to help European industry become more competitive by making the most of available technologies and techniques. The Innovation Programme uses a new systems approach to the promotion of innovation, which identifies three interdependent objectives:

- to promote an environment favourable to innovation and the absorption of new technologies by enterprises;
- to stimulate a European open area for the diffusion of technologies and knowledge;
- to supply this area with appropriate technologies.

The human and financial resources available for the programme are clearly not limitless. The projects and the bodies chosen to work with and for the programme are carefully selected. The action lines and the projects are selected to identify and define best practice to allow us to draw lessons which can then be applied by others.

The bodies are selected for their expertise, and for their capacity to pass on the lessons learned in the widest possible sense. The Innovation Programme delivers competitive tools to companies:

- business contacts across Europe
- technology transfer projects
- access to research results
- access to external expertise and competence
- patent and intellectual property services
- financing advice and networking.

The first strand of the Innovation Programme — promotion of an environment favourable to innovation — includes:

- European Innovation Monitoring System (EIMS)
- a financial environment favouring the diffusion of new technologies
- regional actions and support of science parks
- promotion of innovation management techniques
- increasing public awareness of research and technology.

The second strand — the circulation of technologies — includes:

- the Relay Centre network
- European networks and services
- technology transfer projects.

The third strand — the supply of technologies — includes:

- a community information and dissemination service
- assistance in the protection and the exploitation of R&TD results
- technology validation projects.

Further information is available from the following six sources:

1   **EUROPEAN COMMUNITY INFORMATION AND DISSEMINATION SERVICE**

t +352 4301 32248 / f +352 4301 34989

2   **COMMUNITY RESEARCH AND DEVELOPMENT INFORMATION SERVICE (CORDIS)**

CORDIS — the European Union's R&D information service — is the easiest way to access the wealth of results funded by EU science and technology programmes. Through CORDIS you can access:

- details of 400 research programmes either completed or still running
- data on more than 25,000 research projects with contacts for each
- information on results and prototypes.

CORDIS is a large and functional database which may be accessed via the Internet at its website (www.cordis.lu/). The database is a central source of information crucial for any organisation — be it an industrial company, a small or medium-sized enterprise, a research organisation, or a university — wishing to participate in the exploitation of research results, participate in EU-funded science and technology programmes, and/or seek partnerships, CORDIS places key information on all EU research activities at your fingertips.

3   **THE FOURTH FRAMEWORK PROGRAMME**

A supplement of *CORDIS Focus* (the main EU information journal) which includes the status of calls for proposals for the Fourth Framework Programme and the Euratom Framework Programme; contact points for the specific programmes; how to find a research partner through CORDIS and a list of documents available on the CORDIS World Wide Web server. Fourth Framework Programme, *CORDIS Focus*, Supplement no. 8, May 1996. European Commission f +352 4301 32084.

4   EC RESEARCH FUNDING

A guide designed to answer, in clear and simple terms, the questions in everyone's mind as to the value and success of the European Union's activities in the area of research and technological development. Fourth Framework Programme 1994-98 (1996) *EC Research Funding: a guide for applicants,* 4th edition, Brussels: European Commission, Science Research Development.

5   INNOVATION AND TECHNOLOGY TRANSFER

A journal, published every two months in English, French, and German, which keeps you up to date on Innovation Programme news. Subscriptions are free. t +352 4301 32084

6   INNOVATION RELAY CENTRES

The Innovation Relay Centres (IRCs) are advisory offices located in 52 European regions. Their goal is to promote innovation and to encourage exchange of research results throughout Europe, and to provide advice, consulting, and training support which meets the specific needs of a company and its local industrial situation. If you have been thinking about how your organisation can tap into a network of organisations in other European regions, or how it can cooperate on projects and exchange technologies, the European network of the IRCs is your first contact point. Innovation Relay Centres f +352 4301 34129

The European Design Prize The European Community

Design Prize was launched in 1988 by the European Commission with the support of design promotion organisations of member states of that time. The European Design Prize 1997 is an initiative of the European Union's Innovation Programme.

The aim of the revised European Design Prize (EDP) 1997 is to stimulate awareness and use of design as an instrument of innovation and quality. The Prize is used in communications to, and among, small and medium-sized enterprises in Europe. Further to a competitive call for tender, the 1997 edition of the Prize was produced by a consortium of three organisations: Agence pour la Promotion de la Création Industrielle (APCI), Paris; the European Design Partnership, Dublin; and the Netherlands Design Institute, Amsterdam.

The Prizes are awarded to a limited number of successful companies; a preference is given to small and medium-sized industrial companies located and operating in the European Economic Area — not to a particular product, and not to an individual, such as a designer, although successful design teams may be acknowledged in Prize communications. Nominated companies must persuade a European Jury (the 1997 Jury is listed in the following pages) that they have used design, within the innovation process as a whole, to add functionality and quality to products, to improve communication, and to enhance the physical environment within which the company operates. The Jury's principal criterion is that a company has used design to innovate successfully; its members look in particular for innovation that involves the introduction or exploitation of new technology — either in a new product or process, or to upgrade existing products or services.

The following roll of honour acknowledges and celebrates 11 winners of the 1997 European Design Prize; the other 53 finalists; and 11 winners of previous editions of the Prize since 1988. Among the 11 winners in 1997 the Jury also made four special awards to recognise the following achievements: an award for a young technology-intensive company; a 'newcomer's award' for the successful use of design in a sector that traditionally has not used design to innovate; and a 'life-time achievement' award for excellence in the use of design in all aspects of a company's operation.

**THE EUROPEAN DESIGN PRIZE
1997 WAS ADMINISTERED BY
A CONSORTIUM OF**

European Design Partnership
31 Heytesbury Lane, Dublin 4,
Ireland
t +353 1 660 1722
f +353 1 660 1635
bradley@iol.ie

Netherlands Design Institute
Keizersgracht 609, 1017 DS
Amsterdam, The Netherlands
t +31 20 551 6500
f +31 20 620 1031
desk@design-inst.nl
www.design-inst.nl/

**Agency for the Promotion of
Industrial Creation (APCI)**
3 rue de Brissac, 75004 Paris,
France
t +33 1 44 61 72 40
f +33 1 44 61 72 49
apcifr@mail.club-internet.fr

*For further information on
the European Design Prize 1997
please contact:*
Andrew Bradley
European Design Partnership
31 Heytesbury Lane, Dublin 4,
Ireland

**THE EUROPEAN JURY
OF THE EUROPEAN DESIGN
PRIZE 1997**

Flemming Aggergård (DK)
Former CEO of Kompan,
a manufacturer of children's
playground equipment and EDP
winner in 1994.

Lidewij Edelkoort (NL)
Founder and director of Studio
Edelkoort, a highly influential
Paris-based consumer analysis
trend and forecasting company.

Jordi Montaña (ESP)
Professor of Design Management
at Esade, one of Europe's leading
business schools in Barcelona.

David McMurtry (IRL)
CEO of Renishaw plc. He invented
a unique measuring probe in the
early 1970s and then co-founded
Renishaw to exploit the invention
and develop further applications.
Chairman of the Jury.

André-Yves Portnoff (F)
Adviser to the Club CRIN de
Prospective Scientifique et
Technologique. He is the leader of
the course "Innovation et Cultures
Européennes" of DESS Innovation
at Union Européenne d'Angers.
Freelance journalist specialising in
science and industry.

Joachim Sauter (D)
Director of Art+Com, the Berlin-
based new media development and
design company, and a professor at
the Berlin Hochschule der Kunste.
Art+Com specialises in the
development of user interfaces for
high-capacity network
applications.

James Woudhuysen (UK)
Director of World Wide Intelligence
for Consumer Electronics, Philips;
professor of Design Management at
De Montfort University, UK. He was
previously Associate Director at
Henley Centre for Forecasting.

NATIONAL ORGANISERS
The following national design organisations provided support for the implementation of the EDP project. They are appropriate 'first stops' for anyone seeking information about design. Some of these organisations are large and offer a range of advice and information. Others are relatively small. But most will be able to tell you where to go next if they cannot help you themselves.

Austria
Österreichisches Institut
für Formgebung
St. Ulrichplatz 4,
1070 Wien
Karin Hirschberger
t +43 1 523 8782 14
f +43 1 52387 81

Belgium
Institut Belge du Design
Rue Washington 40, B13,
1050 Bruxelles
Thierry Van Kerm
t +32 2 6401200
f +32 2 6401428

Denmark
Danish Design Centre
H.C. Andersens Bd 18,
1553 Copenhagen V
Birgitta Capetillo
t +45 33 14 66 88
f +45 33 32 00 48

Finland
Design Forum Finland
Fabianinkatu 10,
00130 Helsinki
Anne Stenros
t +358 9 629290
f +358 9 611918

France
A.P.C.I.
3 rue de Brissac,
75004 Paris
Jacqueline Febvre
t +33 1 44 61 72 40
f +33 1 44 61 72 49

Germany
Rat für Formgebung
Messegelände, Postfach 15 03 11,
60063 Frankfurt/Main
Hans Höger
t +49 6974 7919
f +49 6974 10911

Greece
Hellenic Product Design Centre
Xenias 16,
11528 Athens
Gregory Adamopoulostel
t +30 1 7491385
f +30 1 7715128

Iceland
Design Center
Hallveigarstigur 1, PO Box 1450,
121 Reykjavik
Arni Johannsson
t +354 5115555
f +354 5115566

Ireland
European Design Partnership
31 Heytesbury Lane, Dublin 4
Andrew Bradley
bradley@iol.ie
t +353 1 6601722
f +353 1 6601635

Italy
A.D.I.
Via Bramante 29,
20154 Milano
Augusto Morello
t +39 2 33100164
f +39 2 33100878
adi@essai.it
www2.essai.it/Adi/

Luxembourg
Luxinnovation
7 Rue Alcide de Gasperi,
1615 Luxembourg-Kirchberg
Gilles Schlesser
t +352 4362631
f +352 432328

Norway
Norsk Designrad
Riddervolds Gate 2,
0256 Oslo
Eva Christensen-Røed
t +47 22 55 80 40
f +47 22 55 93 02

Portugal
Centro Português de Design
Polo Tecnologico de Lisboa,
Lote 8, 1699 Lisboa Codex
Ana Calcada
t +351 1 716 71 71
f +351 1 716 59 17

Spain
DDI
Paseo de la Castellana, 141-I/B,
28046 Madrid
Carmen Cuesta Garrido
t +34 1 5721083
f +34 1 5711564

Sweden
Swedish Industrial
Design Foundation
PO Box 5501,
11485 Stockholm
Torsten Dahlin
t +46 8 783 8321
f +46 8 66120 35

The Netherlands
Netherlands Design Institute
Keizersgracht 609,
1017 DS Amsterdam
Yvonne Janssen
t +31 20 5516500
f +31 20 6201031
yvonne@design-inst.nl
www.design-inst.nl

United Kingdom
The Design Council
Haymarket House,
1 Oxenden Street,
London SW1Y 4EE
Anthony Land
t +44 171 208 2121
f +44 171 839 6033
www.design-council.org.uk/

Winners of the European Design Prize 1997

Artemide S.p.A.
Via Bergamo, 18
20010-I Pregnana Milanese
Italy
t +39 2 935181
f +39 2 93590254
www.artemide.com
Company Managing Director:
Ernesto Gismondi
Year established: 1959
Number of employees: 115
Company turnover (ecu):
42,000,000
*Artemide is a design-oriented
company which manufactures and
markets lighting fixtures. Artemide's
new Metamorfosi lighting system
marks a radical shift in interior
lighting; the remotely controlled
system can create an infinite
number of atmospheres to suit any
mood or occasion.* (See also pp.
300-305)
+ *special award for lifetime
achievement*

Authentics artipresent GmbH
Max-Eyth-Straße 30
71088 Holzgerlingen
Germany
t +49 7031 68050
f +49 7031 680599
www.authentics.de
Company Managing Directors:
Hans Maier-Aichen and
Hanna Irion
Year established: 1988
Number of employees: 65
Company turnover (ecu):
13,803,400
*Authentics designs, manufactures,
and markets plastic articles for
household use, exploiting plastic's
'natural' qualities. The company's
range of products — all made of
polypropylene, a recyclable thermo-
plastic — includes bowls, pitchers,
vases, and containers of all shapes
and sizes.* (See also pp. 366-369)

Bates Emballage A/S
Stigsborgvej 36
9400 Nørresundby
Denmark
t +45 96323232
f +45 98170274
Company Managing Director:
Arne Juul
Year established: 1995
Number of employees: 350
Company turnover (ecu):
5,000,000
*Bates manufactures industrial
sacks and sack-handling machines,
dunnage bags for freight
protection, paper refuse sacks
and complete waste systems.
The company's new Combi System
allows easy and hygienic processing
and collection of household waste.*
(See also pp. 358-365)

Bulthaup GmbH & Co
Werkstraße 6
84153 Aich
Germany
t +49 8741 800
f +49 8741 80309
Company Managing Directors:
Gerd Bulthaup, Günther Schertel
Year established: 1949
Number of employees: 500
Company turnover (ecu):
39,000,000
*Bulthaup develops and
manufactures high-end kitchens
for private and semi-professional
use. The company's philosophy is
one of continuous innovation,
combining insights into changing
trends, demands, and lifestyles with
the latest technological advances.*
(See also pp. 106-113)
+ *special award for lifetime
achievement*

Dyson Appliances Ltd.
Tetbury Hill
SN16 0RP Malmesbury, Wiltshire

United Kingdom
t +44 1666 827200
f +44 1666 827299
Company Managing Director:
James Dyson
Year established: 1993
Number of employees: 420
Company turnover (ecu):
47,821,800
*Dyson develops and manufactures
bagless vacuum cleaners, based on
the revolutionary new Dual Cyclone
technology. The Dyson vacuum
cleaner can maintain 100% suction
(no dust clogging) and eradicates
the drawbacks and inconveniences
of bags.* (See also pp. 72-77)
+ *special 'high-tech start-up' award*

Fiskars Consumer Oy Ab
FIN-10470 Fiskars
Finland
t +358 19 236350
f +358 19 277582
design@fiskars.gcis.com
Company Managing Director:
Stig Måtar
Year established: 1549
Number of employees: 440
Company turnover (ecu):
35,340,000
*Fiskars' classic products are its
scissors in all shapes and sizes.
More recently, Fiskars has brought
to the market a whole range of
(ergonomic) gardening tools. The
series of Handy axes, consisting of
six axes, each for a different purpose, is one of the company's recent
triumphs.* (See also pp. 202-207)

Hörnell Elektrooptik AB
Ernst Hedlunds väg 35
780 41 Gagnef
Sweden
t +46 241 62400
f +46 241 62107
Anders.Grönberg@hornell-
speedglas.se

Winners of the European Design Prize 1997

Company Managing Director:
Klas Nygårds
Year established: 1983
Number of employees: 112
Company turnover (ecu):
13,627,500
Hörnell manufactures welding helmets and respiratory equipment focused on comfort and safety. Its Speedglass welding helmets incorporate automatically darkening welding filters, which turn from light to dark in a fraction of a second. Hörnell has also developed a unique respiratory system, offering protection against welding fumes and particles. (See also pp. 246-253)

+ special newcomer's award

Lafuma S.A.
6, rue Victor Lafuma
26140 Anneyron
France
t +33 475 313131
f +33 475 315726
Company Managing Director:
Philippe Joffard
Year established: 1930
Number of employees: 300
Company turnover (ecu):
45,490,000
Lafuma manufactures and sells products for outdoor activities, such as mountaineering, hiking, and camping, as well as schoolbags and holders for school-going children. Lafuma aims to create ergonomic and technically fine-tuned products for a wide range of activities, and to offer an optimum mix of performance, quality, and affordability. (See also pp. 208-201)

Mediamatic
Postbus 17490
1001 JL Amsterdam
The Netherlands

t +31 20 626 6262 / 624 1054
f +31 20 626 3793
desk@mediamatic.nl
Company Managing Director:
Willem Velthoven
Year established: 1986
Number of employees: 13
Company turnover (ecu): 300,000
Mediamatic provides a forum for discussion and debate in the field of interactive multimedia by means of a magazine and an internet site. The magazine has evolved into a sophisticated international quarterly, and is now published in print, on cd-rom and on-line. Mediamatic has expanded its activities into several related directions and works for clients in the corporate and cultural community offering practical and strategic support at all levels of interactive and traditional publishing. (See also pp.411-415)

Oken S.A.
C/ Strauss, s/n
Pol. Ind. "Can Jardi"
08191 Rubí Barcelona
Spain
t +34 3 5882568
f +34 3 5880345
Company Managing Director:
Joan Tó Padullés
Year established: 1989
Number of employees: 29
Company turnover (ecu):
5,100,000
Oken designs and manufactures seating systems for public areas, such as offices, airports, schools, auditoriums. Oken's seating systems are attractive and comfortable, making use of highly advanced technology. Many of Oken's products are designed by Josep Lluscá, whose experience and skill in balancing the technical with the cultural have played a decisive role

in helping to shape Oken's identity. (See also pp. 152-157)

Oticon A/S
58, Strandvejen
2900 Hellerup
Denmark
t +45 39 17 71 00
f +45 39 27 79 00
www.oticon.com
info@oticon.dk
Company Managing Director:
Lars Kolind
Year established: 1904
Number of employees: 1485
Company turnover (ecu):
125,000,000
Oticon develops and produces high-technology hearing instruments where the amplification continually adjusts to changing sound environments. It has developed the world's first digital hearing aid which makes hearing as natural as possible for the hearing impaired. (See also pp. 254-261)

Finalists 1997

AKG Acoustics
Lemboeckgasse 21-25
A- 1230 Wien
Austria
t +43 1 866540
f +43 1 86654567
Company Managing Director:
Hendrik Homan
Year established: 1947
Number of employees: 450
Company turnover (ecu):
45,777,000
AKG is one of the world's leading specialist manufacturers of high-quality microphones, headphones, telecom products, recording and sound systems for professional use. AKG supplies whole sound systems to a wide variety of customers, ranging from theatres and concert halls to schools and small companies. (See also pp. 272-276)

Allègre Puériculture/Tigex
41, rue Edouard Martell
42100 St. Etienne
France
t +33 4 77818181
f +33 4 77818185
Company Managing Director:
Jean Paul Allègre
Year established: 1988
Number of employees: 80
Company turnover (ecu):
24,000,000
Allègre develops and produces childcare products, especially in relation to food, care and hygiene. With the MBD design agency, Allègre developed the baby bottle with 'anti-drip nipple system'. The company has introduced a formal innovation programme with periodic improvement and expansion of its entire range of products. (See also pp. 58-61)

Amat S.A.
Camino Can Bros, 8
08760 Martorell, Barcelona
Spain
t +34 3 7755651
f +34 3 7753454
Company Managing Director:
Conrad Amat
Year established: 1944
Number of employees: 70
Company turnover (ecu):
9,000,605
Amat specialises in the manufacture and marketing of metal furniture with design at the forefront of their activities. Amat's TOLEDO outdoor chair and table, designed by Jorge Pensi, are made from anodised cast aluminium, a world first. (See also pp. 120-123)

Atlet AB
43582 Mölncycke
Sweden
t +46 31 984000
f +46 31 884686
info@atlet.se
Company Managing Director:
Marianne Nilson
Year established: 1958
Number of employees: 800
Company turnover (ecu):
180,000,000
Atlet develops and manufactures electric warehouse trucks for indoor materials handling. Atlet's new products for loading, unloading, stacking, and picking offer the user high-performance trucks, low operating costs and excellent ergonomics. The revolutionary swivelling driving seat in the Atlet truck reduces strain in various parts of the body to a harmless level. (See also pp. 196-201)

Blatchford & Sons Ltd.
Lister Road
RG22 4AH Basingstoke,
Hampshire
United Kingdom
t +44 1256 465771
f +44 1256 810450
Company Managing Director:
Stephen Blatchford
Year established: 1890
Number of employees: 326
Company turnover (ecu):
21,000,000
Blatchford, manufacturer of artificial limbs since 1890, has recently taken up the concept of a computer-controlled prosthesis. The company's Intelligent Prosthesis Plus contains a tiny microprocessor to control the speed and precise movements of the limb, making the experience of walking more natural and effortless. (See also pp. 294-299)

Burkhardt Leitner constructiv
GmbH & Co
Am Bismarckturm 39
70192 Stuttgart
Germany
t +49 711 255880
f +49 711 2558811
Company Managing Directors:
Burkhardt Leitner and Stephan Leverberg
Year established: 1993
Number of employees: 11
Company turnover (ecu):
3,271,000
Burkhardt Leitner develops and produces exhibition and display systems, basing its design approach on the functionalist tradition of the Bauhaus. Burkhardt Leitner's systems are characterised by high-quality materials and highly flexible modular structures, so that countless variations can be constructed to suit the customer's wishes. (See pp. 100-105)

Burodep office design from/for Europe
Avenue Louise 216
1050 Brussels
Belgium
t +32 26401200
f +32 26401428
Company Managing Director:
Jean-Claude Rogister

Year established: 1971
Number of employees: 35
Company turnover (ecu):
10,785,000
*Burodep develops and organises
projects for the furnishing and
layout of workplaces, such as
offices and institutions. The
company's philosophy is based on
the conviction that a carefully
thought-out working environment
is an essential factor in today's
working climate.*

Cable Print N.V.
J. Cardijnstraat 14-16
9420 Erpe-Mere
Belgium
t +32 53 806001
f +32 53 806008
cp@cablep.be
salescp@cable.be
Company Managing Director:
Marc van de Mosselaer
Year established: 1969
Number of employees: 130
Company turnover (ecu):
13,000,000
*Cable Print develops, manufactures
and maintains automation (self-
service) equipment for financial
organisations and aims to be a
market-driven developer of
interactive products that can be
connected to a network. It has
developed a range of Foreign
Currency Exchange Stations, in
which PICO is the smallest product
currently on the market.*

Cifial-Centro Idustrial de Ferragens, S.A.
Apartado 410
4524 Rio Meão Codex
Portugal
t +351 56 783071
f +351 56 783
Company Managing Director:
Ludgero Marques
Year established: 1928
Number of employees: 470
Company turnover (ecu):

17,500,000
*Cifial has three main product
ranges: a decorative line of taps
and bathroom accessories, brass
fittings, and security locks. Cifial
is one of the few companies in the
field to use the latest technology
with respect to surface treatment:
PVD (physical vapour deposition).*
(See also pp. 124-125)

Daisalux S.A.
Polígono Industrial Jundiz
c/Ibarredi, 4
01195 Vitoria
Spain
t +34 945 290181
f +34 945 290229
daisalux@jet.es
Company Managing Director:
José Antonio Fernández de
Arroyabe
Year established: 1988
Number of employees: 45
Company turnover (ecu):
5,900,000
*Daisalux develops and manufactures
emergency lighting systems. It has
recently launched an innovative
signage system, called Myra,
comprising over 180 pictograms
and a luminaire designed by Josep
Lluscá. Daisalux designs emergency
lighting systems for a wide range of
specific environments.* (See also
pp. 168-173)

DMD
Parkweg 14
2271 AJ Voorburg
The Netherlands
t +31 70 3864038
f +31 70 3873075
Company Managing Director:
Teake Bulstra
Year established: 1993
*Number of employees: 4,5
Company turnover (ecu): 500,000
DMD (Development, Manufacturing,
Distribution) develops and produces
avant-garde interior design concepts
and introduces them on the*

*international market. The company
is a marketer of independent
designers' concepts and functions
as a link between the designer,
the producer and the market.
DMD operates in an international
network of designers, technical
specialists, producers, wholesalers,
and agents.* (See also pp. 126-127)

DVV/LesAP
Livingstonelaan 6
1000 Brussels
Belgium
t +32 22866111
f +32 22867040
Company Managing Director:
Guy Roelandt
Year established: 1929
Number of employees: 949
Company turnover (ecu):
280,470,319
*DVV develops and markets insurance
products, such as savings plans for
specific target groups (parents,
elderly, etc.). Customers are both
private individuals and larger
organisations, both in the profit
and the non-profit sector.
The design of the new logo
symbolises DVV's professional,
dynamic, and modern approach to
insurance products.*

Escofet 1886 S.A.
Ronda Universidad 20
08007 Barcelona
Spain
t +34 3 3185050
f +34 3 4124465
Company Managing Director:
Emilio Farre-Escofet
Year established: 1886
Number of employees: 75
Company turnover (ecu):
10,500,000
*Escofet is a manufacturer of urban
furniture, such as benches,
pavements, and facades.
The city of Barcelona is a key
aspect of Escofet's identity.
The company has successfully*

introduced mass-produced, high-quality industrial products at affordable prices. Escofet's products create a new urban language, making a significant contribution to the quality of life in the modern city. (See also pp. 146-151)

Eurologic Systems Ltd.
Maple House,
South County Business Park
18 Leopardstown, Dublin
Ireland
t +353 1 2958366
f +353 1 2958433
hosullivan@eurologic.com
pmurphy@eurologic.com
jhanly@eurologic.com
jmaybury@eurologic.com
Company Managing Director:
John Maybury
Year established: 1988
Number of employees: 45
Company turnover (ecu):
11,000,000
Eurologic designs, manufactures, and markets a range of high-availability, high-performance data storage systems for computers. Its recent XL 400 series not only incorporates leading-edge technology, but is also an eye-catching and attractive product. (See also pp. 316-319)

Frequentis Nachrichtentechnik GmbH
Spittelbreitengasse 34
1120 Wien
Austria
t +43 1 811500
f +43 1 81150349
compuserve: 100413,3236
Company Managing Director:
Hannes Bardach
Year established: 1947
Number of employees: 200
Company turnover (ecu):
30,000,000
Frequentis produces voice communication systems for air traffic control and uses state-of-the-art technology to develop telephone and radio communication systems, receivers and transmitters, remote control systems, and controller working positions. Frequentis recently developed and installed the first fully digital voice communication system in the world. (See also pp. 226-233)

Gillet Automobiles S.A.
Parc Scientifique Namur-Gembloux
Rue Saucin, 84
5032 Gembloux
Belgium
t +32 81568444
f +32 81568746
Company Managing Director:
Tony Gillet
Year established: 1992
Number of employees: 10
Company turnover (ecu): 552,630
Gillet designs, develops, and manufactures sports cars making use of ultra-light materials and components. The cars are specifically designed to secure adequate structural resistance or stiffness. Gillet produces 15 cars yearly, as well as car-related products.

Groninger Museum
Postbus 90
9700 ME Groningen
The Netherlands
t +31 50 3666555
f +31 50 3120815
Company Managing Director:
Reyn van der Lugt
Year established: 1994
Number of employees: 180
Company turnover (ecu): -
The Groninger Museum is a museum of modern, contemporary and applied arts and also offers an overview of regional archaeology and history. The striking look of the new building — designed by Alessandro Mendini — has attracted huge numbers of visitors. The special character of the museum is also reflected by the way in which the collections are exhibited and the colours of the walls.

Gunnebo Industrier AB
59093 Gunnebo
Sweden
t +46 490 89200
f +46 490 23889
Company Managing Director:
Staffan Grimbrandt
Year established: 1992
Number of employees: 2,500
Company turnover (ecu):
3,000,000
Gunnebo develops, manufactures and markets high-technology products for access regulation and control. Gunnebo specialises in access regulation and control for both private and public areas and has developed a wide range of products and systems at several security levels suited for a variety of situations. In all its products, Gunnebo applies its revolutionary disc-brake technology, resulting in smooth, silent and maintenance-free products. (See also pp. 158-161)

Hirsch Armbänder GmbH
Hirschstrasse 5, Postfach 390
9021 Klagenfurt
Austria
t +43 463 3839
f +43 463 36605
office@hirsch.co.at
Company Managing Director:
Hermann Hirsch
Year established: 1945
Number of employees: 904
Company turnover (ecu):
58,000,000
Hirsch, a manufacturer of watchstraps, has given the watchstrap totally new functional and aesthetic characteristics. The company offers a wide selection of watchstraps, including an exclusive hand-made line providing made-to-

measure straps. The leather collection contains 100 models in 2,000 variations. (See also pp. 96-99)

Holland Railconsult
Postbus 2855
3500 GW Utrecht
The Netherlands
t +31 30 2355856
f +31 30 2357272
Company Managing Director:
J.W. Jol
Year established: 1995
Number of employees: 950
Company turnover (ecu):
75,000,000
Holland Railconsult specialises in the complete design and execution of complex projects, where transport services have to continue normally during the work. Projects include the design of railways, taking into account cultural values and ecological systems.

Holmhed Systems AB
Box 730
93127 Skellefteå
Sweden
t +46 910 88400
f +46 910 88555
Company Managing Director:
Martin Johansson
Year established: 1982
Number of employees: 34
Company turnover (ecu):
7,000,000
Holmhed manufactures the world's smallest demolition robot — MiniCut — which is remotely controlled, lightweight and extremely versatile. It can thus safely access the most hard-to-reach spots and help make demolition work more efficient and economical. (See also pp. 320-323)

Hultafors AB
51796 Hultafors
Sweden

t +46 332 95000
f +46 332 95138
Company Managing Director:
Bo Jägnefält
Year established: 1883
Number of employees: 200
Company turnover (ecu):
22,000,000
Hultafors develops and manufactures hand tools for measuring, axes, crowbars, and hammers. A complete rethink of the concept of the hammer has resulted in the T-block hammer, a new ergonomic tool that reduces accidents and strain injuries. (See also pp. 44-49)

Innovative Technologies Group plc
Road Three, Industrial Estate
Winsford, Cheshire CW7 3PD
United Kingdom
t +44 1606 863500
f +44 1606 863600
admin@innovat.u-net.com
Company Managing Director:
Keith Gilding
Year established: 1991
Number of employees: 129
Company turnover(ecu):
6,700,000
ITG's main field of application is healthcare. It produces, among other products, a complete range of 'intelligent' wound dressings and woundcare products made from natural materials, such as seaweed and chitin. ITG sees the environment as a rich source of ideas for new materials that are not only biodegradable, but also more in tune with our own human tissues. (See also pp. 374-381)

JCB Special Products Ltd.
Harewood Estate, Leek Road,
Cheadle
Stoke-on-Trent, Staffs. ST10 2JU
United Kingdom
t +44 1538 757500
f +44 1538 757590

Company Managing Director:
Michael James Edwards
Year established: 1986
Number of employees: 242
Company turnover (ecu):
78,000,000
JCB manufactures heavy equipment for handling, construction and agricultural sectors. JCB developed the Robot, the world's safest skid steer, which allows the operator to enter and exit through a side door. (See also pp. 190-195)

Limar s.r.l.
Via Landri, 4
24060 Costa di Mezzate (BG)
Italy
t +39 35 683550
f +39 35 681150
LIMAR@spm.it
Company Managing Director:
Giovanni Caporali
Year established: 1986
Number of employees: 15
Company turnover (ecu):
2,027,118
Limar designs, produces and distributes protection helmets for cycling, motorcycling, and skiing. Limar places great emphasis on the visual appearance and shape of their products, without losing sight of the fact that safety and protection always come first.

Magnus Olesen A/S
Agertoft 2
7870 Roslev
Durup
Denmark
t +45 97 592411
f +45 97 592922
Company Managing Directors:
Flemming Olesen and Kjeld Olesen
Year established: 1937
Number of employees: 86
Company turnover (ecu):
10,000,000
Magnus Olesen produces and sells furniture and accessories for public buildings. The company aims to

produce functional and durable furniture that is also pleasant to look at. It places great emphasis on continuous innovation in response to changing trends in architectures and the urban environment.

MDS Telephone Systems
Unit 14 IDA Enterprise Centre,
3 East Wall Road
Dublin
Ireland
t +353 1 8366288
f +353 1 8366492
mds@iol.ie
Company Managing Director:
Declan Gibbons
Year established: 1985
Number of employees: 140
Company turnover (ecu):
10,000,000
MDS designs and manufactures telephones and communication services for small businesses and private individuals. Its products are extremely user-friendly. For example, the MDS payphone coin detection mechanism allows user programming of new coins or coins from adjacent countries without the intervention of a service technician.

Mediacom Ltd.
Unit 3, 19-20 York Road
Dun Laoghare, Dublin
Ireland
t +353 12809708
f +353 12809796
Mediacom@indigo.ie
Company Managing Director:
John Coburn
Year established: 1995
Number of employees: 8
Company turnover (ecu):
1,000,000
Mediacom is active in the world of modern technological applications — video conferencing, multimedia communications, and interactive information systems. Its products are used for corporate conferencing, distance learning, hotels and

telemedicine. (See also pp. 220-225)

Moviluty S.A.
47 avenue des Fleurs
94170 Le Perreux-sur-Marne
France
t +33 1 43241929
f +33 1 43240390
Company Managing Director:
Jacques Colange
Year established: 1963
Number of employees: 6
Company turnover (ecu): 500,000
Moviluty manufactures flexible-shaft machines (handheld electrical tools) for use in a wide range of manual milling, grinding and polishing applications. They can be used on all kinds of material (metal, wood, stone, plastic, glass, etc.) and are as accurate and as easy to use as a ballpoint pen. Customers range from antique restorers to horse dentists.

Neuromag Ltd.
Elimäenkatu 22 A
00510 Helsinki
Finland
t +358 9 394101
f +358 9 39421203
neuromag@neuromag.fi
Company Managing Director:
Antti Ahonen
Year established: 1989
Number of employees: 13
Company turnover (ecu):
3,000,000
Neuromag designs and develops magnetoencephallography (MEG) systems for brain research and clinical studies. Neuromag developed a helmet-shaped magnetometer system which can examine the whole brain simultaneously, and show how various parts of the brain interact at any given moment. (See also pp. 262-265)

Norton S.A.
Rue JF Kennedy
4930 Bascharage
Luxembourg
t +352 50 401 1
f +352 50 41 88
Company Managing Director:
P.J. Bienert
Year established: 1963
Number of employees: 160
Company turnover (ecu):
41,280,987
Norton develops and manufactures equipment for cutting and drilling for the building industry. The company was the first to use the 'Seeded Gel' (industrial ceramic) in a diamond blade and also manufactured the world's first laser-welded blades. The Norton blade is easily recognisable, representing a clear brand image.

Novacor
4, Passage Saint- Antoine
92508 Rueil Malmaison
France
t +33 141390164
f +33 141390199
100242.1454@compuserve.co
Company Managing Director:
Françoise Guery
Year established: 1983
Number of employees: 32
Company turnover (ecu):
2,600,000
Novacor develops and produces ambulatory ECG and blood pressure monitors. The company has developed a system that allows continuous monitoring of heart functioning or blood pressure away from the hospital. Novacor places great emphasis on patient-friendly products. (See also pp. 268-271)

Octatube Space Structures BV
Rotterdamseweg 200
2628 AS Delft
The Netherlands
t +31 15 2569362
f +31 15 2622300

Company Managing Director:
Mick Eekhout
Year established: 1982
Number of employees: 55
Company turnover (ecu):
7,500,000
Octatube designs and produces space frames and lightweight structures for large buildings and shopping malls. Octatube's aim is to advance building technology by developing innovative concepts and systems and implement them in specific projects. Its constructions are consequently highly sophisticated and elegant.
(See also pp. 162-167)

Olympus Winter & Ibe
Kuehnstraße 61, Postfach 701709
22045 Hamburg
Germany
t +49 4066966 0
f +49 4066966 387
Company Managing Directors:
Hans-Joachim Winter and Ichizo Kawahara
Year established: 1954
Number of employees: 383
Company turnover (ecu):
51,000,000
Olympus produces highly specialised medical instruments in the fields of surgery, gynaecology, sino-therapy, arthroscopy and urology for use in key-hole surgery. Due to the high degree of specialisation in this field, Olympus makes no fewer than 1,800 individual instruments.
(See also pp. 276-281)

Optimom
9, Passage de Flandre
75019 Paris
France
t +33 1 40364848
f +33 1 40364300
Company Managing Director:
Joseph Sabban
Year established: 1985
Number of employees: 12
Company turnover (ecu): 800,000

Optimom specialises in the design and distribution of spectacle frames for children and babies. Optimom's Tropique frames are used in combination with a specially developed silicon nose-cushion to ensure a perfect fit. The company is also involved with research into sight-testing for babies.
(See also pp. 266-267)

Össur hf.
Hverfisgötu 105
PO Box 5288
IS-125 Reykjavík
Iceland
t +354 562 1460
f +354 552 7966
Company Managing Director:
Jón Siggurösson
Year established: 1971
Number of employees: 100
Company turnover (ecu):
7,080,000
Össur manufactures prosthetic components to provide prosthetists with modular solutions. The company's products allow a simple fitting procedure. Great emphasis is placed on comfort for the wearer and on allowing a natural gait.

Partek Concrete Engineering Ltd.
PL 33, 37801 Toijala
Finland
t +358 20455 5399
f +358 20455 5300
Lassi.Jarvinen@partek.partek.
mailnet.fi
Company Managing Director:
Leo Sandqvist
Year established: 1992
Number of employees: 125
Company turnover (ecu):
47,000,000
Partek manufactures machinery and production lines for the con-crete industry. The company has been involved in launching innova-tive technologies, such as the low-noise hollow-core compaction tech-nology called 'shear compaction'.

Plustech OY
Lokomonkatu 15, PO Box 306
33101 Tampere
Finland
t +358 204 804691
f +358 204 804690
plustech@alpha.cc.tut.fi
Company Managing Director:
Erkki Kara
Year established: 1992
Number of employees: 18
Company turnover (ecu):
1,100,000
Plustech developed the Walking Forest Machine for timber harvesting, a machine which makes it possible to adjust to rough ground and minimises soil compaction. It is the first off-road machine application of walking technology in the world. (See also pp. 370-373)

Psion PLC
Alexander House,
85 Frampton Street
London NW8 8NQ
United Kingdom
t +44 171 2625580
f +44 171 2587301
Company Managing Director:
David Potter
Year established: 1980
Number of employees: 800
Company turnover (ecu):
113,000,000
Psion develops and produces palmtop computers, also known as 'personal organisers'. It uses the latest developments in the field of computer technology. More and more providers of Internet or modem-based services are making them compatible for use with Psion's palmtop computers, making it possible to use e-mail 'on the move', for instance. 1996 saw the launch of the Series 3c, an updated version of the 3a. (See also pp. 406-409)

Rexite S.p.A.
Via Edison, 7
20090 Cusago (Milan)
Italy
t +39 2 90390013
f +39 2 90390018
Company Managing Director:
Rino Pirovano
Year established: 1968
Number of employees: 45
Company turnover (ecu):
5,235,000
Rexite manufactures home and office accessories, such as clocks, picture frames, desk organisers, clipboards, etc. Rexite's products have unconventional shapes and colours and are mostly made of plastic. (See also pp. 68-71)

Rukka / L-Fashion Group Ltd.
Vesijärvenk. 15
15140 Lahti
Finland
t +358 3 822115
f +358 3 8225296
Company Managing Director:
Pekka Luhtanen
Year established: 1950
Number of employees: 70
Company turnover (ecu):
24,000,000
Rukka makes mainly professional garments for motor cycling and golfing, rainwear for sailing, and garments for cross-country and down-hill skiing, as well as tracksuits and special underwear. An important Rukka feature is the 'breathable impact protector', which is an ergonomically designed protector for motor cycling suits.

ScanView A/S
Meterbuen 6
2740 Skovlunde
Denmark
t +45 44536100
f +45 44536108
Company Managing Director:
Ib Drachmann-Hansen
Year established: 1990

Number of employees: 140
Company turnover (ecu):
20,000,000
ScanView manufactures high-quality, affordable colour scanners. The original aim of the company was to bring professional scanning quality within the reach of new markets by making drum scanners smaller and cheaper. ScanView's most recent product is a high-quality flatbed scanner. (See also pp. 312-315)

Silampos-Sociedade Industrial de Louça Métalica Campos, LDA.
PO Box 4
3700 Cesar
Portugal
t +351 56 851511
f +351 56 851433
Company Managing Director:
Aníbal José da Costa Campos
Year established: 1951
Number of employees: 215
Company turnover (ecu):
1,150,000
Silampos is a leading manufacturer of metallic cookware for domestic use. The company has three main ranges: aluminium cookware, pressure cookers and stainless steel cookware. Special emphasis is placed on technological innovation. Silampos is the only Portuguese company that manufactures and sells cookware with a thermic bottom achieved by means of an impact bonding system.

SkiData Computer GmbH
Untersbergstraße 40
5083 Gartenau
Austria
t +43 6246 8880
f +43 6246 8887
SCSI@skidatamail.com
Company Managing Directors:
W. Kocznar, E. Strohmeier, and C. Windhager
Year established: 1977
Number of employees: 140

Company turnover (ecu):
45,000,000
SkiData develops, produces, and markets electronic ticket and entry systems for ski-lift units, garages, motorway toll stations and trade fairs. All the company's products are based on the principle that tickets should be hands-free and rechargeable, not only for convenience, but also to minimise the problem of litter caused by paper tickets. (See also pp. 306-311)

Stokke Fabrikker A/S
6260 Skodje
Norway
t +47 70244900
f +47 70244990
www.Stokke-furniture.no
Company Managing Director:
Tor Norbye
Year established: 1932
Number of employees: 194
Company turnover (ecu):
33,100,000
Stokke manufactures chairs that stimulate the human being's natural need for movement. Stokke chairs, suitable for for home and office use, are extremely versatile and can be used for sitting in many different positions; the chair simply moves when the weight is repositioned. (See also pp. 62-67)

Swarovski Optik KG
Swarovskistraße 70
Absam
6067 Hall/Tirol
Austria
t +43 5223 5110
f +43 5223 41860
Company Managing Director:
Gerhard Swarovski
Year established: 1948
Number of employees: 350
Company turnover (ecu):
30,000,000
Swarovski manufactures high-precision optical instruments,

especially for professional and outdoor use. The company has developed the world's first rifle scope with integratedlaser range finding. Several of Swarovski's products have been designed especially for use under poor lighting conditions or at night. (See also pp. 212-215)

Trintech Ltd.
Trintech House,
South County Business Park
18 Leopardstown Road
Dublin
Ireland
t +353 1 2956766
f +353 1 2954735
Company Managing Director:
Cyril McGuire
Year established: 1986
Number of employees: 65
Company turnover (ecu):
6,900,000
www.trintech.com
Trintech designs and produces electronic payment systems for large financial institutions. Trintech's corporate objective is to develop and market cost-effective software and hardware solutions to satisfy the evolving transaction automation and management needs of the payment card industry.
(See also pp. 416-419)

TVS S.p.A.
Via G. Galilei 2 Z.I.
61033 Fermignano
Italy
t +39 722 330485
f +39 722 330035
Company Managing Director:
Bertozzini Gastone
Year established: 1970
Number of employees: 254
Company turnover (ecu):
40,462,000
TVS manufactures porcelain-enamelled aluminium cookware for mass distribution. The company introduced the induction cooking

line, a new, ergonomical and modern-looking range, with entirely new shapes. TVS also offers personalised products, made according to the customer's requirements.

Ufesa
Zumurdiñeta, s/n°
31820 Echarri-Aranaz (Navarra)
Spain
t +34 48 460000
f +34 48 460533
Company Managing Director:
Manuel Crespo de Vega
Year established: 1963
Number of employees: 184
Company turnover (ecu):
22,089,190
Ufesa manufactures small household electrical appliances and aims to make innovative articles using its own design and to offer a guaranteed quality at competitive prices. New products include cool-wall type deep-fat fryers, hamburger makers, intelligent-steam-system irons, and oil-filled radiators.

Unifor S.p.A.
Via Isonzo, 1
22078 Turate (Como)
Italy
t +39 2 967191
f +39 2 96750859
unifor@mbox.vol.it
Company Managing Director:
Piero Molteni
Year established: 1970
Number of employees: 195
Company turnover (ecu):
38,500,000
Unifor develops and manufactures office furniture. In cooperation with architects and designers, the company aims to develop innovative office solutions for working environments, however complex they may be. The core of Unifor's product range is the office system Misura, which is continuously updated.

The company's most interesting new development is the free-standing architectural wall Progetto 25.

Vaki Aquaculture systems
Ármúla 44
108 Reykjavik
Iceland
t +354 5680855
f +354 5686930
vaki@itn.is
Company Managing Director:
Hermann Kristjánsson
Year established: 1986
Number of employees: 8
Company turnover (ecu):
1,000,000
Vaki produces the world's first automatic devices for counting and estimating the size of live fish. Vaki's Bioscanner has quickly established itself all over the world as an essential tool in the aquaculture industry. It uses infrared imaging technology to count up to 60,000 fish per hour with an accuracy of virtually 100%. Vaki is currently developing similar equipment to count chickens.
(See also pp. 324-329)

Vinsmoselle S.O.
Route du Vin, 12,
Chateau de Stadtbredimus
5501 BP 40 Remich
Luxembourg
t +352 698314
f +352 699189
Company Managing Director:
Constant Infalt
Year established: 1966
Number of employees: 120
Vinsmoselle is a cooperative society of some 700 wine growers in the Luxembourg Moselle region, which produces and markets white and pinot noir wine and Crémant. Vinsmoselle aims to improve the image of the brand by moving it up-market. They regularly launch new products and ranges onto different segments of the market,

using innovative packaging and communication strategies.

Vitalograph Ltd.
Ennis Industrial Estate,
Gort Road
Ennis, Co. Clare
Ireland
t +353 65 29611
f +353 65 29289
100436.1025@compuserve.com
Company Managing Director:
Bernard Garbe
Year established: 1976
Number of employees: 77
Company turnover (ecu):
14,400,000
Vitalograph designs and manufactures high-quality medical equipment in global healthcare applications. Its main product is lung function testing equipment, and the company now produces pocket-sized, handheld spirometers and software for personal, portable lung function testing. The modular design of hardware and software allows customers to mix and match to suit their specific and changing needs.

Previous winners of the ECDP (1988-1994)

Goof A/S
(Winner in 1988)
Ussröd Mölle
2970 Hörsholm
Denmark
t +45 42 862111
f +45 42 572726
Company Managing Director:
L. Goof
Year established: 1968
Number of employees: 80
Goof develops, produces and sells dental products, in particular tooth scalers and micro-motors. It trades in all European countries.

C. Josef Lamy GmbH
(Winner in 1988)
Grenzhöfer Weg 32
69123 Heidelberg
Germany
t +49 6221 843 0
f +49 6221 843 132
Company Managing Director:
Manfred Lamy
Year established: 1930
Number of employees: 450
Company turnover (ecu):
113,000,000
Lamy manufactures writing instruments and accessories. Lamy places great emphasis on the high practicality of its products and on the use of the very latest writing technology. (See also pp. 54-57)

Tecno S.p.A.
(Winner in 1988)
Via Bigli 22
20121 Milan
Italy
t +39 2 76820341
f +39 2 784484
Company Managing Director:
Franco Starace
Year established: 1953
Number of employees: 301

Company turnover (ecu):
4,000,000
Tecno is an international manufacturer of office furniture. It continuously updates its old products, but also regularly brings new, design-oriented furniture onto the market. Recent products include the Nomos system, designed by Norman Foster and the Kum executive desks and containers by Gae Aulenti.

Abet Laminati
(Winner in 1990)
Viale Industria 21
12042 Bra (CN)
Italy
t +39 172 419327
f +39 172 431571
Company Managing Director:
Fabio Minini
Year established: 1957
Number of employees: 740
Company turnover (ecu):
117,400,000
Abet produces and sells high-pressure decorative laminates for furniture makers, architects, designers, and building firms. The company's most innovative products include TEFOR (100% recycled laminate) and DIAFOS (the first laminate with translucent and three-dimensional effects).

BD. Ediciones De Diseño
(Winner in 1990)
Mallorca 291
08037 Barcelona
Spain
t +34 3 4586909
f +34 3 2073697
Company Managing Director:
Xavier Batlle
Year established: 1972
Number of Employees: 26
BD. Ediciones produces and commercialises design furniture and objects and accessories for decoration. On the one hand, the company makes replicas of historic

furniture designed by great masters such as Gaudí, Terragni, Mackintosh, etc. On the other hand, it makes products using current designs of several designers and architects of worldwide prestige, including Bedin, Sottsass, Mendini, Meyer, Stern, Milá, and Ricard.

Laguiole
(Winner in 1992)
Route de L'Aubrac
12210 Laguiole
France
t +33 565484334
f +33 565443766
Company Managing Director:
G. Boissins
Year established: 1987
Number of employees: 48
Laguiole designs and manufactures high-quality knives. Without sacrificing the craftsmanship involved in making the perfect knife, the firm now produces some 200,000 knives a year. Many new varieties have been contributed by highly acclaimed designers like Starck, Yan Pennor, and Eric Raffy.
(See also pp. 50-53)

S. Siedle & Söhne
(Winner in 1992)
Postfach 1155
78113 Furtwangen
Bregstraße 1
78120 Furtwangen
Germany
t +49 7723 630
f +49 7723 63300/301
Company Managing Director:
Horst Siedle
Year established: 1750
Number of employees: 500
Siedle manufactures high-grade communication systems, such as entryway and in-house telephone systems, intercoms, video cameras and monitors and access-control systems. Siedle has a clear, consistent design approach to its complete product range, which is

also unique in its modular structure, allowing systems to be easily upgraded. (See also pp. 216-219)

Unicon
(Winner in 1992)
Køgevej 172, PO Box 160
4000 Roskilde
Denmark
t +45 4634 6000
f +45 4634 6023
Company Managing Director:
Peter Assam
Year established: 1926
Number of employees: 1700
Company turnover (ecu): 225.000
Unicon produces ready-mixed concrete and precast concrete products. Unicon exploits the rich possibilities of concrete, so that the material assumes the most fantastic shapes. The company draws on the expertise and experience from countries all over the world in its product development. Its projects have included the supply of concrete elements for the tunnel beneath the Great Belt in Denmark and the Sydney Opera House.

Kompan International A/S
(Winner in 1994)
Korsvangen
5750 Ringe
Denmark
t +45 62 621250
f +45 62 625426
Company Managing Director:
Flemming Schandorff
Year established: 1975
Number of employees: 525
Company turnover (ecu):
67,900,000
Kompan develops and manufactures wooden playground equipment. The colourful design is aimed at communicating with children and inspiring them at play. Furthermore, great emphasis is placed on easy maintenance and proper functioning of the equipment.
(See also pp. 142-145)

Luceplan S.p.A.
(Winner in 1994)
Via Ernesto Teodoro Moneta 44-46
20161 Milan
Italy
t +39 2 662421
f +39 2 66203400
luceplan@planet.it
Company Managing Director:
Riccardo Sarfatti
Year established: 1978
Number of employees: 47
Company turnover (ecu):
13,000,000
Luceplan manufactures lighting appliances for domestic use, workplaces, and public buildings. Continuous and rigorous research has given Luceplan's products a strong, innovative impact that pervades all aspects of its lighting: from the study of types to production technology, materials, quality control, and lighting engineering quality.

Vitra International AG
(Winner in 1994)
Postfach 1940
79576 Weil am Rhein
Germany
t +49 6131 51502
f +49 6131 51500
Company Managing Director:
Rolf Fehlbaum
Year established: 1950
Numbers of Employees: 570
Vitra is a well-known and successful manufacturer of high-quality and high-design furniture for offices, the public sector and the home market. Great emphasis is placed on continuous innovation and Vitra's products are developed with the help of famous designers. By commissioning the best creative talents from different countries and cultures, the company has produced a continuous stream of 'classics'.
(See also pp. 114-119)

WHERE TO
GO NEXT

**Books, Periodicals, Websites,
and Organisations**

"There are two kinds of knowledge: that which you know, and that which you know where to get."

SAMUEL JOHNSON.

Help us improve this list. The essence of Winners! is knowledge-sharing. Do please comment on the list that follows — and send us your suggestions for Winners! 2.

Winners! (WTGN)
Netherlands Design Institute
Keizersgracht 609
1017 DS Amsterdam
The Netherlands
t +31 20 5516500
f +31 20 6201031
desk@design-inst.nl

The new economy, the new design

Article
Between two worlds
A superb essay, available as a reprint, on key features of 'the new manufacturing'.
Morton, Oliver, 'Between Two Worlds: a survey of manufacturing technology'. In: *The Economist,* 5 March 1994.
Reprints are available from the Economist Shop in London.
t +44 171 830 7004
f +44 171 930 0304

Website
Bionomics Institute
This organisation makes bankers and mainstream economists uneasy, to put it mildly. It is dedicated to replacing the traditional, mechanistic view of the economy with economy-as-ecosystem thinking.
www.bionomics.org/

Book
Europe's 500
The result of a fascinating survey which sought out 500 of Europe's most dynamic entrepreneurs; it explains how they have created jobs at a time of rising unemployment across Europe.
EFER and European Commission

(1996) *Europe's 500: dynamic entrepreneurs, the job creators.*
EFER, Bessenveldstraat 25, 1831 Diegem (Brussels), Belgium.
t +32 2 716 4838
f +32 2 716 4107

Organisation
Global Business Network
A membership organisation specialising in scenario thinking and collaborative learning about the future. GBN uses its scenario methodology as a 'language' in order to reframe executives' mental models. Their book list, edited by Stewart Brand, is interesting.
www.gbn.org/BookClub/BookClub_Title.html

Book
301 great management ideas
Culled from the pages of *Inc.,* our favourite small business magazine. Here are sometimes small but always interesting ways to be smarter in the marketplace.
Inc. Magazine, *301 Great Management Ideas from America's most innovative small companies.* Boston: Goldhirsh Group, Inc.

Book
Hidden order
The father of genetic algorithms explains, in a clear and entertaining manner, important

properties of complex adaptive systems, especially those based on computers. Along the way he provides invaluable insights into economics, ecology, biological evolution, and thinking.
Holland, John Henry (1995) *Hidden Order: how adaptation builds complexity*. Reading, Massachusetts: Addison Wesley.

Periodical
Inc. magazine
Inc. Magazine combines upbeat profiles of successful entrepreneurs with practical 'how to' tips and well-researched surveys. 95 percent of the stories are North American but it is still highly recommended for all managers, and for designers interested in a regular and upbeat look at the new economy.
Inc. Magazine, 18 issues a year. Subscriptions: P.O. Box 51534, Boulder, CO 80323-1534, USA. www.inc.com/

Organisation
Lets
Local Economy Trading Schemes are proliferating like crazy; but so far these ultra-grassroots service exchange cooperatives are run manually. What happens when they use computers, encryption, and the Net?
Letslink UK, 61 Woodcock Rd, Warminster, Wilts BA12 9HD, UK.
t +44 1985 217 871

Organisation
Netherlands Design Institute
This think-and-do tank in Amsterdam develops scenarios about key issues of the new economy (age, customisation, connectivity, etc) and undertakes research projects to test them. The Institute's core business is workshops and pilot projects which help companies, designers, and researchers learn from each other.

Netherlands Design Institute, Keizersgracht 609, 1017 DS Amsterdam, The Netherlands.
t +31 20 5516500
f +31 20 6201031
desk@design-inst.nl,
www.design-inst.nl/

Periodicals
New Scientist and Science
A double subscription to the *New Scientist* and *Science* is strongly advised for managers and designers: these magazines are at the same time on top of scientific developments, and critical of 'scientism'. They always ask: what are these developments for? And what will their social and cultural consequences be?
New Scientist, 51 issues a year. Subscriptions: IPC Magazines Ltd. Oakfield House, 35 Perrymount Road, Haywards Health, West Sussex RH16 3DH, UK.
t +44 1444 445555
f +44 1444 445599
enquiries@newscientist.com
Planet Science:
www.newscientist.com/
Science, American Association for the Advancement of Science (AAAS), 52 issues a year. Subscriptions: 1200 New York Avenue, NW, Washington, DC 20005, USA.
t +1 202 326-6501
science_editors@aaas.org
ScienceOnline: www.sciencemag.org/science/home/

Books
New thinking in design and **Redefining designing**
The first book contains in-depth conversations with thirteen design theorists who have forged new ground in user-responsive designs. These thought-provoking conversations illuminate not just the theory of user-responsiveness, but also how it can be realised

across a truly diverse medium of disciplines. The second book evaluates design in terms of human experience rather than the physical form of products.
Mitchell, Thomas C. (1996) *New Thinking in Design: conversations on theory and practice.* New York: Van Nostrand Reinhold. Mitchell, Thomas C. (1993) *Redefining Designing: from form to experience.* New York: Van Nostrand Reinhold.

Book
Out of control
Kevin Kelly, Internet guru and executive editor of *Wired,* chronicles the dawn of a new era in which the adaptability and autonomy of living organisms become the model for human-made systems and machines – everything from telecommunications to manufacturing processes, drug design, and the global economy. Literary equivalent of the 'wear jeans on Friday' rule at IBM.
Kelly, Kevin (1994) *Out of Control: the new biology of machines.* London: Addison Wesley Inc.

Book
Re-thinking the future
A clever publishing idea: 'the best bits' pulled together from business gurus' books. They examine the changing role of the business leader, and the powerful influence of corporate culture, in a post-industrial world of increasing uncertainty.
Gibson, Rowan (1996) *Rethinking the Future: business, principles, competition, control, leadership, markets and the world.* London: Nicholas Brealey Publishing.

Book
Re-thinking work
One of the most pressing dilemmas of post-industrial society is that of

work. This highly intelligent book is the latest working paper of Eco Plan, a Paris-based think-tank that plays a catalytic role in attempts to develop positive new ideas and approaches in the area of work.
Britton, Eric (1996) *Re-thinking Work: an exploratory investigation of new concepts of work in a knowledge society*. 2nd edition, Paris: EcoPlan International. www.the-commons.org/new-work/nw-home.htm

Book
Risk society
A pioneering analysis of the crisis of late twentieth-century techno-logical society. The author, a sociologist, proposes a more reflexive form of modernisation. This manifesto sold more than 70,000 copies in Germany when it was originally published there.
Beck, Ulrich (1992) *Risk Society: towards a new modernity*. London: Sage.

Website
Santa Fe Institute
A multidisciplinary research and education centre, founded in 1984, whose huge intellectual influence belies its modest size. Pursuing emerging science, SFI's researchers, who include some of the most important new scientists, seek to catalyse new collaborative, multidisciplinary projects that break down the barriers between traditional disciplines.
santafe.edu/

Periodical
Sloan Management Review
Less well-known but hipper than the *Harvard Business Review*, the *SMR* always seems to run at least one article that explains big stories from the information economy clearly and well.
Sloan Management Review,

Massachusetts Institute of Technology, 4 issues a year. Subscriptions: Sloan Management Review, P.O. Box 55255, Boulder, Co, 80323-5255, USA.
t +1 303 678 0439
f +1 303 661 1816

Article
The chaordic organisation
Its title is ghastly, but this is a credible account of the new economy – mainly because the author has been there and done it (the author is founder president and CEO emeritus of Visa International).
Hock, Dee W., 'The Chaordic Organization: out of control and into order'. In: *World Business Academy Perspectives*. Washington, DC: World Business Academy, 1994.

Book
The empty raincoat
Charles Handy, Britain's guru of the new economy, reaches here for a philosophy beyond the mechanics of business organisations, beyond material choices. As Handy puts it, "The empty raincoat is, to me, the symbol of our most pressing paradox. If economic progress means that we become anonymous cogs in some great machine, then progress is an empty promise. The challenge must be to show how the paradox can be managed".
Handy, Charles (1994) *The Empty Raincoat: making sense of the future*. London: Hutchinson.

Book
The new business of design
Redefining the idea of design in the light of new developments in business and technology. These essays gathered together by US creativity expert John Kao, examine the relationship between design and business, explore new roles for designers, and ask

questions about the place of the design profession in a changing world. We have not seen John Kao's new book *Jamming*, but the website is very slick (www.jamming.com/).
Kao, John (ed.) (1996) *The New Business of Design*. New York: Allworth Press.

Book
The second curve
The president of the Institute of the Future seems to have written this book rather hastily. But it's still worth a read. His theory is deceptively simple: you must ride the first curve – a company's traditional business carried out in a familiar corporate climate – to the all-important second curve. (Charles Handy, who wrote about curves earlier, also did so less breathlessly.)
Morrison, Ian (1996) *The Second Curve: managing the velocity of change*. London: Nicholas Brealey Publishing Ltd.

Book
The seven cultures of capitalism
Two of the most interesting intellectuals currently writing on business discover that cultural habits and traditions of economic excellence influence every business decision. To understand these habits is to help us gain control over our business behaviour.
Hampden-Turner, Charles and Alfons Trompenaars (1993) *The Seven Cultures of Capitalism: value systems for creating wealth in the United States, Japan, Germany, France, Britain, Sweden and the Netherlands*. London: Currency Doubleday.

Books
The skin of culture and **Brainframes**
Highly original vision of electronic

media and the nature of reality in a world increasingly wired to technology. The author, who is director of the McCluhan Programme in Toronto, says we are about to create a collective mind that will exceed the capabilities of any individual human. (And who am I, a humble singularity, to disagree?) His earlier book *Brainframes* is also worth tracking down.

Kerckhove, Derrick de (1995) *The Skin of Culture: investigating the new electronic reality*. Toronto: Somerville House Publishing.
Kerckhove, Derrick de (1991) *Brainframes: technology, mind and the business*. Baarn: Bosch & Keuning, BSO/Origin.

Book
The third culture: beyond scientific revolution
"An eye-opening look at the intellectual culture of today – in which science, not literature or philosophy, takes centre stage in the debate over human nature and the nature of the universe." In an easy-to-digest format, Brockmans interviews hot scientists about their latest scientific theories and research.
Brockmans, John (1995) *The Third Culture: beyond scientific revolution*. New York: Simon & Schuster.

Book
What machines can't do
Smart machines may not hold the key to industrial renaissance; skills and context probably matter more. By examining four successful manufacturing enterprises, Thomas reveals the complicated social and political dynamics that surround the design and implementation of new production technology. An academic but significant text.
Thomas, Robert J. (1994) *What*

Machines Can't Do: politics and technology in the industrial enterprise. Berkeley: University of California Press.

Age and demographics

Report
Ageing, technology, ergonomics and design abstracts
An overview of articles from scientific and design journals relevant to gerontechnology and design for older people.
More information: Jan Rietsema, t +31 40 2474658
f +31 40 2443335
j.rietsema@bmgt.tue.nl
Hanny Westerik,
t +31 40 466350
f +31 40 466850
westerik@edc.nl

Organisation
Design for Ageing Network (DAN)
This European network of research and teaching organisations encourages the exchange and dissemination of information, ideas, and expertise about design and ageing, and fosters international collaboration on project work. There is a mail order publications list.
Roger Coleman (DAN coordinator), Royal College of Art.
t +44 171 584 5020
f +44 171 584 8217
r.coleman@rca.ac.uk
DAN website:
www.valley.interact.nl/dan/

Report
Designing for our future selves
The results of an action-research project at the Royal College of Art which explored the implications for design and industry of the ageing population around the world.

Royal College of Art (1994) *Designing for our Future Selves*. London: RCA.

Website
SeniorNet
An online organisation based in the United States that encourages adults age 55 and older to use computer technologies further to enrich their lives and the lives of others. www.seniornet.org/

Book
Transgenerational design
A practical and unpatronising guide to the realities of ageing. Professor Pirkl explores changes in abilities that occur throughout one's lifetime, and explains how to make intelligent decisions during the design, production, marketing, promotion, and selection of consumer products used by an ageing population with a wide range of abilities.
Pirkl, James Joseph (1994) *Transgenerational Design: products for an ageing population*. New York: Van Nostrand Reinhold.

Product differentiation

Book
Creativity for managers
As change grows ever more unpredictable, creativity is emerging as a core management skill. Flaky books on the subject abound; but this one, published by Britain's impressive Industrial Society, is solid, enlightening, even creative.
Barker, Alan (1996) *Creativity for Managers*. London: The Industrial Society.

Book
Great inventions, good intentions
A book to read by the fire, or on

the beach. More than 500 drawings filed by industrial designers and independent inventors with the US Patent Office from 1930-1945, one of the great periods in American invention and design.
Baker, Eric and Jane Martin (1990) *Great Inventions, Good Intentions: an illustrated history of American design patents*. San Francisco: Chronicle Books.

Book
Hidden champions
Not for the beach; more for the boardroom. Here are the strategies and practices of low-profile, high-performance German companies; these 500 obscure companies, that are nonetheless world-leaders in their particular sectors, share a surprising set of common characteristics. This book is an important antidote to the quick-fix, nouveau-riche school of business publishing.
Simon, Hermann (1996) *Hidden Champions: lessons from 500 of the world's best unknown companies*. Boston: Harvard Business School.

Book
Manufacturing renaissance
20 articles from the Harvard Business Review on manufacturing strategy and practice. The book is directed mainly at managers in big companies; but, since they are also the main clients of many small ones, it is a useful collection.
Pisano, Gary P. and Robert H. Hayes (eds.) (1995) *Manufacturing Renaissance*. Boston: Harvard Business School.

Book
The art of the long view
We cannot predict the future, but we can tell stories about it. This influential book on scenario planning shows executives, managers, entrepreneurs, and

individuals how to think about eventualities which might affect their own future well-being and that of their organisation.
Schwartz, Peter (1991) *The Art of the Longview: scenario planning – protecting your company against an uncertain world*. London: Century Business.

Book
The evolution of useful things
Petroski looks with affection and awe at how everyday artefacts – from forks to paperclips and zippers – came to be as they are.
Petroski, Henry (1992) *The Evolution of Useful Things*. San Francisco: Knopf.

Book
The monster under the bed
How any high-tech, low-tech or no-tech company can discover new markets, and create new sources of income, by building future business on a knowledge-for-profit basis – and how, once it does, the competitors must follow or fail.
Davis, Stan and Jim Botkin (1995) *The Monster Under the Bed*. New York: Simon & Schuster.

Book
The pursuit of Wow
The American management guru Tom Peters once famously remarked that "there is no such thing as a product business anymore" – which one suspects he will come to regret. Tom Peters is not an expert on small companies, but he is terrific value when it comes to upbeat revivalism in describing the big picture, and case studies within it. His recent books – including this one – are focused on design.
Peters, Tom (1995) *The Pursuit of Wow: every person's guide to topsy-turvy times*. San Francisco: Random House.

Customisation and logistics

Website
Cranfield centre for logistics and transportation
An international focal point for advanced teaching and research in the field of logistics and transportation and the movement of materials, products, and people.
www.cranfield.ac.uk/public/som/cclt/cclt.html

Article
Customizing customization
Beautifully clear essay from the *Sloan Management Review* which explains that customisation is best thought of as a continuum of strategies. While some industries favour customisation, and some foster standardisation, others mix the two in their products, processes, and customer transactions, in intriguing ways.
Lampel, Joseph and Henry Mintzberg (1996) 'Customizing Customization'. In: *Sloan Management Review*. Massachusetts Institute of Technology, Fall 1996, Volume 38.

Website
Integrated supply chain management
A website with information about topics and speakers at a management seminar in 1997. The organisers claim that Supply Chain Management promises to do for productivity and efficiency in the 1990s what 'Just-in-Time' did for inventory control and responsiveness in the 1980s.
www.gscm.com/

Book
Intelligent manufacturing
Workmanlike account of how appropriate use of information technology, underpinned by

effective management techniques, can simplify, integrate, and automate the manufacturing process without necessarily requiring high investment or complex systems.
Underwood, Lynn (1994) *Intelligent manufacturing*. New York: Addison-Wesley Publishers.

Book
In the age of the smart machine
A noted Harvard social scientist argues in this celebrated treatise that advanced information technology fundamentally changes the nature of work and the dynamics of the workplace.
Zuboff, Shosana (1984) *In the Age of the Smart Machine: the future of work and power*. London: Basic Books.

Book
Mass customization
Mass customisation in its historical context; and some ideas about what managers should do about it. An informative chronicle of mass customisation as the successor to mass production.
Pine, B. Joseph (1992) *Mass Customization: the new frontier in business competition*. Boston: Harvard Business School Press.

Website
The Internet guide to transportation
A well-organised, comprehensive listing of Internet sites related to transportation, logistics, and shipping. Topics: aviation, maritime, trucking, rail.
www.iac.co.jp/~bobj/guide.htm

Book
The one-to-one future
Mildly breathless, but they did (we think) coin the term one-to-one. Peppers, an advertising executive, and Rogers, a marketing academic,

set out their 'new marketing paradigm' in detail. A one-to-one competitor focuses on 'share of customer' rather than the mass-marketer's 'share of market'. The strategies here work better for small companies than for big ones.
Peppers, Don and Martha D. Rogers (1993) *The One to One Future: building relationships with one customer at a time*. New York: Doubleday.

Book
The strategy of distribution management
Managerial issues surrounding the not-yet-glamorous but extremely important subject of logistics. Discusses greater cost-effectiveness in distribution – the obscure art of moving products from the supplier, through the company, its factories and warehouses and out to the customer. The integrating factor is the need to anticipate and meet customer demand.
Christopher, Martin (1986) *The Strategy of Distribution Management*. Oxford: Butterworth-Heineman Ltd.

Urban equipment

Website
City search
Cities are listed like consumer products on this website.
www.citysearch.com/

Website
Doors of Perception 2 @ Home
What happens to 'home' when the Internet connects it to the world? Speakers representing many disciplines – from archaeology to virtual reality – addressed this topical question at one of the celebrated Doors conferences.
www.design-inst.nl/

Book
Edge city
The geographical, economic, and sociological forces that have produced the 'new downtown': the 'edge city' – new urban job centres in places that only thirty years before had been residential suburbs or even corn stubble. The book is a provocative introduction to demographic and business patterns that are likely to become important as the twenty-first century edges nearer, even though it failed to anticipate the re-urbanisation of old cities that is now under way.
Garreau, Joel (1991) *Edge of the City: life on the new frontier*. New York: Doubleday.

Organisation
Glasgow 1999
The cultural flagship of Europe's most competitive city? Glasgow 1999, The Terrace, Princess Square, 48 Buchanan Street, Glasgow G1 3JX.
t +44 141 227 1999
f +44 141 248 8754
lighthouse@easynet.co.uk
www.glasgow1999.co.uk

Book
Home
The way we think about 'home' is the culmination of several hundred years of development. With humour and insight, Rybczynski discusses such essential issues as privacy, domesticity, efficiency, and ease; he examines the social and cultural factors that promote them, and proves those concepts to be as much human inventions as easy chairs and wall-to-wall carpeting.
Rybczynski, Witold (1988) *Home: a short history of an idea*. London: Heinemann.

Book
Industrial design in the urban landscape
Essays and design projects, following a workshop in Amsterdam, that explore the question: can industrial design make a meaningful contribution to something so sprawling and unstable as a city? De Balie and Sandberg Institute (1996) *Industrial Design in the Urban Landscape*. Amsterdam: Rob Stolk.

Book
Regions of the new Europe
A relocation specialist's evaluation of the factors which materially influence an incoming company's choice of location. Does a site match long-term strategic aims? Will it fit the customer and supplier base? Will it bring competitive advantage? Lots of obscure but fascinating data and comparisons.
Ernst & Young and Corporate Location (1995) *Regions of the new Europe: a comparative assessment of key factors in choosing your location*. 3rd edition.

Book
The condition of postmodernity
A noted professor of geography at Oxford University casts a critical eye on notions of 'here' and 'now'. Harvey, David (1990) *The Condition of Postmodernity: an enquiry into the origins of cultural change*. Oxford: Blackwell Publishers.

Book
The 100 mile city
London, Paris, New York, Tokyo, and Los Angeles are the ultimate 100 mile cities, set apart by an economic supremacy derived from their size, power, and ambitions. Deyan Sudjic, an incisive observer of architecture in the widest cultural sense, has written a graphic portrait of standardised, monolithic, corporate urban sprawls that are the outward expression of a new society. Sudjic, Deyan (1992) *The 100 Mile City*. London: HarperCollins.

Book
World class
What do companies look for when they think of moving to a new city? Another heavy business book, but quite readable. Entertaining critique of the snootiness of Bostonians. Moss Kanter, Rosabeth (1995) *World Class: thriving locally in the global economy*. New York: Simon & Schuster.

Book
Zone
Extraordinarily pretentious but nonetheless exciting anthology: "an attempt to draw a picture of the city faithful to the precepts of the Chinese masters". The design of this publication established the critical reputation of Bruce Mau, one of the world's trendiest graphic designers. Crary, Jonathan, et al. (eds.) (1992) *Zone (Incorporations)*. New York: Urzone Inc.

Usability and safety

Website
Alertbox
A good place for news and discussion of current human-computer interaction issues. www.sun.com/columns/alertbox.html

Periodical
Applied ergonomics
Practical applications of ergonomic design (human factors) and research concerning office, industry, consumer products, and information technology. Topics include accident prevention and work safety; noise, vibration, temperature, and lighting; product design and evaluation; human-computer interaction; work organisation and job design. *Applied Ergonomics: human factors in technology and society*, 6 issues a year. Subscriptions: Elsevier Science, P.O. Box 211, 1000 AE Amsterdam, The Netherlands.
t +31 20 485 3757
f +31 20 485 3432
onlinfo-f@elsevier.nl
www.elsevier.nl:80/inca/publications/store/3/0/3/8/9/

Book
Bodyspace
A thorough account of how data relating to human dimensions should inform the design of products and environments. It's a bit light on the mind side of things, but other books here deal with that.
Pheasant, Stephen (1996) *Bodyspace: anthropometry, ergonomics and design*. 2nd edition, London: Taylor & Francis.

Book
By design: why there are no locks in the bathroom doors in Hotel Louis XIV and other object lessons
One of North America's most insightful and readable design critics explains the context and processes by which everyday artefacts are designed to be usable – or not.
Caplan, R. (1982) *By Design: why there are no locks in the bathroom doors in Hotel Louis XIV and other object lessons*. New York: St. Martin's Press.

Book
Computers as theatre
A study of the art/craft/business of optimal interfaces, *Computers as*

Theatre takes an original look at our imperfect relationships with our machines, then points the way to improving things.
Laurel, Brenda (1993) *Computers as Theatre*. 2nd edition, Reading, Mass.: Addison-Wesley Publishing Company.

Book
Designing designing
John Chris Jones is an unsung British visionary who strives to develop processes that make users the drivers – not the object – of design. The book consists of essays, interviews, plays, poems, photographs, collages, and quotes (it's probably only available as a library loan).
Jones, John Chris (1991) *Designing Designing*. London: Architecture Design and Technology Press.

Book
Designing the user interface
Professional textbook of interaction principles and techniques. Features computer-supported cooperative work (CSCW) and information retrieval, with closing remarks on the social and individual implications of information technology.
Schneiderham, Ben (1992) *Designing the User Interface: strategies for effective human computer interaction*. 2nd edition, Reading, MA: Addison-Wesley.

Website
Ergonomics on the Web
ErgoWeb is the place for ergonomics (human factors) on the World Wide Web. With subscription access to a sophisticated set of ergonomic job evaluations, analysis, design and redesign software; ergonomics information; products; case studies; instructional materials; standards and guidelines; communication opportunities;

ergonomics-related news.
www.ergoweb.com/

Organisation
European Consumer Safety Association (ECOSA)
ECOSA promotes the exchange of knowledge among experts and institutes in Europe, with the aim of improving home, leisure, and product safety in the widest sense of the word. ECOSA organises conferences and meetings, and publishes the *International Journal for Consumer Safety*.
ECOSA Secretariat, Consumer Safety Institute, P.O. Box 75169, 1070 AD, Amsterdam, The Netherlands.
t +31 20 5114500
f +31 20 5114510

Book
Fitting the task to the human
The fifth edition of this classic book on the rudiments of occupational ergonomics.
Kroemer, Karl (1996) *Fitting the task to the human*. 5th edition, London: Taylor & Francis.

Organisation
ICE Ergonomics
Ergonomics information for designers, manufacturers and suppliers of goods and services, policy makers, and enforcement agencies within the EU. There are four sections: transport ergonomics, consumer products, vehicle safety research, and industrial and commercial ergonomics.
ICE Ergonomics, Swingbridge Road, Loughborough, Leicestershire, LE11 0JB, UK.
t +44 1509 236161
f +44 1509 610725
www.gmtnet.co.uk/ice/

Website
Interaction design
One of the major professional

websites, based in the United States; targeted at user interface practitioners from all fields, not just design; produced by the Association of Computing Machinery (ACM). Also worth visiting for its Special Interest Group in Computer-Human Interaction (SIGCHI).
ACM, New York.
t +1 212 8697440
f +1 212 8690481
interactions@acm.org
Interactions:
info.acm.org/pubs/magazines/interactions/
ACM: www.acm.org/sigchi/

Book
The art of human computer interface design
Interesting texts by fifty of the major thinkers and explorers in the field – not-yet-dated look at some of the most exciting developments in interface design. Technologies such as cyberspace, animation, multimedia, speech recognition, and the philosophical and psychological background to creating effective interfaces, are explored.
Laurel, Brenda (ed.) (1990) *The art of human computer interface design*. New York: Addison-Wesley Publishing Company.

Book
The design of everyday things
A classic. Donald Norman reveals how smart design is the new competitive frontier, and describes how some products satisfy customers while others frustrate them. Norman analyses our everyday use of technological artefacts, such as phones and light switches, and explains psychological theories of action, errors, and memory.
Norman, Donald A. (1988) *The design of everyday things*. New York: Basic Books.

Book
Things that make us smart
The interaction between human thought and the technology it creates. Norman argues for the development of machines that fit our minds, rather than minds that must conform to the machine.
Norman, Donald A. (1993) *Things that Make us Smart: defending the human attributes in the age of the machine*. New York: Addison-Wesley Publishing Company.

Book
Turn signals are the facial expressions of automobiles
Donald Norman (yes, he's one of the best writers on this subject) describes the plight of humans living in a world ruled by a technology that seems to exist for its own sake, oblivious to the needs of the people who create it. A book about our love/hate relationship with machines, as well as a persuasive call for the human-isation of modern design.
Norman, Donald A. (1992) *Turn Signals are the Facial Expressions of Automobiles*. New York: Addison-Wesley Publishing Company.

Book
Usability engineering
Serious handbook by a leading expert on usability technique and usability evaluation methods. Good bibliography.
Nielsen, Jakob (1993) *Usability Engineering*. Boston: Academic Press.

Organisation
US Consumer Product Safety Commission
The US Consumer Product Safety Commission (CPSC) "protects the public against unreasonable risks of injuries and deaths associated with consumer products". The CPSC has jurisdiction over about 15,000

types of consumer products. One of the biggest product-safety web-sites, useful for product recalls and up-to-date news, and for its library.
US Consumer Product Safety Commission, Washington, D.C. 20207, USA. www.cpsc.gov/

Website
User interaction design
An interaction design profes-sionals' website produced by Raghu Kolli and The Netherlands Design Institute: practical, fast-changing information on interaction design, books, websites, mailing lists, people, jobs, tools, etc. Also contains links to many other sites, publications and people.
www.io.tudelft.nl/uidesign/

Technology and the Body

Article
A Cyborg manifesto
"Late twentieth-century machines have made thoroughly ambiguous the difference between natural and artificial, mind and body, self-developing, and externally designed. Our machines are disturbingly lively, and we are frighteningly inert." Strangely academic in tone for such a visceral subject.
Haraway, Donna J., 'A Cyborg Manifesto: science, technology, and socialist-feminism in the late twentieth century'. In: *Simians, Cyborgs, and Women: the reinvention of nature* (1991) London: Free Association Books.

Article
Controlling computers with neural signals
Electrical impulses from nerves and muscles can command computers directly, a method

that aids people with physical disabilities. And after that? Lusted, Hugh S. and R. Benjamin Knapp, 'Controlling Computers with Neural Signals'. In: *Scientific American*, October 1996, pp. 58-63.

Periodical
Journal of telemedicine and telecare
Peer-reviewed papers on all aspects of telemedicine and telecare. Telecare is a subset of telemedicine, specifically relating to the delivery of health care by means of tele-communications technology, and is especially relevant to community care. A huge market for those designing services.
Subscriptions: Royal Society of Medicine Press Ltd., 1 Wimpole St., London W1M 8AE, UK.
t +44 171 290 2928,
ajpubs@aol.com,
www.healthworks.co.uk/hw/publish er/RSM/RSM16.html

Periodical
Medical & biological engineering & computing
Technical papers on biomechanics, biomedical engineering, clinical engineering, computing and data processing, modelling, instrumen-tation, medical physics and imaging, physiological measure-ment, rehabilitation engineering, transducers and electrodes.
Subscriptions: The Institution of Electrical Engineers (IEE), Savoy Place, London WC2R 0BL, UK.
t +44 171-240 1871
postmaster@iee.org.uk
www.iee.org.uk/publish/journals/pr ofjrnl/profjrnl.html

Website
Medical informatics
Big list with links.
www.santel.lu/SANTEL/medinf/ medinf.html

Website
MedWeb
Many links, also very big.
MedWeb - Biomedical Internet
Resources:
www.gen.emory.edu/MEDWEB/med
web.html
MedWeb - Bioethics:
www.gen.emory.edu/medweb/medw
eb.bioethics.html

Book
Microsystem technology
The Netherlands Study Centre for
Technology Trends analyses the hot
topic of microsystems, also known
as micromechanics or
nanotechnology. The book covers
instrumentation, medical
applications, consumer products
and agriculture.
Klein Lebbink, Gerben (1994)
*Microsystem Technology: exploring
opportunities*. Alphen aan de Rijn:
Samson Bedrijfsinformatie.

Website
Plastic surgery
Just in case you think our analysis
of this subject is exaggerated,
check out this strange site.
www.surgery.com/topics/face.html

Book
**The biomedical engineering
handbook**
Core knowledge from all applied
biomedical engineering subjects:
biotechnology, biomaterials,
physiology as it pertains to
engineered devices, ethics, genetic
engineering, medical image
processing, and historical aspects
as well as traditional subjects.
Over 2,000 pages with
contributions from more than 250
experts; more than 1,000 figures,
tables, and illustrations
Bronzino, Joseph D. (ed.) (1995)
*The Biomedical Engineering
Handbook*. Washington:
CRC Press.

Book
The Cyborg handbook
Verges on ultra-theory in places,
but these chapters are balanced by
contributions from NASA
engineers, prosthetic designers and
the like.
Gray, Chris Hables (ed.) (1995)
The Cyborg Handbook. London:
Routledge.

Microchips and smart materials

Website
Chip directory
Everything you need to know about
chips, and a lot that you don't.
www.civil.mtu.edu/chipdir/

Organisation
Domus Academy
One of Europe's more lively and
original design research centres,
Domus Academy draws on the
powerful resource called 'Italian
design' to speculate about what
we might actually do with smart
materials. Other programmes look
at fashion, the design of services,
interaction design, etc. Marco
Susani is director of research,
Frida Doveil runs the materials
programme.
Domus Academy, Edificio 1/C,
Milanofiori, 20090 Assago, Italy.
t +39 2 8244017
f +30 2 6554470

Website
**Electronics engineers toolbox
(IEE)**
A resource for design engineers in
the areas of embedded systems,
DSP, real-time, and other industrial
applications.
www.cera2.com/

Article
Invasion of the micromachines
The operation and possible future

applications of micromotors
(MEMS) are explained in this
article. It is also made clear that
there are still a lot of problems to
be solved before micromachines
can be applied in real products.
Hogan, Hank, 'Invasion of the
Micromachines'. In: *New Scientist*.
29 June 1996, No. 2036.

Book
Mechatronics
The concepts which underpin the
mechatronic approach to engineering design plus, in detail, its principal components: sensors and
transducers; embedded microprocessors; actuators and drivers - the
contents page alone is 11 pages.
Bradley, D.A., et al. (1991)
*Mechatronics: electronics in
products and processes*. London:
Chapman and Hall.

Book
**Mutant materials in
contemporary design**
The catalogue of a startling
exhibition at New York's Museum
of Modern Art which included an
intriguing array of products made
of innovative plastics, ceramics,
fibres and composites, rubber and
foam, glass, wood, and metals.
Paola Antonelli (1995) *Mutant
materials in contemporary design*.
The Museum of Modern Art, New
York: Harry N. Abrams.

Website
Nanothinc
Scientists, researchers, educators,
consumers, buyers, and sellers all
converge on this website for
information, services, and products
relating to nanotechnology.
www.nanothinc.com/

Book
**Plastic: the making of a
synthetic century**
Stephen Fenichell spins the mar-

vellous tale of synthetics - where and why they were produced, the people who dedicated themselves to perfecting them, the companies who sold them to an eager public through some of the most effective and outrageous marketing campaigns in history, and their impact, both positive and negative, on every aspect of our lives.
Fenichell, Stephen (1996) *Plastic: the making of a synthetic century*. London: HarperCollins.

Website
Preparing for nanotechnology
The Foresight Institute's goal is to guide emerging technologies so that they improve the human condition. Foresight focuses its efforts upon nanotechnology, the coming ability to build materials and products with atomic precision.
www.foresight.org/

Website
Smart materials
The results of a workshop at the Netherlands Design Institute that focused on the exploration of the use (and usefulness) of smart materials, as well as the designer's approach to the technology and the user's response. Participants were invited from aerospace, architecture, civil engineering, cognitive science, fashion, medicine, nanotechnology, product design, and robotics.
www.design-inst.nl/activities/3d/smart.html

Websites
SRI Consulting and **Smart materials**
The renowned North American think-tank SRI specialises in information gathering, data collection, technology monitoring, and trend analysis on an international scale. The centre runs

multiclient services and conducts tailored research and consulting projects for government and commercial clients.
SRI Consulting:
www.future.sri.com/index.html
Smart materials:
www.future.sri.com/TM/about_TM/aboutSM.html

Book
The material of invention
The design implications of new design materials are evaluated by one of Europe's most insightful design critics. Professor Manzini's exploration of new possibilities for products is based on a fundamental but inspiring theoretical background and an historical overview. In a final section some well-known designers use his ideas while 'exercising in invention'.
Manzini, Ezio (1986) *The material of invention*. Cambridge, Mass.: MIT Press.

Book
Unbounding the future: the nanotechnology revolution
A comprehensive, easy-to-understand guide that explains what nanotechnology is, and how it will revolutionise our lives. Drexler was the 'inventor' of the term nanotechnology.
Drexler, Eric K., Chris Peterson and Gayle Pergamit (1991) *Unbounding the Future: the nanotechnology revolution - the path to molecular manufacturing and how it will change the world*. New York: Quill, William Morrow.

Book
Vision of the future
This book describes the results of a multi-million ECU project carried out by Philips Corporate Design which explored life and technology in the near future. Lots of ideas

for soft-coloured new products in different 'domains' of life. The website encourages you to respond.
Philips Corporate Design (1996) *Vision of the future*. Bussum: V+K Publishing.
World Wide Vision:
www.philips.com/design/vof/

Ecological limits

Book
A green history of the world
Why did Rome fall? For historian Clive Ponting the answer has urgent relevance for our modern global civilisation: the Roman empire, ever expanding in population and ever evolving in technological complexity, finally exhausted its bountiful natural resources and experienced an ecological breakdown that doomed the society. Geddit?
Ponting, C. (1991) *A Green History of the World: the environment and the collapse of great civilisations*. New York: Penguin Books.

Periodical
Business and the environment
A thorough, practical, and extremely well-informed US newsletter targeted at senior managers; also relevant to Europe. Zero moralising; emphasises pragmatic programmes you can start implementing today. Highly recommended, also for its periodic ISO 14000 updates.
Business and the Environment: monthly global news and analysis. 12 issues a year. Cutter Information Corp., 37 Broadway, Suite 1, Arlington, MA 02174, USA.
t +1 616 641 5125
f +1 617 648 1950
lovering@cutter.com,
www.cutter.com/envibusi/

Organisation
Centre for sustainable design
A small British design research centre that organises the online conference: 'Managing eco design: a business perspective'.
Centre for Sustainable Design, Surrey Institute of Art and Design, Faculty of Design, Falkner Road, Farnham, Surrey GU9 7DS, UK.
t +44 1 252 73 2229
f +44 1 252 73 22 74
spd@cfsd.org.uk or
cfsd@surrart.ac.uk,
www.surrart.ac.uk/cfsd/cfsd.htm

Book
Design for environment
Includes some good case-study examples from leading US companies, and serves nicely as both an introductory and reference source.
Fiksel, Joseph (ed.) (1996) *Design for Environment: creating eco-efficient products and processes.* New York: McGraw-Hill.

Book
Ecodesign
A step-by-step approach to ecodesign, combined with supplements on ecodesign strategies, end-of-life scenarios, methods for life cycle analysis and life cycle costing, green marketing, product oriented environmental policy, ecodesign workshops, worksheets, and ecodesign information providers (250 addresses worldwide) plus literature references.
The authors are from the Centre for Environmental Product Development at Delft University of Technology in the Netherlands.
Brezet, J.C. en G.C. van Hemel (eds.) (1996) *Ecodesign: a Promising Approach.* Paris: United Nations Environmental Program. Delft University of Technology, Section Environmental Product

Development, Jaffalaan 9, 2629 BX Delft, The Netherlands.
t +31 15 2782738
f +31 15 2782956
L.Roos@io.tudelft.nl
www.io.tudelft.nl/research/mpo/index.html

Book
Environmental information for industrial designers
New methods that aid designers in the selection of appropriate environmental strategies; by the resident 'info-eco' expert at the Netherlands Design Institute.
Bakker, C. (1995) *Environmental Information for Industrial Designers.* Delft: University of Technology Press.

Periodical
Environment Business Magazine
A detailed and informative magazine for managers. Environment Business also publishes a newsletter, a business directory, and interesting supplements like the 1996 update from the EU environmental policy guide. They also organise a unique trade fair called Environmental Software Demonstrations.
Further information: Information for Industry Ltd., 18-20 Ridgeway, London SW19 4QN, UK.
t +44 181 9442930
f +44 181 9441982
eb@cix.compulink.co.uk

Organisation
Eternally yours
Strategies that address the psychological lifespan of products and culturally sustainable design. The Dutch design research group's first report is available online.
Stichting Eternally Yours,
P.O. Box 273, 3960 BE
Wijk bij Duurstede.
t +31 343 572189
f +31 343 577430

muis@worldaccess.nl
www.worldaccess.nl/~muis/eternal.htm

Book
Factor four: doubling wealth, halving resource use
A message from respected experts that is novel, simple, exciting – and radical. 'Factor four' means that the amount of wealth extracted from one unit of natural resources can grow by at least a factor of four. The solution lies in using resources more efficiently – in feasible ways. 50 examples of new product developments that have a factor 4 lighter impact on the environment are included.
Hunter, L., A. Lovins and E. von Weiszäcker (1997) *Factor Four: doubling wealth, halving resource use. A report to the Club of Rome.* London: Earthscan Publications Limited.

Book
Green gold
A lively polemic, free of moralising, that berates US business for missing a great opportunity. An argument, for environmentalists and for business, that environmental technologies are necessary for a strong economy.
Moore, Curtis (1994) *Green Gold: Japan, Germany, the United States and the race for environmental technology.* Boston: Beacon Press.

Book
How many people can the earth support?
The key question. This hefty but readable book looks at the main scenarios and concludes that the apparently simple question posed by its title is incomplete: how many people can the earth support, given what kinds of economies and technologies? At

what levels of material well-being? Living in what physical, chemical, and biological environments? With what cultural values? With what social, political, and legal institutions?
Cohen, J. (1995) *How Many People can the Earth Support?* New York: W.W. Norton & Company.

Website and book
Life cycle assessment (United Nations Environment Programme – UNEP)
UNEP delivers information about projects on LCA and Eco-Design, with links to websites on LCA and Eco-design.
UNEP Working Group on Sustainable Product Development: unep.frw.uva.nl/
Lifecycle Assessment: what is it and how to use it (1995), UN Sales No. 96-III-D2. SMI Distribution Services Limited, P.O. Box 119 Stevenage, Hertfordshire, UK.
f + 44 1438 748 844

Organisation and website
02
An international network of environmentally-aware designers. Their website contains a gallery with examples of green product design.
www.wmin.ac.uk/media/02/ 02_Home.html

Book
Packaging and ecology
Comprehensive, expert, and readable guide to safe and environmentally responsible packaging. It considers in detail the interactions of packaging with the environment – including the economics, sociological implications, evolution, and functions of packaging. Life-cycle analysis is discussed with the emphasis on conserving resources and energy.

Lox, F. (1992) *Packaging and Ecology.* Surrey: Pira International.

Book
Product development and the environment
A down-to-earth guide published in Great Britain for managers, which explores the future role of technology in developing greener products.
Burall, P. (1996) *Product Development and the Environment.* London: The Design Council/Gower.

Book
State of the world 1997
State of the World takes the pulse of the planet: its conclusions are so grim that one suspects the result is to demotivate many of its readers. The annual guide is widely used by governments and policy makers, business leaders, and environmentalists.
Brown, Lester R., et al. (1996) *State of the World 1997: a worldwatch institute report on progress toward a sustainable society.* New York: W.W. Norton & Company.
www.worldwatch.org/worldwatch/

Book
The ecology of commerce
Only business worldwide has the power to reverse ecological destruction. The commercial systems of the future must be more like biological systems – self-sustaining, non-wasteful, self-regenerating. Author Paul Hawken (his next book is called *Natural Capitalism*) outlines realistic ways of redesigning commerce, so that everyday acts of work accumulate environmental benefits as a matter of course.
Hawken, P. (1993) *The Ecology of Commerce: how business can save the planet.* London: Weidenfeld and Nicolson.

Organisation
The Natural Step
The Natural Step (TNS) is a new transnational attempt to develop a science-based systems approach to explain the links between ecology and economy; this consortium of enlightened organisations has set out to find a way to plot society's move from an unsustainable, linear model to a more sustainable, cyclical one.
The Natural Step, Amiralitetshuset, Skeppsholmen, 11149 Stockholm, Sweden.
t +46 86780022
f +46 86117311

Book
The new ecological order
An entertaining polemic by a top philosophy professor in France. Luc Ferry examines the ideological roots of the 'Deep Ecology' movement spreading throughout the United States, Germany, and France, and concludes that deep ecology casts aside all the gains of human autonomy since the Enlightenment. His chapter on the Nazis' eco-policy is unsettling, to put it mildly.
Ferry, Luc (1995) *The New Ecological Order.* Chicago: The University of Chicago Press.

Book
The solid side
Leading Italian design theorists contemplate a world dazzled by the promises of non-materialism. The Solid Side asks questions about the true dimension of experience and the endurance of objects, places, and relationships.
Manzini, Ezio and Marco Susani (eds.) (1995) *The Solid Side.* V+K Publishing, Philips Corporate Design.

Book
Wonderful life
This winner of the 1990 Science
Book Prize challenges some of our
most cherished self-perceptions.
Gould, one of our most important
science writers, urges a funda-
mental reassessment of our place
in the history of life on earth.
Gould, Stephen Jay (1989)
*Wonderful life: the burgess shale
and the nature of history*. London:
Penguin Books.

Organisation
**World Business Council for
Sustainable Development
(WBCSD)**
A coalition of international
companies united by a shared
commitment to the environment
and to the principles of economic
growth and sustainable development. The WBCSD aims to develop
closer cooperation between business, government, and all other
organisations concerned with the
environment and sustainable
development.
World Business Council for
Sustainable Development, 160,
route de Florissant, CH-1231
Conches-Geneva, Switzerland.
t +41 22 839 3100
f +41 22 839 3131
info@wbcsd.ch
www.wbcsd.ch/

Organisation
**Wuppertal Institute for Climate,
Environment and Energy**
Germany's (and Europe's)
influential and important
environmental research institute.
It has four divisions: climate
policy; material flows/restruc-
turing; energy and transport; and
'new models of wealth'.
Wuppertal Institute for Climate,
Environment and Energy,
Centre for Sustainable Design,
Wuppertal Institute, Doeppersberg

19, D-42103 Wuppertal, Germany.
t +49 202 2492 0
f +49 202 2492 108
www.xs4all.nl/~foeint/wupper.html

Website
Doors of Perception 3
The third Doors of Perception
conference addressed a big
question: how might information
technology and design help us live
more lightly on the planet? How
can faster information help us
dematerialise products and services
and slow down our consumption of
matter and energy?
www.design-inst.nl/

Website
**Environmental sites
on the Internet**
An almost endless list of
environmental links. If the
amazing proliferation of online
eco-sites is a reliable indicator,
far more people are actively
contemplating fundamental
change than you would think from
watching traditional media.
www.lib.kth.se/ ~lg/envsite.htm
Virtual library on sustainable
environment: www.ulb.ac.be/
ceese/sustvl.html

Website
Environment bookstore
Extensive online environmental
bookstore; the site features a tree-
unfriendly catalogue of 60,000 in-
print or forthcoming environment-
related books, CD-Roms, and other
materials. Orders can be placed by
e-mail. www.nhbs.co.uk/

Website
ISO 14000
Rather limited information on ISO
14000, the environmental
management standard being
developed to provide a worldwide
focus on environmental
management and sustainable

development. www.casti.com/qc/
html/iso14000.html

Website
**Pollution prevention in process
development and design**
Primarily focused on production
processes.
www.seattle.battelle.org/services/e
&s/p2design.htm

The Internet
and business
connectivity

Book
Being digital
One of those books that is so
widely read that people find
themselves trying to make its
predictions come true. A mixed
blessing, given the author's
technology-led mind set (he's head
of Medialab at M.I.T).
Negroponte, Nicholas (1995) *Being
Digital*. New York: Knopf.

Website
CommerceNet
An industry association for Internet
commerce. Connecting nearly 150
companies and organisations
worldwide, including leading banks,
telecommunications companies,
VANs, ISPs, online services, and
software and services companies,
as well as major end-users.
www.commerce.net/

Website
DoorsAll
The proceedings of the four Doors
of Perception conferences (1993-
1996) are only available online.
Published by the Netherlands
Design Institute, DoorsAll contains
the equivalent of a 1,000 page
book, in response to the question:
what are the Internet, information
technology, and multimedia, for?
Includes scientists, designers,

philosophers, gurus, critics, media artists, misanthropes, and true believers, from four continents.
www.design-inst.nl/

Website
EC World resource pages
Links to a variety of information sources on the Web related to Electronic Commerce. Topics covered here include EDI, security, intranets, online marketing, research, resource sites.
ecworld.utexas.edu/ejou/resdir/

Website
Electronic consumer resource center for small businesses and SMEs
Collection of links to various places on the Web which play a role in electronic commerce. The site attempts to filter through the mass amounts of information the Web has to offer in order to bring small business owners a quick and relevant tour of what is happening in Electronic Commerce. A recent section on European initiatives in Electronic Commerce for SMEs has been added.
www.gwis2.circ.gwu.edu/~rwill/

Website
Electronic markets & electronic commerce
More relevant content in two visits to this site than hours spent surfing. Good resource when you know what you are looking for.
www.pitt.edu/~malhotra/Elecomm.htm

Website
European WWW business awards
An award that aims to raise awareness, particularly among SMEs in Europe, for the many business opportunities opened up by the World Wide Web.
www.ispo.cec.be/EW3BA/ew3ba.html

Book
Going digital
A selection of surveys previously published in *The Economist* on tele-communications; the computer industry; the Internet; manufacturing technology; retailing; defence technology; the future of medicine; the frontiers of finance; artificial intelligence. Some are already rather dated, but it's strong in parts.
The Economist (1996) *Going Digital: How new technology is changing our lives.* London: Profile Books.

Website
Hotbot
The ultimate (for the moment) web search engine. The total url is "Hotbot". Try it and see!

Periodical
Information strategy
A monthly magazine aimed at senior managers. A lot of the content is good, but the magazine's rather downmarket design and presentation makes it look like a cheap trade rag.
Information Strategy: Europe's magazine for business advantage, 12 issues a year. Subscriptions: P.O. Box 14, Harold Hill, Romford, RM3 8EQ, UK.
t +44 1708 381 555
f +44 1708 371 872
isedit@info-strategy.com
www.info-strategy.com

Book
New community networks
This is a unique contribution to the literature on social uses of technology. The book provides practical 'how-to' advice and discusses the rationale, concerns, and directions of socially directed technology.
Schuler, Douglas (1996) *New Community Networks: wired for change.* New York: ACM Press.

Website
Project 2000
Getting a statistical hold of the Internet is 'like pinning down a greased watermelon in a swimming pool'. Project 2000 research objectives are to enrich and stimulate the knowledge base on the role of marketing in new media environments, provide a principal point for the discussion and exchange of these ideas, and impact business practice in this emerging area. Worth visiting are: 'Marketing in hypermedia computer-mediated environments', and 'Commercial scenarios for the web'.
www.2000.ogsm.vanderbilt.edu/

Book
The children's machine
Some areas of human activity – medicine, transportation, entertainment – have changed beyond recognition in the wake of modern science and technology. One that most definitely has not changed is school. Why? Seymour Papert set out a vision of how it could. Seymour Papert (1993) *The Children's Machine: rethinking school in the age of the computer.* New York: Harper Collins Publishers.

Book
The electronic word
An extremely lucid exploration of tomorrow's literacies. Unchecked by the inherent limitations of conventional print, digitised text has introduced a radically new medium of expression.
Lanham, Richard A. (1993) *The Electronic Word: democracy, technology, and the arts.* Chicago: The University of Chicago Press.

Book
The Internet strategy handbook
Written for managers facing the challenge of devising an Internet

strategy that will bring their companies recognition and competitive advantage – by Internet pioneers in the companies that have been there. Includes cost-benefit analyses and discussions of critical issues such as staff training and secure commercial transactions.
Cronin, Mary J. (1996) *The Internet Strategy Handbook: lessons from the new frontier of business.* Boston: Harvard Business School Press.

Book
The rough guide to Internet & World Wide Web
This streetwise British paperback promises to make you an Internet guru in the shortest possible time. In plain English, with no hint of techno-jargon, it explains how to work with the Internet. Plus a 600-site web directory, a guide to Usenet discussion groups, and a cyberspace glossary.
Kennedy, Angus J. (1995) *The Internet & World Wide Web: the rough guide 2.0.* London: Penguin Books.

Book
World Wide Web marketing
Interviews with marketing managers at Sun, Hewlett Packard, and other high-profile companies. Introduces Web marketing techniques and explains what works and what doesn't, and how to integrate the Web into your overall marketing and business plans.
Sterne, Jim (1995) *World Wide Web Marketing: integrating the Internet into your marketing strategy.* New York: John Wiley & Sons.

Designing online

Book
Creating killer web sites
A thoughtful guide to building third-generation websites: sites driven by design deployed to provide visitors a complete 'experience' employing real-world metaphors and models of consumer psychology. Siegel provides especially good information about page layout and handling text and type faces.
David Siegel (1996) *Creating Killer Web Sites: the art of third-generation site design.* New York: Hayden Books.
www.amazon.com/exec/obidos/

Website
David Siegel
Web design 'casbah' with a lot of attitude. Includes the 'High Five' awards for website design, 'Severe Tire Damage' (an interactive manifesto) and 'WebWonk' (tips for writers and designers online).
www.dsiegel.com/home.htmlWeb

Book
Designer's guide to the Internet
A look at the Internet from a designer's perspective with practical suggestions, directions, and insights for creating design-related services on the Internet.
Zender, Mike, et al. (1995) *Designer's guide to the Internet.* Indianapolis: Hayden Books.
www.zender.com/designers-guide-net/

Book
Designing business
One of North America's most successful and commercial web designers has teamed up with Adobe to create a thoughtful account of online architecture and design processes. Almost too well-produced: the flow-charts are so

beautiful that they are more like artworks than approachable maps. An enclosed CD-Rom contains interactive prototypes and projects.
Mok, Clement (1996) *Designing Business: multiple media, multiple disciplines.* San Jose: Adobe.

Book
Film theory and criticism
The best collection anywhere on film theory. This raises the question: who will be the Eisenstein of the Internet? Quite fascinating.
Maast, Gerald (1992) (ed.) *Film theory and criticism.* Oxford: Oxford University Press.

Book
Interactivity by design
Another smart book from Adobe. It focuses on real-world scenarios – not just tools – and presents the process of interface design as the sum of clearly defined parts; a system of critical decisions and tasks leading to interfaces that work.
Kristof, Ray and Amy Satran (1995) *Interactivity by Design: creating & communicating with new media.* San Jose: Adobe Press.

Book
Multimedia graphics
36 top multimedia projects from a dozen countries provide a sourcebook of this fast-growing phenomenon.
Velthoven, Willem and Jorinde Seijdel (eds.) (1996) *Multimedia Graphics: the international sourcebook of interactive screendesign.* Amsterdam: BIS.

Website
The hub club
Sponsored by the Arts Council in the United Kingdom as a forum for multimedia creatives.
www.sonnet.co.uk/hub/

Book
Thinking it through
Another in the new 'white paper' series from Apple. This is a practical guide to planning, designing, and building a World Wide Web site in order to establish an effective presence on the Web. Very intelligently and clearly done.
Informing Arts (1996) *Thinking it Through: a practical guide for planning a successful web site, for publishing, marketing, and new media professionals*. Apple, 1 Infinite Loop, Cupertino, California 95014.

Website
Yale University web style manual
An online manual which describes design principles used to create the pages within the Center for Advanced Instructional Media's (C/AIM) World Wide Web site.
info.med.yale.edu/caim/StyleManual_Top.HTML

How to use design

The best way to exploit the many benefits of design is to get acquainted with the design industry and the way it thinks and behaves. The following books and organisations have been selected (from among several thousand candidates) as the best, most up-to-date, and most useful places to start.

Background

Book
A pattern language
One of the most influential and interesting books ever written about design and architecture. To design their environments, people always rely on certain 'languages', which, like the languages we speak, allow them to articulate and communicate an infinite variety of designs within a formal system which gives them coherence.
Alexander, Christopher (1977) *A Pattern Language: towns, buildings, construction*. New York: Oxford University Press.

Book
Industriekultur: Peter Behrens and the AEG
An account of how a radically new technology, with fantastic long-term potential, needed to be introduced to a nervous and conservative public. Today it is information technology – then it was electricity.
Buddensieg, Tilmann (1984) *Industriekultur: Peter Behrens and the AEG, 1907-1914*. Cambridge: MIT Press.

Book
Looking closer
Contemporary graphic design criticism by most of the more perceptive of today's critics and practitioners.
Bierut, Michael, William Drenttel, Steven Heller & DK Holland (eds.) (1994) *Looking Closer: critical writings on graphic design*. New York: Allworth Press.

Book
The nature & aesthetics of design
An insightful and literate exposition of what 'good design' might mean. David Pye's classic text investigates the scientific nature of function; the priority of economy; physical components and manufacturing technique; and the utilitarian and aesthetic roles of design.
Pye, David (1978) *The Nature & Aesthetics of Design*. London: The Herbert Press.

Book
The new typography
Full English translation of Jan Tschichold's classic treatise on typography, originally published in Berlin in 1928.
Tschichold, Jan (1996) *The New Typography*. Northweald: Zwemmer.

Book
The reflective practitioner
A leading M.I.T. social scientist and consultant examines five professions – engineering, architecture, management, psychotherapy, and town planning – to show how professionals really go about solving problems. The unarticulated, largely unexamined process is the subject of Schön's original book, an effort to show how 'reflection-in-action' works and how this vital creativity might be fostered in future professionals.
Schön, Donald A. (1984) *The Reflective Practitioner: how professionals think in action*. Aldershot: Gower.

Design industry today

Book
Company image & reality
One of the best books ever written on how companies 'speak'. David Bernstein analyses all aspects of corporate communication. Not only the obvious ones – corporate ads and corporate identity – but the equally important and usually neglected areas of staff and community relations.
Bernstein, David (1989) *Company Image & Reality: a critique of corporate communications*. London: Cassel.

Report
Design across Europe
A statistical and analytical

background briefing on the European design market. Netherlands Design Institute (1994) *Design Across Europe: patterns of supply and demand in the European design market.* Amsterdam: Netherlands Design Institute.
t +31 20 5516500
f +31 20 6201031
desk@design-inst.nl

Book
Design protection
The leading UK expert explains design protection, from patenting inventions to protecting styles and brands. It also outlines the latest European legislation.
Johnston, Dan (1995) *Design Protection: a practical guide to the law on plagiarism for manufacturers and designers.* 4th edition, Hampshire: The Design Council.

Papers
Managing product development into the 90's
Six rather well-written booklets in the series of Managing into the 90's, published by the Department of Trade and Industry in Great Britain, on product development; product creation; design for effective manufacture; total product management; organising product design and development; and managing the financial aspects of product design and development. *Managing product development into the 90's.* The Enterprise Initiative, Department for Enterprise. For reprints: Mediascene Ltd., PO Box 90, Hengoed, Mid Glamorgan, CF8 9YE, UK.
t +44 1443 821877

Book
No more teams!
No More Teams! (previously published as *Shared Minds*) confronts the faddish clichés of teams to

explain how creative relationships really work. Includes practical tools and techniques for tapping the interpersonal power of collaboration.
Schrage, Michael (1995) *No More Teams! Mastering the dynamics of creative collaboration.* London: Doubleday.

Book
Teams & technology
If teamwork is the key to effective organisations, information is the key to effective teamwork. The authors, who are authorities in this area, show managers how to develop new information systems that support collaborative work, build teams that take advantage of technological potential, and create an organisation with a structure and policies that support the synergy of teams and technology.
Cohen, Susan and Bikson, Tora and Mankin, Don (1996) *Teams & Technology: fulfilling the promise of the organization.* Boston, Mass.: Harvard Business School Press.

Book
The new guide to identity
Wally Olins has spent many years honing his corporate identity sales pitch to some of the world's most hard-bitten CEOs. This, his latest version, deals with theory and practice and examines identity both as a strategic and a tactical tool in a wide range of contexts. Throughout the book, identity is treated not only as a mechanism for branding but also as a significant tool for change management.
Olins, Wally (1995) *The New Guide to Identity: how to create and sustain change through managing identity.* Aldershot: Gower.

Book
The successful management of design

Among a plethora of turgid and unhelpful books on design management, this one stands out as clear, helpful, and recognisably based on the real world. Probably because it is informed by the tough world of building and construction.
Gray, Collin, Will Hughes and John Bennet, 1994. *The Successful Management of Design: a handbook of building design management.* Centre for strategic studies in construction, University of Reading, Whiteknights, PO Box 219, Reading RG6 2AW, UK.
t +44 1734 318 190
f +44 1734 750 404

European organisations
(See also page 443)

Organisation
Agency for the Promotion of Industrial Creation (APCI)
A Paris-based French production and communication bureau that creates exhibitions, events, and publications.
APCI, 3 rue Brissac, 75004 Paris.
t +33 1 44 61 72 40
f +33 1 44 61 72 49
apcifr@mail.club-internet.fr

Organisation
Bureau of European Designers' Associations
Represents the major professional asssociations; source of expertise on pan-European copyright and IPR. Operates a register of associations.
Bureau of European Designers' Associations, PO Box 91526, 2509 EC The Hague, The Netherlands.
t +31 6 546 23781
f +31 70 3831466
beda@bart.nl

Newsletter
Business & design
A newsletter, published by the
industry association of British
design companies, that focuses on
client-related issues.
Business & Design, 4 newsletters a
year. The Chartered Society of
Designers, 32-38 Saffron Hill,
London EC1N 8FH.
t +44 171 831 9777
f +44 171 831 6277

Organisation
European Design Centre (EDC)
The EDC initiates and maintains
applied research programmes and
develops activities for education,
the profession, the world of
industry and commerce, and
governmental bodies.
European Design Centre,
Schimmelt 32, 5611 ZX Eindhoven,
The Netherlands. P.O. Box 6279,
5600 HG Eindhoven.
t +31 40 2466350
f +31 40 2466850
box@edc.nl

Book
European design guide
Alarmingly heavy, and you need
some expertise to extract the
information you need, but this
is nonetheless a comprehensive
list of more than 1,500
promotional organisations, unions
and professional associations,
awards and competitions,
newspapers and magazines,
directories and indexes of
designers, educational institutions,
trade shows and events; it includes
even a list of designer tourist
attractions.
A.P.C.I (1994) *Design: European
Design Guide.* Paris: A.P.C.I.

Organisation
Netherlands Design Institute
This think-and-do tank in
Amsterdam develops scenarios

about key issues of the new
economy (age, customisation,
connectivity, etc.) and undertakes
research projects to test them.
Netherlands Design Institute,
Keizersgracht 609, 1017 DS
Amsterdam, The Netherlands.
t +31 20 5516500
f +31 20 6201031
desk@design-inst.nl
www.design-inst.nl/

Website
PIRA
This research centre undertakes
an impressive array of future-
oriented investigations into all
aspects of printing and packaging.
www.pira.co.uk

Organisations in the United States

Organisation
American Center for Design
The American Center for Design
promotes excellence in design
education and practice.
Their newsletter *Statements*
addresses the following six
areas: new trends; strategic
design; professional practice;
education, methodology and
tools; history, criticism, and
theory.
Statements, 3 issues a year.
American Center for Design,
325 West Huron Street,
suite 711, Chicago, Ill. 60610.
t +312 787 2018
f +312 649 9518
acded@aol.com

Website
**American Institute
of Graphic Arts**
A smart website run by this
recently remodernised and now
dynamic professional association
in the United States. Of particular

interest to professional designers,
but worth a look by managers to
see how the design industry is
repositioning itself. Includes also
dial-up bulletin-board discussions,
general information, and events
listings.
www.dol.com/AIGA/

Website
Corporate Design Foundation
A non-profit educational
institution in the United States
that explores design/business
aspects of product design,
communication design, and
architecture. Publishes quarterly
glossy magazine called *@Issue,*
which contains intelligent,
industry-relevant pieces.
www.cdf.org/

Periodical and Organisation
Design Management Institute
An international journal published
in Boston. By 'design management'
they refer mostly to the work of
managers in large corporations
who buy design services. The
journal's attempts to equate
design with corporate strategy
tend to be tendentious. But it
fulfils a role, and the organisation's annual conference is
popular and well-attended.
The Design Management Institute,
107 South Street, Suite 502,
Boston, MA, USA. www.dmi.org/
Design Management Journal,
4 issues a year. The Design
Management Institute.
t +1 617 338 6380
f + 1617 338 6750
dmistaff@designmgt.org

Journal
Fast Company
Slightly frantic (the mood of
American entrepreneurialism) but
well-connected enjoyable and
much-discussed new magazine
about trendy young companies in

the new economy. It's put together by ex-editors of the *Harvard Business Review*. You need it to keep on top of the US scene.
Fast Company, 77 North Washington Street, Suite 401 Boston, MA 02114 1927 www.fastcompany.com/fastco/home.htm

Journal
Red Herring
A lively and well-informed North American monthly (but with international coverage) for the venture capital community which is dedicated to providing a first look at emerging technology companies. The magazine is one of the places where stock market crazes for new high-tech companies start.
t +1 415 865 2277
f +1 415 865 2280

Graphic design

Book
Envisioning information
More than 400 illustrations enlighten practical advice about how to explain complex material by visual means, with vivid examples that illustrate the fundamental principles of information display.
Tufte, Edward R. (1990) *Envisioning Information*. Connecticut: Graphics Press.

Book
Information architects
How to communicate efficiently. Using over 100 examples of information design, the book reveals the heart of a good explanation, showing that inside everyone, beneath every clever application of technology and style, lies a disciplined process of logic and common sense.

Wurman, Richard Saul and Peter Bradford (eds.) (1996) *Information Architects*. Zurich: Graphis Press.

Book
The visual display of quantitative information
250 illustrations of the best (and a few of the worst) statistical charts, graphics, and tables, with a detailed analysis of how to display quantitative data for precise, quick, and effective analysis.
Tufte, Edward R. (1983) *The Visual Display of Quantitative Information*. Connecticut: Graphics Press.

Book
Typography now two: implosion
Poynor describes the new typography as a 'genre': the book itself is an example of the new typography.
Poynor, Rick (1996) *Typography Now Two: implosion*. London: Booth-Clibborn Editions.

Seven glossy design magazines

To get the best out of designers, it will help to know what turns them on, what their influences are, and what they are talking about. These are the most intelligent and best-produced design magazines of the moment. If you are a dentist, put them in your waiting room to ensure a stylish atmosphere.

Axis
An international and glossy review of contemporary design, published from Tokyo, with English texts. Contains profiles of designers and design studios, news of current trends, and reviews of exhibitions.
Axis, 6 issues a year, Japanese/English. Axis Inc., 5-17-1 Roppongi Minato-ku, Tokyo 106, Japan.
t +81 03 3587 2781
f +81 03 3586 5246

Blueprint
Influential British magazine about architecture and design.
Blueprint, 11 issues a year. Subscriptions: Freepost, LON8209, London NW1 0YT, UK.
t +44 171 706 4596
f +44 171 479 8515

Design Report
International in coverage, with a bias towards German design. Contains long, well-illustrated articles, shorter news items, profiles, interviews, conference reports, book and exhibition reviews, and details of current and forthcoming exhibitions, conferences and seminars. Scope: industrial design, furniture design, vehicle design, design theory, design education, and design history.
Design Report, 12 issues a year, German (summaries in English).

MACup Verlag GmbH, Große
Elbstraße 277, 22767 Hamburg,
Germany.
t +49 040 391 09 01
f +49 040 39 10 91 50

Domus

Published in Milan, this extremely
high-quality magazine is
sometimes ahead of its time,
sometimes behind it (it's weak on
new media and the new economy).
The principal subjects covered are:
architecture, industrial design,
furniture design, lighting design,
interior design, environmental
design, and its historical and
theoretical aspects.
Domus, 11 issues a year,
Italian/English. Editoriale Domus,
via Achille Grandi 5/7, 20089
Rozzano, Milan, Italy.
t +39 2 824721
f +39 2 8255033

Form

High-modernist review of
contemporary German design with
long, well-illustrated articles,
profiles, interviews, book and
exhibition reviews, reviews of new
products, conference reports, and
news of current and forthcoming
exhibitions, conferences and
seminars.
Form, 4 issues a year, German
(summaries in English). Verlag
Form GmbH, Hanauer Landstraße
161, 60314 Frankfurt am Main,
Germany.
t +49 69 94 33 25 0
f +49 69 94 33 25 25

ID Magazine of International Design

Recently voted the best small
magazine in the United States,
ID's coverage is international but
biased towards the USA. Contains
long, well-illustrated articles,
profiles, interviews, book and
exhibition reviews, a listing of
current and forthcoming
exhibitions, conferences and
competitions, conference reports,
and classified advertisements.
*ID Magazine of International
Design,* 12 issues a year. Design
Publications Inc., 330 W. 42nd St.,
New York, NY 10036.
t +1 212 447 1400
www.idonline.com/

View on Colour

The colour forecasting bible is
published by trend magnate
Lidewij Edelkoort in Paris, with art
direction by Anthon Beeke, one of
Europe's most original visual
designers. The magazine is
extremely well produced, extremely
expensive, and extremely chic.
View on Colour, 2 issues a year.
United Publishers, 30 Boulevard
Saint Jacques, 75014 Paris, France.
t +33 1 43 31 15 89
f +33 1 43 31 77 91
upsa@FranceNet.fr

*We would like to thank the
following people for additional
advice in selecting the resources:*
Prof. J. Buijs (TU Delft), D. Dirne
(TU Eindhoven), R. Goossens (TU
Delft), Carolien van Hemel (TU
Delft), René Hoefnagels (TU Delft),
Sytze Kalisvaart (TNO), A. Korbijn
(STT), D. Maatman (TNO), Bart
Meijer (TU Delft), Johan
Molenbroek (TU Delft), R. Niesing
(Erasmus University Rotterdam),
Prof. W. Oppedijk van Veen (TU
Delft), Tamar van de Paal (Philips),
Prof. K. Robers (TU Delft), Arnold
Vermeeren (TU Delft), Prof. R. van
Wijk van Brievingh (TU Delft).

Learning Resources
Centre